ECONOMIC INEQUALITY IN CANADA

Lars Osberg

Economic Inequality in Canada

Lars Osberg
Associate Professor
Dalhousie University

Butterworths
Toronto

HC
120
.I5
082

Economic Inequality in Canada
© 1981 Butterworth & Co. (Canada) Ltd.

Printed and bound in Canada

The Butterworth Group of Companies

Canada:
Butterworth & Co. (Canada) Ltd., Toronto and Vancouver

United Kingdom:
Butterworth & Co. (Publishers) Ltd., London

Australia:
Butterworths Pty. Ltd., Sydney

New Zealand:
Butterworths of New Zealand Ltd., Wellington

South Africa:
Butterworth & Co. (South Africa) Ltd., Durban

United States:
Butterworth (Publishers) Inc., Boston
Butterworth (Legal Publishers) Inc., Seattle
Mason Publishing Company, St. Paul

Canadian Cataloguing in Publication Data

Osberg, Lars.
    Economic inequality in Canada

(Urban economics series)
Bibliography: p.
Includes index.
ISBN 0-409-85727-0

1. Income distribution — Canada. I. Title.
II. Series.

HC120.I5082   339.2'2'0971   C81-094311-5

Printed by Hunter Rose
Cover design by Julian Cleva

For Frances,
    For Many Reasons

Contents

Preface

The aim of this book is to present an up-to-date description of the extent of economic inequality in Canada and to outline existing theories as to its causes, and policies for its change. It is to be hoped such a book will prove useful to general readers interested in the issues surrounding economic inequality, as well as to students in both economics and sociology courses. To my mind, the study of economic inequality is one of the most fascinating and important areas of economics. If some of the readers of this book develop a greater interest in the values, the facts, and the causes of economic inequality, and in how it could be changed, this book will have accomplished its purpose.

In writing a book of this sort however, one accumulates debts in many directions. Many of the ideas developed in this book were first presented to students in classes in labour economics, and income distribution and poverty at Dalhousie University and the University of Western Ontario. Their comments and questions over the past five years have forced the clarification of many points, even if the original presentation may have been obtuse. Edgar Friedenberg, Ken Scott and Phillip Welch were kind enough to introduce me to areas of literature in medicine and education with which I was unfamiliar. Charles Beach, Alan Harrison, Ian Irvine and Michael Wolfson made available some of their own work, which would otherwise have been difficult to obtain. Monique Dancause, Mary Simms and Jura Smith put up with the pressure of unrealistic deadlines and remained in good cheer throughout. Thanks must also go to my colleagues at Dalhousie, Michael Bradfield, Robert Comeau, Christian Marfels, Al Sinclair, and Fred Wien who commented on various chapters of the first draft. James Davies' very helpful comments on the first draft produced major alterations and substantially improved the final result. Finally, I must especially thank John Cornwall, who provided patient "therapy" on virtually the entire manuscript. Naturally, since I did not always take all the advice which was offered to me I cannot implicate any of the above in the final product, for which I take sole responsibility.

Chapter 1

Introduction

1.1 Equality — A Value or a Description?

Few areas of economics are as contentious as a study of economic inequality. In part, this is because at the same time that "equality" is for many a deeply-held value about how society should be, "inequality" is a description of how society is. The most straightforward definition of economic inequality is probably, "differences among people in their command over economic resources" (although to be useful one must be more specific about which economic resource and how it is measured).[1] In this book, we do not enter the debate on whether society *should be* economically equal or unequal or how a just degree of economic inequality should be defined. Rather, the emphasis here is on description and analysis — description of the extent of economic "inequality" in Canada and analysis of its causes. A full discussion of what "ought to be" is clearly not omitted because it can be viewed as an unimportant topic; it is left out solely because there is more than enough material involved in the description and analysis of economic inequality to fill this, or indeed a much larger, book.

Most people's interest in the extent and causes of inequality stems, however, from the value which they place in "equality." Such a value is traced by many writers to religious roots that, "all men are equal in the eyes of God," since regardless of "superiority in the arts which bring wealth and power, judged by their place in any universal scheme, they are all infinitely great or infinitely small" (Tawney, 1952:38). The value of equality finds expression in such classic statements as the American Declaration of Independence: "We hold these truths to be self-evident, that all men are created equal, that they are endowed by their Creator with certain unalienable rights, that among these are Life, Liberty and the pursuit of happiness."[2] Equality is thus a very powerful ideal, closely connected to

---

[1] Whether such differences can be justified or whether people in similar circumstances receive equal rewards is considered here to be the issue of "equity," but for a different approach, see Atkinson (1975:5).

[2] Not all societies, of course, may prize equality. Tawney (1952) has written of the "religion of inequality" as it persists in England, while Lipset (1966) contrasted U.K. and U.S. attitudes to inequalities of status and authority. Canada appears to be an intermediate case.

(but not identical with) the criteria of equity, fairness and justice by which we judge the moral authority of existing and potential social institutions.

But what does "equality" mean? If it means "equality of result" in the economic sphere, is this equality of annual income, of lifetime income or of lifetime "utility," which includes non-monetary rewards? If it means equality of opportunity, is this an "equal start" in any race, however defined? Or is it an equal start in a contest whose prizes are set to maximize the utility of the least well-off participant (Rawls, 1971)? Or is it the conception that although people "differ profoundly as individuals in capacity and character, they are equally entitled as human beings to consideration and respect, and that the well-being of a society is likely to be increased if it so plans its organization that, whether their powers are great or small, all its members are equally enabled to make the best use of such powers as they possess" (Tawney, 1952:35)?

Each of these conceptions of equality would lead to a very different ideal society. There is a world of difference, for example, between a society which defines "equal opportunity" as identical expenditure on the education of all children and one which defines it, a la Tawney, to mandate compensatory educational programs for the handicapped and the disadvantaged. If equality is one's goal, it clearly matters a great deal how one defines it.

A major theme of Chapters 2 and 3 is, however, that for the purposes of description and analysis, it also matters a great deal how one defines the extent of inequality. Pure "description," uncontaminated by values, is probably an unobtainable goal. There are many empirical definitions of economic "inequality," each of which emphasizes more or less heavily particular aspects of inequality. As Chapter 2.2 discusses, some statistical measures will emphasize more heavily differences between the extremes and the middle groups of a distribution, while some will emphasize more heavily inequality among the middle groups. Some variables (such as wealth, Chapter 3) are distributed more unequally than other variables (such as income, Chapter 2). Which variable, and which measure, one chooses to describe will clearly affect one's perception of economic inequality. In Chapter 2, we focus on the distribution of annual income, while Chapter 3 discusses the distribution of economic power, wealth and riches, and lifetime income. One's view of which variable is the most important to study will depend, at least partially, on one's values — i.e., on which definition of "inequality," as a description of where society *is* makes sense in terms of one's conception of "equality" (i.e., where society *should be*).

Indeed, definitions are important even if one does not value "equality" and wishes only to analyse the reasons why the wages of working Canadians varied in 1979 between $5,500 and $778,000[3], or why the top

---

[3]The 1979 Nova Scotia minimum wage was $2.75 per hour — at 40 hours per week for 50 weeks that is $5,500. Edgar Bronfman received $778,979 in 1979 as President of Seagram's (Robinson, 1980).

1 per cent of adults own an average of $887,000 while the bottom 40 per cent have an average wealth of about $1,000 (see Table 3-3). There are a variety of explanations for these phenomena and some variables (such as "economic power" and its inequality) may be crucial components of one theory, although they do not make sense in the context of another. Indeed, even the "facts" one selects to explain are intimately related to one's theoretical perspective. Some "facts" (e.g., the inequality of lifetime consumption paths as described by Irvine (1980), or the rate of surplus value as described by Wolff (1979)) are only understandable within a particular theoretical context. Other "facts" (such as the inequality of wealth or riches — see Chapter 3) may have subtly different definitions, whose rationale depends partially on the theory they are part of, and whose measurement produces different perceptions of the extent of the economic inequality around us.

Since it is a truism that the personal acquaintances of most people tend to be other people with similar habits, attitudes and backgrounds, these differences in theoretical perspective can have important practical consequences. Given a sufficiently circumscribed set of personal experiences it is quite possible for the logic of a theory, reinforced by the pleasures of complacency, to overwhelm an individual's other sources of information and convince him/her that economic inequality is "really" quite small and not worth troubling about. Such a perception does not, of course, alter the reality which faces other people. Although low income is a fact of life for many Canadians, society's perception of the extent of poverty will, for example, be influenced by which of the definitions of a "poverty line" used in Canada we choose to adopt. Chapter 4 therefore outlines these methods of defining poverty (which are ultimately based on a different analysis of the nature of deprivation) and their connection to the general issue of inequality.

1.2 Economic Theory — The Problem of Choice

It is therefore far from easy to separate values from descriptions and descriptions from analyses. It is, however, essential to try if one is to make an informed choice among the various research traditions which seek to explain economic inequality. A major theme of Chapters 5 to 9 is that a variety of explanations exist. Chapter 5 discusses alternative explanations of the division of national income between the owners of "labour" and of "capital" while Chapters 6 to 8 present critical summaries of the different theories available of the determination and distribution of labour earnings (Chapter 9 offers a tentative summary).

In Chapters 6 to 9, a distinction is drawn between theories which explain the determination of individual earnings and those which explain the distribution of earnings. It is argued that only under fairly extreme assumptions can some theories of earnings determination serve as theories of the earnings distribution. Our confusion of the two sorts of theories can perhaps be partly ascribed to the ambiguity of the term "distribution." Sometimes the word is used in the sense of the distribution of a given amount of goods among different people and sometimes it is used in the statistical sense of a frequency distribution of a variable over a population. It is in this second sense that the term "distribution" is used here.

Only under particular assumptions, however, can a theory which explains, for example, why a more highly-educated individual usually receives a higher salary be generalized to a theory of the impact of a general increase in education on the distribution of earnings (see 7.3.3, 8.2.2 and 9.1). It may make sense, when looking at how education will affect an individual, to assume that the market demand for education (either as a credential or as a productive input) remains unchanged. It makes much less sense to assume that a general change in the distribution of education will leave market values unchanged. Thus, generalizations of the impact of the distribution of education (or other variables) on the distribution of earnings require a general equilibrium approach — i.e., both a theory of supply and one of demand. A theory of earnings determination can, therefore, explain why the earnings of two individuals are unequal, but it may not be able to explain the "inequality" of earnings — i.e., the distribution of earnings of the entire population.

Chapter 6 discusses "chance" as a theory of earnings distribution, the role of ability and socio-economic background in earnings determination and the influence of sex on earnings. Chapter 7 presents the "human capital/neoclassical" perspective on individual and family earnings, on the distribution of earnings and on the inter-generational transmission of earning power. Chapter 8 outlines the "neo-institutional" and "radical" views. In some respects the differences among these theories are very profound—in Chapter 12 we outline some of their differences on appropriate public policy to deal with inequality. In other respects, however, their differences are surprisingly slight, since as bodies of applied theory their predictions must conform to the same underlying empirical events of the real world. Some events therefore acquire a different terminology in different theories, but retain the same consequences. (One can, for example, assert that the advantages children from upper-income families have when they enter primary school (see 6.3) are due to early human-capital investments in "child quality" by their parents (see 7.4), or to their "class background" (see 8.4). Either way they tend to do better in school as a result.) Given the great differences in theoretical starting points and methodologies, it is extremely interesting that the "human capital" and "radical" analyses agree on two important predictions — that left to itself, a capitalist market system will produce neither equality of result nor equality of opportunity in the labour market.

1.3 Other Issues

Anyone who starts a book on economic inequality will inevitably acquire a certain humility by its end. The topic is as vast as any in economics, and with considerably more implications than most for a wide range of other disciplines. Psychology, biology and genetics tell us of the "inequalities" we can expect to find in the human organism; sociology and politics emphasize the inequalities in the relationships of human social animals; history reminds us that the inequality of the present is conditioned by the inequalities of the past, while ethics points out that as moral beings we all must make judgments on inequality. All of these disciplines remind us that "economic man" is but one of humanity's dimensions, and in all of these disciplines inequality has been greatly studied — often with frequent reference to economic inequalities. One cannot, and should not, avoid making some connections to these other disciplines in a book on economic inequality, but for the most part, they have been left as unexplored avenues.

Even within economics, "inequality" is so broad a topic that any discussion that does not spread over several volumes will leave many stones unturned. There is no discussion here, for example, of regional inequalities, very little on the impact of trade unions on inequality, and nothing on economic inequality in non-capitalist societies. Even among those subjects which are discussed, it is apparent that any of them could well receive far more extensive treatment, and readers will have their candidates for the ones which should have. The selection of topics and emphases are entirely the responsibility of the author — in addition to those already discussed, the issues of property, of growth, and of government intervention seemed to him the most important.

Chapters 6 to 9 emphasize the determination and distribution of earnings because that is the primary source of income for most Canadian families. Chapter 10 discusses the acquisition of property — the theory and evidence surrounding both the "life-cycle" view that most families acquire their property by individual saving from labour earnings, and the radical view that most property is inherited. As an empirical matter, there is no necessary contradiction between the two views if a relatively small minority of families own a majority of a nation's wealth (and inherit most of it) while the rest of the population (i.e., the majority of families) save their wealth (if any) from labour earnings. There is, however, an ethical issue involved since the social institution of property has generally been justified as a reward for individual exertion. Since the ownership of property is also at the centre of the "socialism versus capitalism" debate, Chapter 10 concludes with a discussion of the ethics of the institution of property and the possible policies which might change its distribution.

Economic inequality among Canadians is only a small part of the much greater economic inequality among all the peoples of the world. Chapter 11 discusses world-wide economic inequality and the link between economic inequality, and economic growth and development. Sociologists and political scientists would argue that the link is profound and that unequal societies which lack an ideology to legitimate inequality face a continual tension between institutionalized values and social reality. As Knight remarked:

> In the distribution of economic resources atomistic motivation tends powerfully toward cumulatively increasing inequality. For all productive capacity — whether owned property or personal qualities — is essentially "capital," a joint creation of pre-existing capacity (or the result of "accident"). And those who already have more capacity are always in a better position to acquire still more, with the same effort and sacrifice. This applies about as much to personal capacity as to property, though the latter is a more convenient way of passing on "unearned" advantage to heirs or successors. It is a gross injustice — by one of several conflicting norms of justice generally accepted in liberal society. But it is also the main reliance for the motivation of accumulation in all forms, hence of progress. (1951:20)

The political and sociological issue is then whether it is the fruits of economic growth which render economic inequality socially tolerable. The economic issue is whether economic inequality is a precondition for economic growth, i.e., whether reductions in equality are purchased at the cost of reductions in growth.

If Canadian society is to choose greater or less inequality, government will be the agent of that choice. Chapter 12 therefore considers the current impact of government policies on the Canadian distribution of income and the potential impact of a number of alternative policies. It will be seen that great disagreements exist about the desirability of particular policies — disagreements which stem from different conceptual understandings of the economy and in particular from the debate outlined in Chapters 7 and 8. One is therefore brought back to the problem of choice, since one must choose which analysis of the economy appears most reasonable if one wishes to advocate particular policies to affect it. In this choice, I can offer both a bias and a consolation — a bias that the reader should make an informed choice, based on criteria which he or she is prepared to defend intellectually, and a consolation, that even if one's choice turns out to be "wrong," one can be sure there are knowledgeable and intelligent people who share it.

Chapter 2

Income Inequality

In this chapter, we examine the distribution of annual income among Canadian family units. Any discussion of distributional issues must begin by defining:
(a) distribution of what?
(b) distribution among whom?
(c) distribution how measured?
Section 1 therefore presents the definitions of "income" and "family unit" which are necessary to get the discussion under way. Section 2 examines alternative measures of the extent of inequality, while section 3 compares the current inequality of the Canadian income distribution with that prevailing in other nations.

It should be stated at the outset that income inequality is only a part of economic inequality. Statistics on the distribution of annual income among existing family units present only a "snapshot" of a complex and moving process. Some things (such as wealth or leisure) are left out of the picture entirely, some things (such as income or family composition) may change drastically before the next snapshot is taken, and still other aspects of the picture (such as fringe benefits) are very blurred and out of focus. These omissions are the subject of Chapter 3, but as we shall see there is plenty of complexity even in the snapshot which income distribution statistics present.

2.1 Definitions

2.1.1 What is Income?

Economists usually distinguish between wealth and income by arguing that the former is a stock and the latter is a flow, but underlying *both* is the broad concept of "control over the use of society's scarce resources" (Simons, 1938: 58). Wealth is then the total extent, at a point in time, of an individual's access to resources. Income (minus consumption) is the amount by which wealth changes during a given period of time. Or, as Hicks put it, income is "the maximum value a person can consume during a period and still be as well off (as wealthy) at the end of the period as he was at the beginning" (Hicks, 1946: 75). "Income" can thus come to a person in many ways — as cash, as goods, as services for which one does not have to pay, as gifts, or as increases in the value of assets which one already owns.

A broad concept of income would come close to measuring flows of economic welfare, but this is extremely difficult to measure in statistical surveys. In practice, Statistics Canada estimates "money income" — i.e., receipts from wages and salaries, net income from self-employment, investment income, government transfer payments, pensions, and miscellaneous incomes such as scholarships or alimony. Excluded from this measure of income are gambling gains and losses, inheritances, gifts, capital gains or losses, the value of fringe benefits, income in kind (such as free meals, living accommodations, or food and fuel produced for one's own use) or the value of services received from government or other individuals during the year. The great advantage of using Statistics Canada data on money income to measure income distribution is their availability. The disadvantage is that one cannot be sure that omissions at the upper end of the income scale (e.g., capital gains and executive "perks") balance omissions at the lower end of the income scale (e.g., medical services received by the elderly), and to the extent that they do not balance, published statistics on money income may be misleading.

Table 2-1

PERCENTAGE DISTRIBUTION OF INCOME
BY INCOME GROUPS — 1978

Income Interval	Family Units (Families & Unattached Individuals)	Families	Unattached Individuals
Under 3,000	5.6	1.4	15.9
3,000 - 4,999	9.1	3.0	24.0
5,000 - 6,999	6.7	5.3	10.3
7,000 - 8,999	6.6	5.4	9.4
9,000 - 10,999	6.2	4.9 ⎫	
11,000 - 12,999	5.5	5.2 ⎬	21.5
13,000 - 14,999	6.0	6.1 ⎭	
15,000 - 16,999	6.1	6.4 ⎫	
17,000 - 19,999	9.1	10.6	
20,000 - 24,999	13.1	17.0 ⎬	18.8
25,000 - 29,999	9.4	12.4	
30,000 - 34,999	6.4	8.6	
35,000 and over	10.0	13.7 ⎭	
	100%	100%	100%
Median Income	16,358	20,963	6,979
Average Income	18,547	22,397	9,159

Source: Statistics Canada 13-207 (1980)

2.1.2 Distribution Among Whom?

In this chapter we will be referring to the distribution of money income among *family units*. Family units are the focus because we are concerned with the distribution of current economic welfare, i.e., the distribution of potential consumption. We assume that income is pooled within family units for the purpose of consumption. This may not always be true. We must also be aware that unattached individuals count as a family of one, so the number of family units is the number of unattached individuals plus the number of families.

There are no single "always correct" answers to the questions of which recipient unit and which measure of income to choose. A concern with the distribution of economic well-being would imply that one should examine the distribution of income from all sources among *consuming* units (i.e., family units); a concern with discrimination in the labour market would imply that one should examine the distribution of earnings among individual members of the labour force. The choice of whether to use individuals or family units therefore depends on the question at issue.[1]

The economic well-being of a family unit with a given income clearly depends on how many mouths there are to feed with a given income.[2] A particularly important distinction is that between families and unattached individuals. Table 2-1 presents separately income distribution data for families, unattached individuals, and family units (i.e., families and unattached individuals together). In part because many unattached individuals are either young people who have not fully entered the labour

---

[1]The importance of seemingly minor changes in the definition of recipient unit is illustrated by comparison of the distributions of income using the "census" and "economic" definitions of "family" in Canada. An "economic" family is defined as "a group of individuals related by blood, marriage or adoption, who share a common dwelling unit," while the "census" definition is more restrictive and refers only to the nuclear family — i.e., either a husband and wife (with or without children who have never married) or a parent with one or more children who have never married living together in the same dwelling. By the "economic" family notion a parent and married children sharing a house would be considered one family, but by the more restrictive "census" definition they would be considered to be operating separately. Clearly the census definition implies that more people would be considered to be independent units than under the economic family definition. In 1977, use of the census concept of family would imply that 700,000 Canadians who were part of economic families would be counted as unattached individuals (Statistics Canada, 13-208). Since these people have incomes very much below the average and appear to live with relatives primarily for economic reasons, counting them as separate family units (i.e., using the "census" definition of family) inflates the number of family units in the lower end of the income distribution. The Gini index of inequality (defined in 2.2.2) for family units using the census family concept is therefore higher (.410) than the Gini index of inequality for family units using the economic family concept (.388). Fairly small definitional changes can therefore produce apparently quite large changes in measured inequality. In the text, we use only the economic family concept as a basis for defining the family unit.

[2]We will consider this issue again in Chapter 3.9.

market or older people who have left it, the average income of unattached individuals is very much below the average income of families. Income inequality among all family units is therefore somewhat greater than income inequality among families of two or more people. An "unattached individual" is defined as a person living alone or in a household where they are not related to any other household members. They form a somewhat troublesome category since one might suspect that some fraction of them can lay claim, in practice, to family resources, although they may not share a common dwelling unit. On the other hand, many unattached individuals who have no family (e.g., elderly, single women) are among the poorest people in Canadian society. Since it is impossible in practice to distinguish between these two cases, the "family unit" is an unavoidable compromise.

2.2 Measuring the Inequality of Income

2.2.1 Quintile Shares

An obvious way of measuring the inequality of income distribution is to calculate the share of the total income of a society which is received by the "poor" and by the "rich." If we lined up the whole population in order of income from poorest to richest and then divided the line into five equal groups, each group would be called a "quintile." Table 2-2 gives the share of different quintiles of Canadian family units in the total income of Canadian family units for various years since 1951.[3] An equal distribution of income would imply that each quintile received 20 per cent of total Canadian family incomes — i.e., the poorest 20 per cent of family units would receive 20 per cent of the total income, as would the richest 20 per cent of family units. By contrast, one can note that during the period in which these statistics have been collected, the share of the poorest 20 per cent has remained roughly constant at around 4 per cent of total income while the share of the richest 20 per cent of family units has remained roughly constant around 42 per cent of total income. If anything, there has been some tendency to a decline in the share of the poorest 20 per cent[4]. Statistics on the 1930s are fragmentary, but appear to indicate a somewhat higher level of income inequality (see Ostry, 1979: 292). Income inequality appears to have decreased during World War II.

---

[3]In Table 4-3 one can note that, by coincidence, the 1977 Statistics Canada "revised" poverty lines implied that 19.7% of Canadian family units lived in poverty. By this criterion, in that year, the poverty population is therefore approximately equal to the bottom quintile of the Canadian income distribution.

Note that money income includes transfer payments such as old age pensions, welfare or family allowance, but is calculated before tax. See Chapter 12 for a discussion of the net impact of government.

[4]If one ignores unattached individuals and considers only families, the share of the poorest 20 per cent increases somewhat (to approximately 6 per cent) but exhibits the same constancy over the postwar period.

Table 2-2

INCOME SHARES OF CANADIANS
— FAMILIES AND UNATTACHED INDIVIDUALS —
VARIOUS YEARS

Year	Lowest 20%	Second Quintile	Third Quintile	Fourth Quintile	Top 20%
1951	4.4	11.2	18.3	23.3	42.8
1957	4.2	11.9	18.0	24.5	41.4
1961	4.2	11.9	18.3	24.5	41.1
1965	4.4	11.8	18.0	24.5	41.4
1967	4.2	11.4	17.8	24.6	42.0
1971	3.6	10.6	17.6	24.9	43.3
1975	4.0	10.6	17.6	25.1	42.6
1976	4.3	10.7	17.4	24.7	42.9
1977	3.8	10.7	17.9	25.6	42.0
1978	4.1	10.4	17.6	25.2	42.7

Sources: Podoluk (1968: 294)
Statistics Canada 13-207-(1980: 85)

This constancy of income shares since World War II should be some-thing of a surprise, since a great deal has happened in the Canadian economy in the last 30 years. Real per capita personal income has considerably more than doubled, the labour-force participation of married women has more than tripled, the number of families composed of only one person has increased by roughly 40 per cent and, recently, inflation has played havoc with money wage rates and the returns from different assets. All these factors could be expected to affect income shares. Having two family members in paid employment, for example, pushes the money income of many families into the middle-class range. The rise in female labour-force participation therefore tends to decrease inequality, if measured in money income terms (see MacLeod and Horner, 1980:17). Measured in terms of economic well-being, however, the decrease in inequality is far less, since working in the labour market means a decrease in time available for other things. Goods that were previously produced at home (e.g., meals, child care) must now be purchased (see Chapter 7.4). On the other hand, the increase in single-person households might mean that income inequality is now overstated since it may be a sign of affluence that young workers or retired parents set up their own (low income) household rather than continue to live at home.

Henderson and Rowley (1977, 1978) have performed a series of "standardizations" for family unit size, age, sex, and education of family head, and the number of male and female earners, in an attempt to see how much of the observed increase in dollar income inequality between 1965 and 1975 can be accounted for by these factors. Using some measures of income inequality almost all of the observed inequality increase appeared to be due to these demographic changes; but under other assumptions standardization could only account for 60 per cent of the increase in income inequality.[5] Analysis of the trend of inequality therefore depends in a fundamental way on how one measures the extent of inequality.

Table 2-2 gives a fairly good picture of the income shares of Canadians, but it requires five numbers to describe the income distribution at any given point in time. This method could be improved by examining the shares of each decile (i.e., each 10 per cent) of the Canadian population, but that would require even more numbers. All these numbers can appear confusing if one is looking for an answer to the seemingly simple question of whether income inequality is "greater" or "less" now than in 1951, or "greater" or "less" in Canada than in the United States or Britain. Economists yearn to answer such seemingly simple questions and have therefore been fascinated for years with the search for an index of inequality which could summarize the income distribution in a single number.

2.2.2 The Gini Index of Inequality

One of the most popular indices of the extent of inequality was also one the earliest proposed. In Figure 2.1, if one graphs the cumulative percentage of family units along the horizontal axis and the cumulative percentage of income which is received by those families along the vertical axis, one has what is known as a Lorenz curve (Lorenz, 1905). In fact, Table 2-2 enables us to find four points on the Lorenz curve for 1978, since A is the point where the poorest 20 per cent of family units received 4.1 per cent of total income, B is the point where the poorest 40 per cent of family units received (4.1 + 10.4 =) 14.5 per cent of total income, C is the point where the poorest 60 per cent get (14.5 + 17.6 =) 32.1 per cent, and D represents the fact that the poorest 80 per cent of Canadian family units received (32.1 + 25.2 =) 57.3 per cent of total Canadian family income. If Table 2-2 was the only data we had available, we could draw an approximation to the Lorenz curve (i.e., a polygon) by simply connecting the points O, A, B, C, D, and Y. Such an approximation would be rather crude, and clearly could be improved if data were available on a larger number of income intervals. Where the incomes of individual respondents are reported, the Lorenz curve can be drawn exactly.

Corrado Gini (1912) proposed that the extent of inequality in a society

---

[5]MacLeod and Horner (1980) found that over the period 1954 to 1975 the impact of changing family composition in apparently increasing the Gini index of inequality was very slightly greater than the apparent decrease caused by increasing female labour force participation.

Figure 2-1 THE GINI INDEX OF INEQUALITY

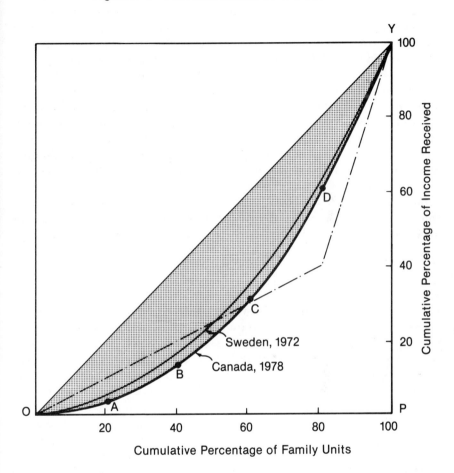

might be measured by the ratio of the area between the Lorenz curve and the line OY (shaded in the diagram) and the area of the entire triangle OPY. If everyone had equal incomes, each quintile of the income distribution would receive exactly 20 per cent of total income and the Lorenz curve would coincide with the diagonal OY — hence the shaded area would disappear and the Gini index would be 0. By contrast, a situation of "perfect inequality" where one person had all the income and everyone else had none would imply that the Lorenz curve lies along the line OP for virtually all its length, and the area between it and the diagonal would be almost exactly equal to the area of the entire triangle OPY — hence the Gini index would be very close to one. The real world falls between these two extremes. In 1977 the Gini index for the distribution of total money income among Canadian family units was 0.388.[6]

The Gini coefficient for Sweden is 0.346 and the Lorenz curve for Sweden lies entirely inside the Lorenz curve for Canada — hence one can say unambiguously that the Swedish income distribution is more equal than Canada's. Unfortunately, this unambiguous situation is relatively rare and it is more common for the Lorenz curves of different societies (or the same society at different points in time) to intersect. In this case interpretation of the Gini coefficient becomes much more problematic, as the following example (admittedly extreme) may indicate.

Suppose there were a society (call it "Adanac") in which the top 20 per cent of families all had annual incomes of $55,638 while all other families had annual incomes of $9,273. This would mean that the bottom 80 per cent of families share equally 40 per cent of total income (each of the bottom four quintiles getting 10 per cent) while the top quintile shares equally the remaining 60 per cent of total income. These figures have been picked so that average income of Adanac ($18,547) is the same as the average income of Canadian family units in 1978. Remembering that each of the four bottom quintiles of Adanac receives 10 per cent of total income, one can compare its income distribution with that of Canada in 1978. (see Table 2-2). Both the poorest and the richest quintile would receive a larger share of total income in Adanac than in Canada — the poorest would get 10 per cent instead of 4.2 per cent and the richest would get 60 per cent instead of 42.7 per cent. The second quintile would be approximately equally well-off but the third and fourth quintiles would be significantly less well-off. Is Adanac "more equal" or "less equal" than Canada? The Lorenz curve for this mythical society is drawn as the dashed line in Figure 2-1 and one can note that it lies above the Lorenz curve for Canada over approximately the bottom three quintiles before crossing and lying below it for the remainder. One might well think that a society where 20 per cent of families have incomes six times the incomes of the remaining 80 per cent would be a much more unequal society than Canada, but in fact the numbers in this example have been chosen so that the Gini coefficient of this mythical society is 0.4, i.e., approximately the same as Canada's![7] Societies which are very similar

---

[6]The Gini coefficient can be calculated as

F2:1
$$G = \frac{1}{2\overline{Y} \cdot n \cdot (n-1)} \cdot \sum_{i \neq j}^{n} \sum^{n} |Y_i - Y_j|$$

where: (1) Y_i and Y_j are the incomes of the ith and jth family units
(2) Y is average income
(3) n is the number of family units

For a further discussion, see Marfels (1972a).

[7]The "economic" definition of family implies a Gini index of 0.388, the "census" definition implies a Gini of 0.411. Their average is 0.3995.

in terms of average income and Gini coefficient can have very different income distributions.

One may adopt the Gini index as an indicator of the extent of income inequality, but the interpretation which one places on it will depend on the mechanism which produced that distribution of income and the values by which one judges both the mechanism and the ensuing distribution. A caste society in which the top 20 per cent of families were able to pass their incomes of $55,638 on to each succeeding generation while all other families inherited an annual income of $9,273 would be judged by most to be extremely unfair. If the income distribution of Adanac were determined by a truly random lottery in which each person had the same 20 per cent chance of winning an income for life of $55,638 it would be more "fair" in the sense that all individuals at least had an equal opportunity of joining the privileged classes. In both the above examples annual income is a good indicator of total lifetime income, but where this is not the case income inequality may be a poor indicator of the extent of economic inequality.

In our society, old people are generally poorer than average, but in African societies which are organized along an "age set" principle, old people enjoy much greater status, authority and income than average. If Adanac were organized along the principle that the youngest 80 per cent of the population had annual incomes of $9,273 while the oldest 20 per cent had annual incomes of $55,638, the Gini index of inequality of *annual* incomes would still equal 0.4, even though (assuming equal lifetimes) each person could expect, eventually, to become wealthy and everyone would, over their lifetimes, receive the same total income. This example may be as unrealistic as "Adanac," but it illustrates the importance of looking beyond annual income to broader ideas of economic inequality (see Chapter 3).

In many cases, a picture is worth a thousand words and a useful picture of the income distribution in Canada is that of Figure 2.2. In it, annual dollar income is shown along the horizontal axis and the percentage of all family units which are in that income class is measured vertically. As is typical of income distribution in most countries, the resulting graph shows a large hump concentrated among lower incomes and a long tail extending out to the right denoting the small percentage of families which receive high annual incomes. Indeed, one cannot both preserve the scale of the diagram and include everyone in it, as those individuals with incomes as high as $100,000 or $200,000 (although only a small fraction of the entire population) are simply off the page entirely! The dividing lines between the income quintiles of Table 2-2 are marked in Figure 2-2 as A, B, C, and D.[8] One can

---

[8]The income shares of various groups can be read off Figure 2-2. For example, if the total area under the graph represents 100 per cent of personal income, the area under the graph over the interval OB then represents the share of total personal income received by the bottom 40 per cent.

Figure 2-2   INCOME OF CANADIAN FAMILY UNITS

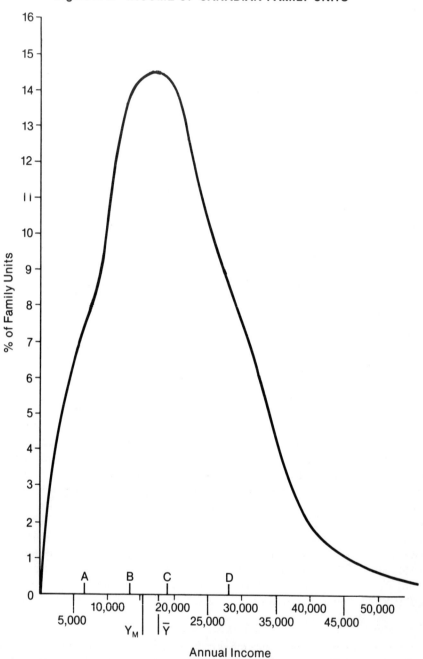

Source: Statistics Canada 13-207, 1980:57

note that the bottom four quintiles span intervals of more or less $6,000 each, but the top 20 per cent includes everyone from associate professors to multimillionaires. It takes only a few very high incomes to pull up the arithmetic average of incomes fairly substantially, hence average income ($\bar{Y}$) is approximately $2,000 higher than median income (Y_m — the income which separates the poorest and richest halves of the population). Jan Pen (1971) paints a fascinating word picture of the income distribution of individuals when he likens it to a parade of people whose heights are proportional to their income, and who all must pass a certain point in an hour — it takes 48 minutes before one sees marchers of average heights (income) and the parade grows with agonizing slowness until giants of 27 feet loom up at one minute to go. From then on, their height increases with dizzying rapidity; in the last few seconds of the march come businessmen and executives a hundred-feet tall, while the final marcher (a multi-millionaire) is some thousands of feet high.

More concretely, the 1978 Canadian data indicate that 20 per cent of Canadian family units had total family money incomes less than $6,564, 40 per cent had incomes under $13,072, 60 per cent were under $19,600 and 80 per cent were under $27,741 (Statistics Canada, 13:207, 1980:85). Since hourly wages are more familiar to many people, one can calculate that if each family unit had one earner (and no income from any other source), a "normal" 2,000 hours per year (50 weeks per year x 40 hours per week), would mean that the bottom quintile would consist of those earning $3.25 per hour or less, while the next quintile's wages would lie in the range $3.25 to $6.50, and the third and fourth quintiles would range up to $9.80 and $13.90 per hour respectively. Of course, in reality the bottom quintile is heavily dependent on transfer payments and the number of earners, and hours worked differs greatly across families. Especially in the lower quintile (the poverty population) many families are retired or otherwise out of the labour force (see Table 4-3). Many families in the middle-income groups are only there because they have two (or more) earners. Unemployment, even for part of the year, means that wages which might appear high on an hourly basis (e.g., in construction) must be spread over slack periods as well. And, of course, in thinking in terms of hourly wages one must remember that family units differ in size, and what is "good money" to a college student who lives at home or shares rent with room-mates is bare subsistence if the same wage must support a family.[9]

2.2.3 The Coefficient of Variation

Those who have a statistical background will recognize Figure 2-2 as a

---

[9]High rates of inflation render the dollar figures cited here inappropriate quite rapidly. But since the overall income distribution has changed relatively little, a rough approximation of current values can be obtained by "scaling up" by the rate of inflation. The 1979 figures would be roughly 1.09 times those cited.

frequency distribution, and perhaps will wonder if a statistical measure such as the variance of this distribution can be a good index of the inequality in it.[10] Unfortunately, the variance of the income distribution is not a particularly good measure of inequality. Most economists have argued that a measure of income inequality should be "scale free" in the sense that it should be unaffected by equiproportionate changes in all incomes (such as might occur if inflation affected everyone equally) or by changes purely in the size of the population (such as might occur if two separate, identical, societies were merged). One can, however, "normalize" the variance so that it is unaffected by such changes by dividing its square root by the average income. The resulting measure is called the "coefficient of variation."[11] Like the Gini coefficient, the coefficient of variation is unaffected by "scale." Both measures also have the desirable characteristic that they will decrease (i.e., show less inequality) if income is transferred from a richer individual to a poorer individual.[12]

Using the idea of transfers, let us examine the responsiveness of the Gini ratio and the coefficient of variation to changes in the income distribution which occur at different points in the income distribution. Hypothetically, consider two possible transfers: (a) a transfer of $100 of annual income from the Smith family, who have an annual income of $100,000, to the Jones family, who have an annual income of $99,000; (b) a transfer of $100 in income from the Gray family, annual income $18,000 to the White family, annual income $17,000. Since the coefficient of variation is calculated from the variance, which in turn depends on the *absolute difference* between an individual family income and the average income, and since the same *size* of transfer ($100) is involved in both cases, both the Smith-Jones transfer and the Gray-White transfer would produce the same size of change in the coefficient of variation. The Gini ratio, however, depends on the Lorenz curve which expresses the *cumulated percentage of income received by families.* Hence the size of the change in the Gini ratio is affected by the number of families who have incomes between the incomes of those who are involved directly by the transfer. Since very few families have incomes in the range $99,000 to $100,000 while a great many

---

[10]The variance of a distribution is calculated as

$$F_{2:2} \qquad Var(Y) = \frac{\sum_{i=i}^{n} (Y_i - \overline{Y})^2}{n}$$

[11]

$$F_{2:3} \qquad CV = \frac{\sqrt{Var(Y)}}{\overline{Y}}$$

[12]This is known as the "principle of transfers." Obviously, the transfer of income must be less than half the original difference between their incomes, as otherwise the transfer would simply reverse the original inequality.

are in the range of $17,000 to $18,000, the Gini ratio will decline by considerably less if $100 is transferred from the Smiths to the Joneses than if $100 is transferred from the Grays to the Whites. If, therefore, one wishes to measure the extent of changes in the inequality of income distribution one must remember that the Gini ratio is more sensitive to changes which occur in the middle ranges of the income distribution than among the very poor or the very rich, while the coefficient of variation is more sensitive to changes in the upper-income ranges.

The choice of a measure of income inequality cannot, therefore, be "value free." In addition to the problem of choosing which economic variable (e.g., income, earnings or wealth) and which population (e.g., families, individuals or household units) one is concerned with, there is also the problem of which statistical measure one wishes to use to summarize the inequality of that variable among that population. Basically, one must "choose one's index of inequality to be sensitive to changes (in the income distribution) of that type with which one is primarily concerned" (Champernowne, 1974: 806), since different indices of inequality will emphasize more heavily changes in different parts of the income distribution.[13]

2.2.4 Theil's Index of Inequality

If we knew that a society contained one hundred families and had an equal distribution of income, you would not be surprised to learn that each family received 1 per cent of total income. "Surprise" is a key concept in information theory since when a message is completely predictable it conveys no information (i.e., it does not surprise). When a message tells you something you did not already know (i.e., it surprises you) it conveys information. Similarly, when income is equally distributed or nearly so, income for any individual is predictable. When income is unequally distributed, however, it is less easy to predict the income of any randomly chosen individual and a message which tells us what that individual's income is has information

---

[13]It is worth noting that some measures of inequality that have been proposed are completely insensitive to certain sorts of transfers. For example, measures of inequality such as the "Kuznets" measure, which are based on the relative mean deviation do not change at all when income is transferred from a poor person to a richer one, as long as both individuals are on the same side of the average income level. Worse still, a measure such as the variance of the logarithm of income may actually show the perverse result of an apparent decrease in inequality when a transfer of income occurs from a rich person to an even richer one and for that reason is a poor indicator of the extent of income inequality. In the text we consider only measures of income inequality which satisfy the "principle of transfers." None of these measures can, however, escape the problem of "Adanac" vs. Canada — that very different societies may appear the same if we only use one number to measure their inequality. Love and Wolfson (1976), Sawyer (1976), Rossi (1979), Cowell (1977), and Champernowne (1974), provide surveys of the characteristics of alternative income inequality measures.

content. Theil (1967: 90-134) has therefore proposed that the inequality of income distribution be measured with the aid of some concepts developed in information theory to measure the average information content (surprise) of a series of messages.[14]

Often, income distribution data are available only on a group basis — i.e., one knows that the n individuals in a society are divided into g groups where n_g denotes the number of people in group g and Y_g denotes the average income of that group. The formula for the Theil index of inequality then becomes somewhat more complex.[15] But one of the great advantages of the Theil index of inequality is its property of decomposition, i.e., the straightforward way in which inequality in a total society can be broken down into the components of inequality which exist between and within different social groups.[16] In fact, Shorrocks (1980), Cowell (1980), and Marfels (1972b) have independently shown that if one wishes a measure of total inequality which can (a) be decomposed into between-group inequality and within-group inequality, (b) which is "scale-free," and (c) which respects the principle of transfers, only the Theil measure will do.

Like the Gini ratio and the coefficient of variation, the Theil index satisfies the "principle of transfers" in that a transfer of income from a richer to a poorer person implies a decrease in the index. The size of the change in the Theil index of inequality for any given transfer of income, however, depends on the *ratio* of the incomes of the individuals involved in the transfer.

---

[14]When data on individual income are available the Theil index of inequality is calculated as

F2:4
$$R = \frac{1}{n\overline{Y}} \sum_i Y_i \log\left(\frac{Y_i}{\overline{Y}}\right)$$

[15]   F2:5
$$R = \sum_g \left(\frac{n_g Y_g}{n\overline{Y}}\right) \cdot R_g + \frac{1}{n} \sum_g \left(n_g \frac{\overline{Y_g}}{\overline{Y}} \log \frac{\overline{Y_g}}{\overline{Y}}\right)$$

Fortunately, this equation has the easy interpretation that the first term in it represents the inequality which exists within group g (R_g), weighted by that group's share of total income, and the second term in it represents the inequality which exists between groups, calculated by the Theil formula. (If we only have data on the income of groups we are often forced to assume incomes within that group are identical. E.g. $R_g = 0$). Up to this point, we have been quite general — the total population could be divided into G groups on the basis of income intervals, regions of the country or age or sex of household head.

[16]Neither the Gini ratio nor the coefficient of variation can be decomposed into between-set and within-set components of inequality. Thus, when Paglin (1975) attempted to decompose the trend of total inequality in the United States by age groups he used the Gini ratio, but the resulting so called Paglin-Gini ratio was based on an incorrect decomposition — as Nelson (1977), Danziger (1977) and others were quick to point out. The Paglin-Gini has been applied to Canadian data by Armstrong et al. (1977, 1979) but does not deserve serious consideration.

2.2.5 Atkinson's Measure

Implicitly, the choice between the Gini ratio, coefficient of variation and the Theil index as measures by which to rank the inequality of societies inevitably implies value judgments. Of course, if one is comparing two societies whose Lorenz curves do not intercept (i.e., the Lorenz curve for one lies completely inside the Lorenz curve of the other) Atkinson (1970), has shown that the choice of an inequality index is relatively unimportant since they will all give the same ranking. A choice of inequality index is important, however, when Lorenz curves intersect, as they commonly do. Out of 66 comparisons of countries, Atkinson found that in 50 cases the Lorenz curves crossed. This implies that the choice of inequality index may reverse the ranking of societies. For example, measured by the Gini index of inequality the Netherlands may be seen as more equal than Sweden, but measured by the coefficient of variation Sweden may seem more equal than the Netherlands. Choosing among these two indices of inequality in such a case will necessarily involve a value judgment, as we will wish to use the coefficient of variation if we consider inequality between the middle class and the very rich to be especially important while we will wish to use the Gini index if we wish to give more weight to the inequality among the middle classes.

Atkinson has argued that since value judgments are unavoidable, we should make them more explicit — i.e., we should specify our "social welfare function." In particular, he argues that one might want to be specific about the degree of "inequality aversion" with which one approaches the issue of the income distribution. He sees "inequality aversion" as the price which society is willing to pay in order to decrease income inequality. Atkinson argues that if we are considering taking one dollar from a rich person and giving a proportion x to a poor person (the remainder being lost in the process, for example, in administrating the transfer). We ought to ask "at what level of x do we cease to regard the redistribution as desirable?" If all the income lost by the rich actually gets to the poor (i.e., x = 1) then anyone at all concerned about inequality sees redistribution as desirable. If only a small fraction (say 20 per cent) gets to the poor, presumably only those who are very concerned about inequality will see the transfer as desirable." What is crucial is how far one is prepard to let x fall below 1 before calling for a stop" (Atkinson, 1975:49). Another way of putting it is to say that society would be equally well off if all incomes were the same, even if these equal incomes were only x percent of current average income. If we argue for a low value of x, we are highly "inequality averse" — i.e., we believe society would be equally well-off with an equal distribution of income, even if its average were only (for example) two-thirds of current average income.

Notice that we have introduced the idea of "society" having different degrees of welfare. Economists often argue that social welfare depends on the incomes of the individuals which make up a society, and that the way in which social welfare depends on individual income can be expressed as a "social welfare function."[17] If we prefer one society to another solely because its index of inequality is lower, we are implicitly saying that the social welfare of the first is greater than that of the second. Our ranking, however, may depend on the index of inequality which we chose — hence the choice of index implicitly involves a choice of a social welfare function.

Atkinson's measure of inequality requires that we should specify "e" — our degree of "inequality aversion"[18]. Specifying a high value of e will imply that we are most concerned with the share of the bottom end of the income distribution, while specifying a relatively low value of e means that we are particularly sensitive to changes in distribution at the top end.

2.3 International Comparisons

The various measures of section 2.2 may indicate how much income inequality exists in a society, but by themselves they are mere numbers, and cannot say whether this degree of inequality is "a lot," or "a little." Such statements are relative ones and involve a comparison either between the inequality of this society and that existing in other societies or between current inequality and past or possible future inequality. Comparisons between countries that are broadly similar in their level of economic development and social organization (i.e., rich and capitalist) are helpful in answering such "reformist" questions as whether it is possible to make changes in the income distribution, within a familiar social and political framework. More fundamental questions, such as what impact socialism would have on Canada's income distribution, cannot be answered with statistics alone.[19]

---

[17]In Atkinson (1970) the social welfare function is required to be "additively separable and symmetric," i.e., social welfare depends not on who is well-off but only on the amount of individual utility, and the utility of an individual depends only on his own income, and not on that of others. This formulation rules out envy or altruism, and, one must say, imposes social values of its own. Some (e.g., Sen, 1973; Dasgupta, 1972) have therefore criticized this formulation of a social welfare function.

[18]   F2:6 $$I = 1 - \left[\sum_i \left(\frac{Y_i}{\bar{Y}} \right)^{1-e} \cdot \frac{1}{n} \right]^{\frac{1}{1-e}}$$

where

F2:7 $$X = \frac{1}{2^e}$$

[19]The nations of Eastern Europe have often been called "state capitalist" rather than "socialist" but even the statistics on their income inequality cannot easily be compared to those of the OECD nations, due partially to the much greater importance in the former of "in-kind" income (e.g., housing provided at very low rentals). Whether "perks" and special privileges are available in greater measure to upper level executives in "Eastern" or "Western" countries is also an issue which has received little rigorous examination.

Even comparisons of inequality among capitalist countries are fraught with many difficulties. Countries differ slightly in the definitions they use of income and of household. They differ as well in the extent of coverage of their population and of income which their statistical authorities succeed in achieving. Errors and omissions also differ in importance. When a survey of households is conducted (as in Canada), poor memories or modesty may prevent some respondents from giving an accurate estimate of their annual income. Where taxes are concerned, natural modesty tends to be reinforced by a certain financial incentive. There is a strong suspicion that upper-income groups tend to understate their income rather more than lower-income groups and that some types of incomes are particularly susceptible to being understated (e.g., income from rents, dividends, small businesses or self-employment are poorly reported — salaries are generally fairly accurate).

One can check these suspicions of under-reporting by adding up the income which individuals do report and checking the total against aggregate estimates of income from GNP statistics. Sawyer (1976:513) argues that in 1972 in Canada, statistical authorities appear to succeed in counting 95.5 per cent of wage and salary income, 93.4 per cent of entrepreneurial income, and 76.3 per cent of property income in the income distribution statistics. The British authorities did somewhat better, but the French reported coverage of only 88.9 per cent of wage and salary income, 34.4 per cent of entrepreneurial income and 35.4 per cent of property income (perhaps because the concept used in France is income declared to the tax authoritties). Since higher incomes are correlated with greater wealth (although not perfectly; see Table 3-2) and since property income is more heavily under-reported, it seems likely that these omissions are on balance concentrated in the upper tail of the income distribution. Hence the true picture would be one of greater inequality than that statistically reported (especially in France).

Comparisons across societies of the distribution of family money income are particularly affected by variation in family size and structure (see Kuznets, 1976). Societies differ widely in such social norms as the appropriate age at which children should leave home to establish separate households, and in the degree to which aged parents reside with their married children or separately. Different social norms and differences in the cost of maintaining separate households cause the proportion of single-person households to differ very widely among nations — from a low of 6.6 per cent in Spain to high of 45.4 per cent in the Netherlands (Sawyer, 1976:18). Since small households tend to have considerably lower incomes than average, a society which has a large proportion of single-person households will tend to have an income distribution which shows a large number of households at low income levels. Its distribution of economic welfare may, however, be just as equal as in a society where young workers and older retired people stay in the family unit and add their (low) incomes to the household total.

Correcting for such differences in the distribution of household size, Table 2-3 presents the results of Sawyer (1976) for the OECD nations (also adjusted for the impact of direct taxes). He cautions, "it is only when the international differences are large that unequivocal statements on inter-country degrees of inequality can be made." His caution arises partly because of the statistical deficiencies of the data, and partly because it was impossible for him to account for variations in the impact of indirect taxation and government expenditure across nations.

Table 2-3

INTERNATIONAL INCOME INEQUALITY — POST-TAX, "STANDARDIZED" HOUSEHOLD SIZE

	Year	Share of Income Received by Income Quintiles					Inequality Indices			Atkinson	
		1	2	3	4	5	Gini	Theil	C.V.	e=.5	e=1.5
Australia	1966/67	4.8	12.2	17.8	24.1	40.9	.354	.091	.065	.106	.329
France	1970	4.2	9.7	16.2	22.8	47.1	.417	.126	.081	.143	.401
Germany	1973	6.5	10.3	14.9	21.9	46.3	.386	.110	.078	.118	.299
Japan	1969	5.1	12.4	16.8	21.7	41.9	.336	.084	.068	.092	.247
Netherlands	1967	9.1	14.5	17.5	22.5	36.3	.264	.050	.050	.057	.167
Norway	1970	6.6	13.0	18.9	24.7	36.9	.301	.064	.055	.076	.236
Spain	1971	4.2	10.2	16.8	24.0	45.0	.397	.113	.076	.132	.383
Sweden	1972	7.3	14.1	19.0	24.7	35.0	.271	.051	.048	.063	.201
United Kingdom	1973	6.1	12.2	18.4	24.0	39.3	.327	.076	.060	.088	.261
U.S.A.	1972	4.9	10.9	17.5	24.6	42.1	.369	.097	.068	.113	.338
Canada	1972	5.2	12.0	18.0	24.2	40.5	.348	.087	.063	.103	.320
Average		6.0	12	17.5	23.5	41.0					

(*Coefficient of variation calculated from decile shares)
Source: Sawyer, 1976: Tables 10, 11

Nevertheless it is fairly clear that the Netherlands, Sweden and Norway are the most equal of the OECD nations, while the most unequal are France and Spain. By the Gini index of inequality, the Netherlands is the most equal, but by the coefficient of variation measure (which emphasizes high incomes) Sweden is. Interestingly, using Atkinson's measure with a low "e" value (i.e., emphasizing the top end of the distribution), Canada is more equal than Germany, but if we emphasize inequality among the poor (high "e") Canada is more unequal than Germany. Nevertheless, on most indices, Canada appears to rank approximately mid-way, not as unequal as the United States but more unequal than the United Kingdom.[20] The middle

---

[20]Note that by adjusting for family size we eliminate the difference between income inequality calculated on a "census" or "family" basis.

quintiles of our income distribution are relatively close to the OECD average, but it is noteworthy that in Canada the poorest 20 per cent of households are considerably less well-off than in the social democracies of Western Europe. The fraction of national income going to the poorest 20 per cent in Sweden is, for example, 40 per cent higher than in Canada. The least well-off quintile in the Netherlands receives a share of national income fully 75 per cent greater than that they would receive in Canada. These are large differences, especially from the point of view of the poor.

2.4 Summary and Conclusions

(a) Definitions are important in a study of inequality. Different definitions of *what* is being distributed among *whom* will affect our perceptions of the extent of inequality. For example, measuring inequality of annual money income among Canadian family units measures only one aspect of economic inequality, but even here the use of a "census" rather than an "economic" definition of family will reveal an apparently higher degree of inequality. In the text we referred to "economic" families since this is probably most appropriate for comparisons of economic well-being, but there is no "always correct" definition. The "correct" definitions with which to organize data depend entirely on what question one wants to ask of the data.

(b) Examination of income quintile data reveals that the distribution of money income among Canadian economic family units has remained fairly constant over the post-World War II period. This is a surprising and highly important finding, since a great deal has happened over the same period which might have been expected to change the income distribution.

(c) Detailed examination of income distribution statistics may reveal some differences (or no differences), but in general one should be very cautious of such statements as "country X is more equal than country Y" or "country X is more equal (or unequal) now than it was some years ago." It may be that such statements are unambiguously true but it may also be the case that they depend on the use of a particular measure of inequality and would be contradicted by other measures of inequality. The Gini coefficient is more responsive than other measures to changes in distribution among the middle classes, while the coefficient of variation emphasizes more heavily inequality between the top and the middle of the income (or wealth) distribution. Atkinson's measure may be specified so as to emphasize either the high or the low end of the distribution. The Theil measure of inequality should be used when one wishes to "decompose" aggregate inequality into that inequality which exists *within* groups and that inequality which exists *between* groups. In analysing inequality, one should therefore choose the measure of inequality which is most sensitive to the type of inequality in which one is primarily interested; and that choice must depend, again, on the issue at hand.

(d) Comparing income distributions internationally is made more difficult by the considerable differences in statistical sources and social structures which exist, even among developed capitalist nations. Nevertheless, it appears that most measures of inequality would place Canada "in the middle rank" of OECD nations — "more equal" than some and "less equal" than others.

Chapter 3

Economic Inequality

3.1 Introduction

Chapter 2 discussed the distribution of annual income among Canadian family units, but noted that for many purposes this is an inadequate description of economic inequality in Canadian society. Economic inequality can be broadly conceived of as differential command over resources, but it has many different facets. How will the aspect of economic inequality which we choose to emphasize affect our perception of the extent of inequality? How will it colour our understanding of its causes?

In this chapter, we consider the distribution of economic power, of wealth and riches, and, to the extent that one can estimate it, of lifetime income and consumption. All of these topics are highly controversial. Data limitations are particularly important elements of the controversy underlying the discussion of economic power and of wealth. In addition, discussion of the inequality of lifetime consumption usually takes place within the context of assumptions which may not be universally accepted. This chapter will not, naturally, provide the last word on any of these issues, as they have a depth and a history which render resolution impossible for many generations to come, but it does attempt to outline the main features of current Canadian knowledge.

3.2 Economic Power — The Ownership and Control of Canadian Industry

The Canadian industrial structure is, to a very large degree, dominated by foreign ownership and a relatively small number of great family fortunes. Of the 100 largest industrial firms of Canada — as identified by the *Financial Post* in 1979 — 52 can be classified as foreign-owned, 20 as controlled by identified Canadian families, and nine as government-owned Crown corporations. These 100 corporations had total sales in 1979 of $118 billion. The 97 per cent of all Canadian businesses classified as "small" (i.e., with sales of less than $2 million) numbered some 640,000 in 1979 and had total sales of $109 billion (Gooding, 1980; *Financial Post*, 1979). As Marfels (1976) has shown, concentration levels in Canadian industry are significantly higher than in counterpart sectors in the U.S. Indeed, comparison with seven other developed countries, in a sample of nine industries, gives Canada" a clear overall lead" for the most concentrated industrial structure.[1] The vast majority of the dominant firms of Canadian industry are controlled by foreigners or by specific Canadian family interests.[2]

Both foreigners and the very wealthy are, however, excluded from most Canadian statistics on the distribution of wealth, since these statistics originate in a series of sample surveys of households, which necessarily exclude foreigners and which largely omit the very rich, since they are too few in number to be adequately captured in random samples of the general population. Discussion of the economically powerful must, therefore, rely on fragmentary data on particular wealthy individuals and families (e.g., Newman, 1975; Clement, 1975), and the occasional study of corporate interconnections (e.g., Niosi (1978), Statistics Canada, 61-517).

3.2.1 The Great Family Fortunes of Canada

Great family fortunes are clearly an important part of the Canadian picture, as the largest of them are very large by any standards. Figure 3-1 outlines the holdings of a branch of the Bronfman family in 1975. It is extremely difficult for an outsider to estimate the worth of these holdings, partly because they are continually changing.[3] One can get some idea, however, of the scale involved by noting that the assets of the Cadillac-Fairview subsidiary were $1.05 billion in 1978 and that the sale of the U.S. oil properties of the subsidiary company, Texas Pacific Oil Company, netted $2.3 billion in 1980.[4] Table 3-1 provides a partial list of the major companies controlled by the Weston, Black, Thomson, Desmarais and Irving families. Other families whose companies make the top 100 industries are the Schneider, Webster, Mara, Gordon, Bentley, Prentice, Sobey, McLean and Child families. Among the top 50 merchandisers of 1979 one can count 20 foreign-controlled enterprises and 26 family firms. In addition to those families already mentioned, they include the Eaton, Steinberg, Wolfe

---

[1]Australia, Germany, France, Japan, Sweden, Switzerland, U.S.A. — the smaller populations of Australia, Sweden and Switzerland indicate that our relatively limited domestic market cannot totally explain our high degree of industrial concentration.

[2]The picture is even clearer for the second hundred industrials on the *Financial Post* list (total sales 78/79 of $18.9 billion) — 64 are foreign-controlled, 20 controlled by identifiable families or estates, 9 are Crown corporations and 7 are either widely held or controlled by unknown groups of investors.

[3]Newman (1978:17) estimates "at least $7 billion" and provides a highly readable account of the origins of this vast fortune in bootlegging during Prohibition in the U.S. Table 3-1 does not include the holdings of Edper Investments (Trizec Corp. (58.26 per cent), Brascan (51 per cent), Mico (99.69 per cent) and 136 others) which is controlled by a different branch of the family.

[4]The Bronfmans retained the 4.2 million acres of oil properties held by Texas Pacific outside the United States. *Globe and Mail,* Report on Business, 8-4-80.

Table 3-1

ILLUSTRATIVE LIST OF CANADIAN COMPANIES
CONTROLLED BY FIVE CANADIAN FAMILIES (JULY, 1979)

Weston	Black	Thomson	Desmarais	Irving
B. C. Packers	Massey-Ferguson	Thomson Newspapers	Power Corp.	Irving Oil
Loblaws	Perkins Engines	Hudson's Bay Co.	Laurentide Financial	Saint John Shipbuilding
Weston Bakeries	Argus Corp.	Simpson's	Canada Steamship	Saint John Pulp and Paper
Bowes	Standard Broadcasting	Zellers	Davie Shipbuilding	Consolidated Fisheries
Neilson	Dominion Stores	Scottish & York Insurance	Consolidated Bathurst	Kent Homes
Super Valu	General Bakeries	McCallum Transport	Kingsway Transport	Chipman Timber
Nabob	Hollinger Argus	Fields Stores	Montreal Trust	Atlantic Truck & Trailer
Eddy Paper	Labrador Mining	International Thomson	Great West Life	N. B. Publishing
Donlands Dairy	CFRB, CJAD	Woodbridge	Voyageur Colonial	First Maritime Mining
& 166* others	&70* others	& 119* others	& 208* others	& 156* others

(* = approximate number)
Source: Statistics Canada 61:517 and Calura, special tabulation.

Figure 3-1 BRONFMAN FAMILY HOLDINGS — 1975

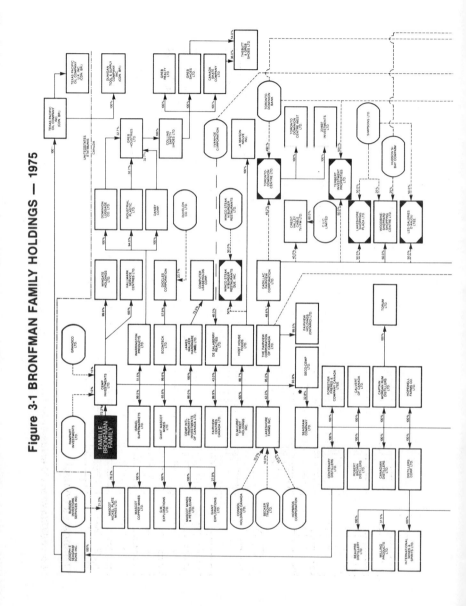

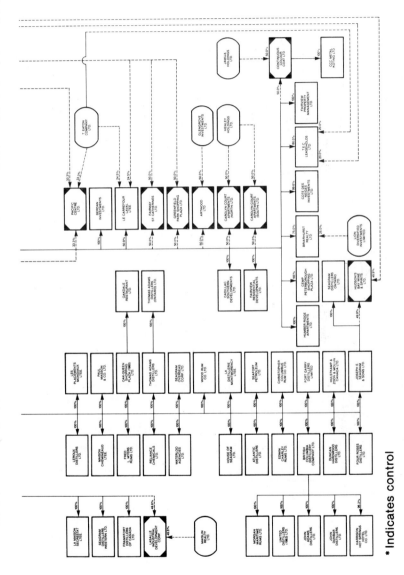

* Indicates control

Source (Statistics Canada 61 — 517)

(Oshawa Group), Billes (Canadian Tire), Woodward, Scrymgeour (Westburne), Kay, Posluns (Dylex), Cohen (General Distributing), Richardson, Reitmans, and Birks families (and a dozen others). Other sectors show the same picture. As many have noted (e.g., Porter, 1965: 241), it is a very different picture from the U.S., where dispersal of stock ownership has produced, much more frequently, a separation between ownership and control.[5] After examining the 146 private Canadian-owned companies which had assets of more than $100 million in 1975, Niosi (1978:167) concludes, "Of the 136 companies for which we possess information, 68 per cent are controlled by individuals, groups of associates or by families."[6]

Although these families control, in some cases, billions of dollars in assets and hundreds of millions in annual investment,[7] the probability of any of them being selected in the random sample of 15,000 families from the Canadian population on which wealth distribution statistics are based is nearly zero, and the probability of their co-operating in such a survey is almost certainly even less. Their holdings do not therefore, appear in the statistics cited in Table 3-2 and 3-3 which follow.[8] They do, however exist.

3.2.2 The Distribution of Economic Power

Do the very rich have "economic power"? If so, how might one measure it? To answer this we have to attempt some definition of "power," which is not an easy task. A dictionary definition is "control, authority, or influence over others," so as a starting point one might define "economic power" as "that control, authority or influence over others which arises from the ownership of property." Defined in this way, it is obvious that the owner of a firm employing, say, 5,000 people has control, authority and influence over a great many people, and that economic power is very unequally distributed, since he can control their work and can often fire any of them, while they individually, can do little to affect him. Sometimes, however, he *cannot* fire particular employees (e.g., if they are protected by a union and a collective agreement). In this case his authority is constrained, as it is also constrained in his dealings with other corporations and with the government.[9]

---

[5]Nyman and Silberston (1978: 97) have however argued, "ownership interests control, in one way or another, the majority of large U.K. industrial companies."

[6]Since several "managerial" firms (e.g., CP, Bell) are among the largest, 57 per cent of the $109 billion in corporate assets in these 136 firms was in management controlled firms, 43 per cent in family, group and individually controlled firms (Niosi, 1978:80).

[7]In July 1980, Edper (Edgar and Peter Bronfman) controlled Brascan, which had about $1 billion on hand for investment, due largely to the sale of its Brazilian properties. Brascan's subsidiary, Western Mines, had "between $500 million and $600 million of its own to invest." *Globe and Mail,* Report on Business, July 22, 1980.

[8]As a result, their investment incomes do not appear in the statistics of Chapter 2. In 1978, income distribution statistics did not include 25 per cent of total investment income (13-207: 33).

[9]All "power" is of course constrained to some degree.

The real issue then is not whether economic power exists or whether it is unequally distributed, but the degree to which it is constrained. What one might call the "Chicago" position argues that economic power is so constrained as to be practically meaningless, amounting only to the power to make bad business decisions and be driven from the market place. In this view, a perfectly competitive market with no externalities and no distortions offers no alternative to the owner but profit-maximizing behaviour (i.e., a unique course of action.) It is therefore seen as uninteresting that the Thomson family, through their ownership of Zeller's, Simpson's and The Hudson's Bay Co., controls some $2.8 billion in department store sales (30.4 per cent of the market — see Gray, 1980) as well as having substantial media and newspaper holdings. The consumer, or rather consumers in aggregate, determine through decentralized individual decisions what will sell, and those who do not provide it at minimum cost go bankrupt. Hence economic power, in anything but a very transitory sense, is not an issue.

Galbraith (1967) is less convinced of market perfection and argues that the economic power of the technostructure of large corporations is essentially constrained only by other large economic actors, such as big unions and big government (he saw owners as an ineffectual breed). A "political economy" perspective sees fewer effective constraints on economic power since it regards middle managers as having little independence of action, and views government as essentially subject to the manipulations of large corporations. This perspective expects that individuals will use all the resources at their command, both political and economic, to advance their interests, which are both political and economic. The economically powerful have, in this view, some conflicting interests, such as which company should get approval to build a pipeline, and some common interests, such as opposition to a redistribution of wealth. Their aim in politics is to ensure that government is in the position of arbitrating their conflicting interests while safeguarding their common interests. The "political economy" viewpoint then sees great economic power as inevitably conveying political influence. Campaign contributions, corporate lobbying,[10] the potential rewards which a business career can offer someone after their civil service or political career, personal influence and elite friendships[11], the ability to withold or divert investment from areas where jobs

---

[10] *Dun's Review* (1979: 32), for example, in the U.S. refers approvingly to "the increasingly sophisticated and successful lobbying efforts of big business — as evidenced by such recent Congressional victories as defeat of labour law reform and the passage of legislation to reduce the capital gains tax."

[11] The "political economy" viewpoint would see as entirely predictable Peter Newman's description of the relationship of Pierre Trudeau and Paul Desmarais of Power Corporation (see Table 3-2) "The channels of influence that link Power Corporation and the federal Liberal party carry considerable two-way traffic. For Paul Desmarais, the ultimate expression of power is to feel history as it is being made. It's when he is being consulted by the prime minister and premiers on options before they become policies that he really begins to fulfill every great entrepreneur's dream" (1975: 57).

are needed (see Kimber, 1980), all give political leverage to those who possess economic power.

How might economic power best be measured? Net assets may indicate wealth, but be a poor guide to assets controlled. Corporate control is often possible with much less than majority ownership.[12] In 1979, for example, the Black brothers controlled Dominion Stores (sales of $2.2 billion, 25,492 employees) by holding 100 per cent of Warspite, which held 73.7 per cent of Ravelston, which held 43.46 per cent of Hollinger-Argus, which held 96.18 per cent of Argus Corporation, which held 30.14 per cent of Dominion Stores. Through the Argus Corporation, the Black brothers also controlled numerous mining interests and Standard Broadcasting and their subsidiaries, sometimes by majority and sometimes with minority stock positions. The prorated value of their shareholding in Dominion Stores or their 80 other companies does not approach the value of the assets they can control.[13] Similarly, Paul Desmarais controlled companies with an estimated $7 billion in assets in 1975 (Newman, 1975: 64) via a pyramid of holdings centred in Power Corporation, Canada Steamship Lines and The Investors Group, but his personal net worth in 1980 was estimated at only $75 to $100 million (Booth, 1980). Gross assets controlled are therefore probably as good a measure as one can get of the economic muscle of an individual or family, but economic muscle must be placed in the context of where it is exercised. The Irving fortune, for example, may be smaller than some of the others of Table 3-1, and their influence on the Canadian political system as a whole may not be as large, but their clout within the Maritime provinces (and especially New Brunswick, where the majority of their 166 corporations are situated) is quite considerable.[14]

The definition of economic power as that "control, authority or influence over others which arises from the ownership of property" is somewhat restrictive, however, since not all major Canadian companies are controlled by their owners. The second largest Canadian resident corporate enterprise (after General Motors) is the Canadian Pacific conglomerate (CP Rail, CP Ships, CP Air, Marathon Realty, Pan-Canadian Petroleum, Algoma Steel, Pacific Logging, Cominco and roughly 161 others) which in

---

[12]Most of the "top 200" are foreign-controlled, often 100 per cent owned by their foreign parent. Hence, minority control does not, in aggregate, typify the Canadian scene (Berkowitz, 1976).

[13]The Black brothers initially acquired control of Argus Corporation in 1978. They had acquired 22.4 per cent of the voting shares of Ravelston (which then controlled Argus) from their father and purchased another 47.2 per cent for $18.4 million, about half of which was financed by partners. In a series of complicated manoeuvres, other stockholders were bought out and the corporate structure re-arranged to its current form (see Ross, 1979).

[14]Newman (1975:202) quotes K. C. Irving. "I don't think politics and business mix. New Brunswick is too small for politics." The population of New Brunswick is roughly one-third that of greater Toronto.

1979 had assets of $8.9 billion, sales of $6.3 billion and 106,650 employees (Hughes, 1979). Since its share ownership is widely dispersed, however, effective control rests in its board of directors and especially in its chairman and chief executive officer, Ian Sinclair.[15] Sociologists have therefore tended to define power as "the capacity to mobilize resources" (Clement, 1975:3). Porter (1965) and Clement (1975) have concentrated on the members of the boards of directors of dominant Canadian corporations and have seen them as the economic elite which controls corporate power in Canada.

There is nothing, however, quite like owning the store. Chief executives and directors who do not have a substantial equity share may possess great power in the sense of a capacity to mobilize vast amounts of capital, but it is, to some degree, held at the sufferance of their fellow board members. A hired manager (or a board member) who does not continue to produce results can be replaced. Indeed, other board members have an incentive to replace him, since if he is not replaced the entire corporation can become vulnerable to a takeover bid. Owners do not have these worries. Whether we concentrate on the ownership of industry or on the economic elite which directs it is therefore an important theoretical point. Empirically, however, the numbers of people involved are very small in either case. By either of the above definitions, economic power is very highly concentrated in Canada.

3.3 The Distribution of Wealth and Riches

3.3.1 The Distribution of Wealth

How unequal is the distribution of wealth? In Canada, our data come primarily from the Survey of Consumer Finances.[16] Table 3-2 presents SCF estimates of the distribution of wealth in Canada in 1970 and 1977.

Of course, there is a vast difference between the relatively wealthy (top 10 per cent) and the very rich (top 1 per cent). Davies (1979) has made very careful adjustments to the 1970 Statistics Canada figures to correct for errors and omissions in the initial survey, and estimates that the top 10 per cent of Canadian families owned 58 per cent of all net assets, but of that, roughly a third (19.6 per cent) was owned by the top 1 per cent of families and over two-thirds (43.4 per cent) by the top 5 per cent. He estimates the

---

[15]Sinclair's 1979 salary was $568,515 (Blunn, 1980).

[16]As noted earlier, the relatively small random samples of the population cannot be expected to include any of the ultra rich. Davies (1979: 244) estimates that the 1970 Survey of Consumer Finance underestimated share ownership, in aggregate, by 8 per cent and total wealth by 46 per cent. He argues that the various errors and omissions of the 1970 survey roughly balance, so that, in aggregate, wealth distribution statistics do not require drastic revision — but that they are unreliable if one wishes to estimate ownership patterns on a disaggregated basis.

Table 3-2

THE WEALTH DISTRIBUTION OF CANADA
(AS MEASURED BY THE SURVEY OF CONSUMER FINANCE)
1970 AND 1977

| | Family Units Ranked by Wealth | | | | | | Family Units Ranked by Income -Share of Net Worth- | | |
| | Financial Assets | | Total Assets | | Net Worth | | | | |
Decile	1970	1977	1970	1977	1970	1977	1970	1977	Decile
(Share of) poorest 10%	0.0	0.0	0.0	0.0	-1.0	-0.6	4.4	4.0	lowest income 10%
2	0.1	0.1	0.2	0.3	-0.0	0.1	6.0	5.0	2
3	0.3	0.4	0.6	0.9	0.3	0.6	7.0	6.4	3
4	0.7	0.9	1.4	2.3	1.3	1.7	6.8	6.4	4
5	1.2	1.5	3.2	5.0	3.0	3.6	6.7	7.1	5
6	2.2	2.6	6.3	7.4	5.4	6.0	7.3	7.9	6
7	4.0	4.5	9.6	9.6	8.3	8.6	8.4	9.0	7
8	7.3	8.0	12.7	12.2	11.8	12.0	10.6	10.0	8
9	15.1	15.0	17.5	16.8	17.6	17.5	11.5	12.7	9
(Share of) richest 10%	69.1	67.0	48.5	45.6	53.3	50.6	31.3	31.6	highest income 10%

Financial assets = deposits, cash, bonds, stocks, mortgages, etc.
Total assets = financial assets, business equity, real estate, automobiles
Net Worth = total assets - debts.
Source: Oja, 1980: 352

Gini ratio of the total wealth distribution to be 0.746, which is considerably greater than the inequality of income distribution. If we look at the distribution of wealth *per adult* and update Davies' figures for the growth of GNP between 1970 and 1980 we get Table 3-3.

Neither Table 3-2 nor 3-3 reveals, however, that some forms of assets are very narrowly held in Canada. The Survey of Consumer Finances states that in 1970, 87.7 per cent of Canadian family units reported owning no publicly traded stock at all, while only 3.2 per cent reported owning $5,000 or more (Statistics Canada, 13-547:105). This evidence may be flawed (see Davies, 1979) but it clearly shows that direct stock ownership is restricted to a very small fragment of Canadian society.

Davies (1979:242) has estimated that stock ownership constitutes only approximately 9 per cent of the total assets of Canadian families. Other financial assets include equity in business interests, life insurance and funded pension plans, bonds, and deposits in banks and other financial institutions. For most Canadians, tangible assets such as houses, other real estate, automobiles and consumer durables are the main form of wealth holdings. Davies is considering, of course, wealth as comprehensively

Table 3-3

ESTIMATED WEALTH PER CANADIAN ADULT* — 1980

	Number (1)	Total net worth (Assets-debts) (2)	Share (3)	Per adult (2) ÷ (1)
TOP 1%	165,000	$146,361M	18.8%	$887,040
NEXT 4%	661,000	$187,623M	24.1%	$283,847
NEXT 5%	826,000	$110,549M	14.2%	$133,837
(TOTAL TOP 10%)	(1,653,000)	($444,534M)	(57.1%)	($268,925)
NEXT 10%	1,653,000	$126,120M	16.2%	$ 76,297
(TOTAL TOP 20%)	(3,306,000)	($570,654M)	(73.3%)	($172,611)
NEXT 40%	6,612,000	$200,857M	25.8%	$ 30,377
BOTTOM 40%	6,612,000	$ 6,228M	0.8%	$ 1,002
TOTALS	16,530,000	$778,519M	100.0%	$ 47,097

*i.e., wealth per household ÷ number of adults in household; M = million
Sources: Davies (1979)
         S.C. 91-202
         Bank of Canada 5/80

defined, i.e., the value of *all* assets (minus debts) owned by the household. Were the definition narrower, the share of the top 10 per cent or top 1 per cent would be higher.

3.3.2 The Distribution of Riches

Most students consider discussion of definitions to be a bore and accept them uncritically, impatient to get on to the "real thing." This is a great mistake, as apparently quite subtle differences in initial wordings can be magnified by their subsequent logical development into very different perceptions of the world around us. In 1977, the median wealth of Canadian family units was estimated by the Survey of Consumer Finance to be $22,298 (Oja, 1980: 351), a sum which could easily be accounted for by a car, a small bank balance, and a modest amount of equity in a home.[17] It is likely that many of those Canadians who are in fact in the *top* half of the wealth

---

[17]For example, a house bought for $40,000, with $5,000 down, if property values increase by 8 per cent per year for three years, will given the owner a net home equity of roughly $15,000. Add one fully paid for car and two to three weeks of average family income in the bank and the total may well approach $22,000. Fifty per cent of Canadian family units own less than this, according to the SCF. If the same degree of error was present in the 1977 as in the 1970 survey, this would be a substantial underestimate, but some improvements to the methodology were made and no independent re-estimates have yet been made for that year.

distribution do not consider themselves to be rich. When most people talk of "the rich," they usually appear to mean other people who have a large amount of money (or assets which can be converted to money) which they can spend as they wish. Suppose, therefore, that we had defined "riches" as an individual's stock of discretionary purchasing power, which might seem an unobjectionable, common-sense idea underlying wealth. We would then have had to define the difference between "discretionary" and "non-discretionary," and might well have adopted the idea that "non-discretionary" expenditures on assets are those expenditures which are socially required by one's occupation or work role.

It is a commonplace observation that some occupations require the ownership of tools (e.g., mechanics) or expensive clothing, and that some positions require entertaining, which mandates a certain size of house and quality of home furnishings. More importantly, some occupations, such as fishing or farming, require the possession of assets for which markets in Canada are poorly developed. These assets may be worth a great deal if sold, yet the owners cannot sell without fundamentally changing their occupation and lifestyle. Hence, the owners have a relatively small stock of purchasing power which can be used for personal consumption. The extent to which other ownership patterns are socially required would be a grey area of such a definition, but grey areas also exist in the computation of income in kind or of "wealth" in the standard definition. If we adopted the stock of discretionary purchasing power held by an individual as our idea of riches, we would probably have to exclude from its measurement most consumer durables (e.g., automobiles) and a good fraction of farm real estate and housing stock. We would also have to exclude the "transactions balances" which Canadians hold to finance current purchases.[18] Since most of the assets of the poorest 80 per cent of Canadian families are of exactly these types, the resulting riches would be distributed more unequally than "financial assets" (Column 1 of Table 3-3), which are considerably more unequally distributed than the total wealth of Canadians as conventionally defined. One would then make statements such as: "According to the SCF, over 70 per cent of the riches of Canada were owned by the richest 10 per cent of family units in 1977," rather than saying: "According to the SCF, 50.6% of the wealth (net worth) of Canada was owned by the richest 10 per cent of family units of 1977." Clearly, our idea of the extent of inequality would be considerably altered.

---

[18]Automobiles, farming equipment and some fraction of the housing stock could be seen as some of the intermediate inputs which are required to reproduce a given labour force at their appropriate work sites — i.e., not part of "riches" because if sold by their owners, they would merely have to be replaced.

Table 3-4

CANADIAN FAMILIES[1] WITH NET WORTH OVER $100,000,000 IN 1975
[AS IDENTIFIED BY NEWMAN, *THE CANADIAN ESTABLISHMENT*]

Bronfman (Figure 3-1)	Webster (Burns Foods, F.P. Publications[2] and 130[3] others)	Davis
Weston (Table 3-1)	Rathgeb (Comstock International)	Stewart
Thomson (Table 3-1)	Roman (Denison Mines-uranium)	Harvie (oil)
Eaton (Eaton stores)	Molsons (Molson Breweries and 87[3] others)	Meighen (Canada Trust)[4]
Taylor (Argus)[4]	Richardson (Richardson Securities)	McConnell
Irving (Table 3-1)	Bentley (Versatile Cornat, Canadian Forest Products and 105 others)	Bata (Bata Shoes)
McDougald (Argus)[4]		

[1]In some cases, individuals.
[2]F.P. Publications was sold to Thomson in early 1980.
[3]Approximate numbers, as of July 1979.
[4]Indicates non-control holdings; control relationships identified with S.C. 61-517 and a CALURA special tabulation.

3.3.3 At the Top of the Pyramid

At the summit of the Canadian wealth pyramid sit a very small number of extremely wealthy families. Table 3-4 presents the names and major identifiable corporate interests of those families listed by Newman (1975: 269-295) as having net worth of more than $100 million in 1975. This list is almost certainly incomplete. The Wolfe family of Toronto, for example, owns 100 per cent of the equity of the Oshawa Group of companies. Its 1978-79 sales were $1.3 billion, assets were $287.9 million and the liabilities/equity ratio was 2 (*Financial Post*, 1979, 53; Hughes, 1979). Hence, it appears likely that their personal net worth is in the region of $100 million but one cannot be sure. Newman's list also excludes the reclusive Reichmann family, owners of the privately held Olympia and York Developments Limited, with assets estimated at "as much as $3 billion" (Poole, 1980). How many other Canadian families number among the ultra-rich? Newman identified a further 138 families as having net worth of over $20 million (but this is likely very incomplete). Porter (1965: 274) estimated that the economic elite of Canada in 1955 consisted of 985 people — all of whom were men — with directorships in dominant corporations and financial institutions. Clement (1975: 213) estimated the corporate elite to number 946 in 1972, of whom 282 held multiple directorships — "a very select group."[19] Porter's and Clement's "economic elite" includes, however, key corporate officers whose personal wealth (though substantial) does not approach that of the companies they control.

3.4 Adjustments to Measures of Income Inequality

In Chapter 2 we noted that the distribution of annual money income among family units is a poor indicator of the inequality of economic well-being. It omits income from capital gains, it omits the wealth families may own and it omits consideration of how many people share each family unit's income. Since we really have no reliable information on the incomes of the very rich, we cannot consider how these factors would affect *total* inequality, but we can ask how the distribution of income discussed in Chapter 2 would be affected if we considered the distribution of wealth among "ordinary" families (i.e., those sampled by the SCF) or the fact that family units differ in size.

Obviously, the welfare of a family depends partly on how many mouths there are to feed with a given income. Since some costs (such as rent) do not increase in direct proportion with family size, Wolfson (1979) has adjusted the distribution of income to reflect the number of individuals in each family unit by deflating family income by the number of "adult equivalents" present.[20] This adjustment produces a decrease in the Gini ratio of approximately 5 per cent and a decline in the coefficient of variation of approximately 15 per cent, while the share of the top 5 per cent declines from 16.3 per cent to 16.1 per cent, and the share of the bottom 20 per cent increases from 4.3 per cent to 5.5 per cent (Wolfson, 1979: 137). These aggregate changes in measured inequality conceal, however, substantial differences between age cohorts. The correction of family income for family size tends to increase inequality among younger cohorts, while decreasing measured inequality among older cohorts.

Since owning your own home means that you do not have to pay rent, home owners receive an income "in kind" whose size depends on the equity they have built up in their homes. Allowing for this would not produce much change in the estimated income of younger families with heavy mortgages, but among older families who have paid off their mortgages the

---

[19] An insider's estimate was "Oh, sure, there is an establishment in Canada. It consists of about a thousand wealthy families. It works by exclusion but once in a while a new name pops up, like Paul Desmarais, and then he has to be included in." George Black (Argus Corporation and Canadian Breweries) quoted in Newman (1975:178). It is his two sons, Conrad and Montegu, who now control Argus.

[20] The "adult equivalent" is calculated from the Statistics Canada poverty lines (see Chapter 4) which express the rate at which expenditures on necessities increase with family size. Lazear and Michael (1980) have investigated the implications of alternative weightings for family size in the calculation of the distribution of per capita real income.

saving may be quite a large fraction of money income. On balance, including the imputed income from home ownership tends to produce a somewhat smaller decrease in total measured income inequality than that produced when family size is considered. For the younger age groups the change is minimal. For older cohorts measured income inequality decreases (despite the fact that home equity is more unequally distributed than income) because some groups (such as rural households) tend to be both low in money income and high in home ownership.

Since home ownership is only a part of wealth one should also adjust the estimated income distribution for total net worth. Wolfson computed the value of an annuity which could be purchased with the assets of each family sampled in the 1970 Survey of Consumer Finance, and added that annuity to their annual income for 1969. Since net worth is quite unequally distributed[21] (see Table 3-2), including the annuity value of wealth in a measurement of the income distribution tends to produce a fairly substantial increase in measured income inequality. Since wealth ownership is concentrated in the upper tail of the income distribution (see Table 3-2), measured income inequality shows a sharper increase for indices of inequality (such as the coefficient of variation) which are sensitive to the upper tail of the distribution than for indices (such as the Gini ratio) which are more sensitive to the middle of the distribution. A higher rate of interest means, naturally, that a given amount of wealth will produce more income. The assumption one makes about interest rates is, therefore, also crucial to the estimate one obtains of the impact of wealth on the income distribution.

Considering all age groups, the result of all three adjustments (family size, home ownership and value of wealth) is to record a small decrease (.39 to .36 or .37) in measured income inequality, if inequality is measured by the Gini ratio. If inequality is measured by the coefficient of variation, a small decline (.65 to .64) is evident after all adjustments if the interest rate is 4 per cent. If the interest rate is 10 per cent, however, measured inequality increases by about 20 per cent (from .65 to .79). (Wolfson, 1979: 137). The differences between age cohorts are, however, quite considerable and Wolfson cautions, "It is not simply the case that high income families have large amounts of net worth, with the opposite for low income families" (139). There is a substantial correlation between annual income and net worth, but it is considerably less than perfect, as we can infer from Table 3-2 where the seventh and eighth columns show *income deciles* by net worth. The top *income* decile owns (by SCF estimate) about 31 per cent of wealth, but the top *wealth* decile owns about 51 per cent. Obviously some people who

---

[21]Since Davies' estimate of the top decile's share is 58 per cent while Wolfson uses the SCF figure of 53 per cent, Wolfson may be underestimating the impact of wealth inequality.

are in the top 10 per cent of wealth holders are not in the top 10 per cent of income receivers. Some older families with paid-off mortgages may well possess more net worth than families with higher current incomes, but heavier debts and mortgages.

Possession of assets yields returns both in current interest (or dividend) payments and in capital gains. Both sorts of returns produce an increase in the purchasing power of wealth holders and should be included in a discussion of the impact of wealth on the distribution of income. Capital gains (and losses) on the stock market are especially important for upper-income groups. If, for example, the stock market falls in average value, the owners of stocks will, on average, realize losses on their holdings. Since these are the people at the top of the distributions of income and wealth, the inclusion of capital gains and losses in a measure of income distribution will then mean that indices of inequality will show a decrease. Over a longer period of time, however, stock market gains tend to dominate losses; thus, including capital gains will mean that the measured share of upper-income groups tends to increase. Bhatia (1976) has shown that over the period 1960-64 the inclusion of capital gains would have increased the Gini ratio of the U.S. income distribution by about 5 per cent. Naturally, measurement of the wealth distribution (and especially the share of the top 5 per cent) is even more sensitive to year-to-year vagaries in the stock market.

Capital gains (and losses) can also be very important in an inflationary environment. If inflation is unanticipated it will benefit those who hold most of their wealth as real assets (such as houses or land) and those who have debts fixed in monetary value (e.g., people owing money on mortgages). People who have assets (such as a pension entitlement) which are fixed on dollar amounts will tend to lose. Since most of the poor have little or no debt (presumably because few institutions will lend to them — see Statistics Canada, 13-547: 166) they are unlikely to benefit from the depreciation of the real value of debt. The decline in the real value of pension income will, however, affect older people very heavily. Their decline in welfare will be greater if inflation in the prices of necessities (e.g., heat and food) is greater than inflation in the general price index. Manga (1977) therefore concluded that the old and the poor were the principal losers from inflation in Canada in the 1970-1975 period while the principal gainers were young, middle and upper-middle income groups, especially those who had just purchased homes.[22]

Of course, in the long run, expectations and behaviour become adjusted to inflation, and if inflation is correctly anticipated its distributional

---

[22]If the policy measure chosen to fight inflation is that of allowing aggregate demand to fall and unemployment to rise this unemployment will be concentrated among the working poor — i.e., for them the cure for inflation is worse than the disease.

consequences may almost disappear.[23] The main issue is the speed and accuracy with which expectations of inflation adjust. If inflation is correctly anticipated, mortgage interest rates will, for example, rise to reflect these anticipations. This interest rate rise will erode the benefits of borrowing to buy real estate and will increase the earnings of the pension funds which invest in mortgages. Fully anticipated inflation has few long-run impacts on the real economy. Unanticipated inflation is another matter. Unanticipated inflation imposes on everyone a giant lottery wherein some (e.g., homeowners) gain and some (e.g., pensioners) lose.

Nordhaus (1973) argues that under a variety of assumptions inflation is an equalizing factor in the long-run distribution of economic welfare. Wolff (1979) found that in the 1969-75 inflation in the U.S. the largest gainers were home-owners with large mortgages. Since the real value of stocks fell relative to other assets and since these are largely owned by top wealth-holders, this inflationary period saw a decline in wealth inequality. Minarik (1979) examined the impact of inflation on the U.S. income distribution (comprehensively defined to include capital gains, etc.) and found that inflation hurt primarily upper-income groups, while low-income households suffered only small losses, and the gains and losses of middle-income groups roughly balanced. Tables 3-2 and 2-2 indicate, however, that in Canada the 65 per cent increase in the price level between 1970 and 1977 may have imposed substantial gains and losses on particular individuals, but *in aggregate* the distributions of income and wealth underwent very little change.[24] In practice, the quasi-random reshuffling of individual fortunes is probably the most important consequence of inflation.

3.5 Inequality of Lifetime Consumption

Up to this point we have been, for the most part, simply counting the income and the material wealth of current Canadian families. This has the great advantage of concreteness. Corrections may be required for incomplete surveys or biased responses but fundamentally we are concerned with a currently observable entity. We have, however, omitted "human wealth," or the prospects of future earnings which an individual is likely to receive. If, for example, we look only at people's current wealth and income we might see a bus driver and a medical intern as being in the same economic position; but the latter can look forward to a very much higher income soon after beginning practice. Their economic expectations are thus fundamen-

---

[23]Nordhaus (1973: 492) estimates the "tax on real balances" due to a 1 per cent rise in the inflation rate as involving a dead-weight loss of $0.30 per year per capita.

[24]Again, the possible deficiencies of the SCF must be mentioned — if it under-represents top wealth-holders, who own most stocks, it could not be expected to pick up the effects of rises and falls in stock prices.

tally different. If it is frequently true that families have low incomes now because they are now investing in "human capital" (see Chapter 7), but they will have high incomes in future years when this investment "pays off," then we will overestimate the degree of "true" inequality if we look only at their current incomes.

Unfortunately there is no known way of predicting the future with certainty.[25] In order to estimate the inequality of lifetime earnings we must forecast the earnings individuals are likely to receive in future years, as well as how these earnings will be combined within families. Total future earnings plus current wealth give the total resources which a family will have available over its lifetime. Out of these resources, a family can finance a certain amount of consumption, and if it is the fully-informed, forward-looking, utility-maximizing family of neoclassical economic theory, it will choose an optimal lifetime consumption level (which implies a program of asset accumulation while working, and of dissaving while retired, of the sort discussed in Chapter 10.4).

Irvine (1980) has examined the distribution across Canadian male-headed family units of such consumption levels, adjusted for family size, since he argues that it is a "more meaningful measure of economic well-being."[26] Predicted earnings are estimated on the basis of education, age, area of work, occupation, etc., for men and for those women estimated to be employed. These predicted values are then adjusted, both for non-transitory permanent deviations from predicted income and for transitory variations from permanent income.

Two factors may imply that "lifetime" income exhibits less measured inequality than annual income. In Chapter 7, Figure 7-1 illustrates the case where earnings paths cross; i.e., some occupations may have relatively low pay to start and high pay later on. In addition, variations from year-to-year may mean greater income inequality in any given year than if incomes were averaged over a number of years. If, on the other hand, some individuals commence working with a low salary, which stays low, while others start with a high salary, which gets higher, inequality in annual earnings may be less than inequality in life-time earnings. On balance, Irvine estimates the distribution of lifetime "consumption annuities" to be unambiguously more equal than that of annual money income. The decline in measured inequality is of roughly the same order of magnitude as the decline when

---

[25]Even the individuals concerned may incorrectly estimate future returns from education if they look at the current earnings of older cohorts among whom that education was scarcer. See Welch (1979).

[26]Some sociologists agree — e.g., Rainwater (1974: 36).

income inequality is measured across "economic" rather than "census" families (see Chapter 3.1).[27]

The simulation model of Davies (1980: 23) examined the distribution of the present value of lifetime resources of young couples, comparing the distribution of life earnings to the distribution of life earnings plus inheritances (see Chapter 10). His base-run estimate was that the top quintile would receive, from earnings and inheritances, 40.4 per cent of the lifetime resources available while the bottom quintile would receive 5.3 per cent. Irvine's methodology starts from characteristics of respondents to the 1970 Survey of Consumer Finances, but ignores the possibility of inheritance. He estimates the share of the top quintile in lifetime consumption annuities to be 36 per cent and the share of the bottom quintile to be 6.8 per cent. Looking simply at annual income in Irvine's sample, one would have said that the share of the top 20 per cent of families was 38.5 per cent and the share of the poorest 20 per cent of families was 5.3 per cent (Irvine, 1980: Tables 2 and 4). The underlying difficulties of earnings estimation, representativeness of the samples, and data reliability ought to caution us against placing too exact an interpretation on these numbers; they ought to be seen as approximate estimates. Hence, it is the stability of shares of total income, rather than their fairly minor changes, which is the most remarkable. It appears that lifetime earnings, (or lifetime resources available or lifetime consumption annuities) are somewhat more equally distributed than annual income across Canadian families, but not much.[28]

3.6 International Comparisons

International comparisons of the distribution of wealth are even more hazardous than comparisons of income distributions, since very few countries publish statistics on the distribution of wealth that are even mildly reliable. The U.S. and the U.K. are exceptions, but comparison of their figures on wealth distribution with Canada's is impeded because they

---

[27]For the population under consideration (male-headed family units) the Gini index for annual money income is .3294 while the Gini index for consumption annuities is .2949, a fall of roughly 10 per cent. The fall in coefficient of variation is 21 per cent, and that in measures which emphasize heavily the lower tail is even greater (i.e., the Atkinson measure where e = 2). But since the population covered excludes female-headed families whose incidence of poverty is particularly high (see Table 4-3) and since there is, among other things, no provision for family dissolution, generalizations of these results to the lowest income groups should be very cautiously made. Orcutt (1976: 93) emphasizes Morgan's (1974) point "Changes in family composition, along with labour force participation, so dominate family economic well-being that nothing else seems to matter very much."

[28]In 1978, considering families alone, the top 20 per cent received 38.6 per cent of annual income and the bottom 20 per cent received 6.2 per cent (Statistics Canada 13-207: 85).

are presented on an individual (not household) basis and are derived by quite a different methodology. As we have noted, the survey method used in Canada to estimate the distribution of wealth tends to leave out the very wealthy and is exposed to the chance of inaccurate answers by respondents.[29] The U.S. and U.K. therefore use the "estate multiplier" method which estimates the wealth distribution of the living from the size of the estates left by the dead.

In any given year, a certain fraction Pa of those people of age "a" die. If they leave an estate, the worth of that estate is evaluated, in the U.S. and U.K., for inheritance taxes.[30] Each decedent can then be held to "represent" a certain number of living persons (i.e., 1/Pa), and the size distribution of estates can be adjusted for the number of living fortunes which each represents, to give an estimate of the size distribution of total wealth. For example, if 1/1,000 of 30-year-olds and 1/10 of 87-year-olds generally die every year, it is assumed that for each estate left by a 30-year-old, 1,000 other similar living people have assets of the same amount as the estate, and for each estate left by an 87-year-old, ten living people have assets of the same size. Adding up the estimated wealth of all age groups gives the total wealth distribution of the society.

Of course, the probability of death Pa depends on more than just age, and to give an accurate picture of how many living people a decedent "represents" one must be as accurate as possible in estimating death probability. Since males and non-whites have lower life expectancies, Pa must be calculated separately by race and sex. Since wealthier individuals tend to live longer, Pa must be adjusted for social class (U.K.) or size of estate (U.S.) (see Harrison, 1979:9).

Corrections are also necessary to account for the fact that wealth for estate tax purposes is not quite the same as wealth for the living. Some assets (such as pensions) may cease on death, while some (e.g., life insurance policies) may change in value. Other assets, such as a business, may be worth less in the open market than as a going concern. Other corrections must be made for property held jointly with one's spouse, but a major problem with the estate-multiplier method is that many people leave either no estate at all on death[31], or an estate that is too small to be evaluated for estate duty purposes.

The estate-multiplier method is therefore best able to estimate the share of top wealth-holders in total wealth, since their total wealth (as derived from the estate-multiplier method) can be expressed as a fraction of

---

[29]"Response error" can occur if the respondent forgets to include a particular asset, if he or she cannot accurately estimate its worth (e.g., family heirlooms) or if there is a desire to deceive.
[30]There is no federal estate tax or succession duty in Canada and most provinces likewise have no inheritance tax. Hence the estate-multiplier method cannot be used in Canada.
[31]In the U.S. some 55 to 60 per cent of individuals receive no inheritance at all (Blinder, 1973).

the nation's total wealth (as derived from balance sheet totals and national income figures). Table 3-5 presents the results of Harrison (1979: 28).

Table 3-5

THE DISTRIBUTION OF WEALTH — USA AND BRITAIN

	Share of the Top		
	1%	5%	10%
USA 1969 (individuals)	25.1%	43.7%	53.0%
Britain 1970 (individuals)	30.1%	54.3%	69.4%

The greater inequality of wealth in Britain may, Harrison suggests, be due to the larger role played there by inheritance. Here, however, is the Achilles heel of the estate tax method since it relies on the presumption that the wealthy do not anticipate their demise with sufficient foresight to avoid death duties.[32] Where succession duties are heavy, "estate planning" can become a minor art form, where lawyers and accountants create intricate mazes of foundations, fiduciary trusts, lifetime interests and trusts between grandparents and grandchildren, whose ultimate aim is to ensure that each generation dies legally penniless yet materially comfortable. Cooper (1979) details some of the intricacies of preferred stock recapitalization, charitable split-interest trusts and other devices which have enabled some families of immense wealth (e.g., the duPonts, with a fortune of roughly $500,000,000) to reduce estate taxation to nuisance levels. He concludes that the U.S. estate tax is largely a voluntary tax, paid only by those who do not really want to avoid it. Titmuss (1962, Ch. 5) reached a similar conclusion for Britain. One must therefore, suspect that an unknown fraction of the wealth of the rich escapes Table 3-5.[33]

3.7 Summary

To answer the question, "How much economic inequality is there?" one must first specify:

(a) inequality of what;
(b) inequality among whom;
(c) inequality how measured.

---

[32]Gifts made within three (U.S.) or seven (U.K) years of death are taxed as part of the estate. However, as Gerald Grosvenor, Sixth Duke of Westminister who made his first will at 18 and whose family fortune of between £200 million and £500 million is safely in the hands of 11 family trusts, puts it, "The whole concept is planning ahead in case I fell in front of a number eight bus" (J. Cunningham, 1979).

[33]Whalley (1974) used stamp duty statistics in the U.K. to estimate that perhaps 7 per cent of wealth passing between generations was as tax exempt gifts and thus, escaped estate duty. This exempt wealth is "probably" concentrated among the top percentiles. Cooper emphasizes that such outright gifts are only one of many tax avoidance methods and have the significant disadvantage, unlike trusts, of a surrender of control.

Our perception of economic inequality will depend on these specifications, and our perception of inequality may change when different authors, using slightly different specifications, suggest amendments to the measurement of inequality. Of course, these different measurements may offer different perceptions of inequality but they do not change it. In this chapter we have outlined many of the amendments to the measurement of inequality which are necessary once one moves beyond the simplistic use of annual income as a criterion. One can consider these to be different dimensions of inequality, and the dimension one emphasizes should depend largely on the problem at hand.

Those interested in political science or the political economy of policy formulation will probably be most interested in the distribution of economic power. Those interested in social-class attitudes will emphasize lifetime income and consumption. Government policymakers who, for example, want to know whether encouraging home ownership increases or decreases inequality, will be interested in including the value of home ownership in measures of income inequality. These are all dimensions of inequality, but since the most sophisticated economic studies (e.g., Davies, Irvine, Wolfson) have only been done once, one cannot really answer the question that is most interesting to many — i.e., "what is the *trend* of economic inequality in Canada? Is it increasing, decreasing or remaining constant?" It is by this sort of global question that many judge existing social and political institutions, but unfortunately, we do not yet know whether movements (or lack of movements) in each of the dimensions of inequality are correlated or necessarily linked.

Those figures that are available over a period of time in Canada show either a constant level of wealth inequality or a slight tendency to increased family income inequality (see MacLeod, 1980). In the U.S., Henle (1980) has noted a "slow but persistent" trend to greater inequality among the earnings of men over the last 20 years, while female earnings inequality showed no real trend.[34] Whether the inequality of comprehensively defined family income or lifetime command over resources shows a similar long-run trend is, as yet, not known.

---

[34]Female earnings are more unequal than male, as well as being lower. A trend to greater inequality of male earnings was evident in aggregate, and when earnings were disaggregated by full-time year-round workers and others in total and by occupation and industry.

Chapter 4

Poverty and Inequality

Material welfare has no significance except in its relation to men's feelings and as an element in the psychological state called happiness. And the extent of a man's happiness depends on the number and intensity of the desires which he is able to satisfy relative to the number and intensity of those which he is not able to satisfy . . . . in the search for material welfare, our modern civilisation under conditions of industrial progress is continually manufacturing new and previously un-wanted sources of pleasure, so that the old luxuries become the new necessities, alike for those who can and those who cannot afford them. Hence where there is a great inequality of purchasing power, a continuous increase in the statistical total of goods and services produced per head will no doubt enable a larger and larger proportion of the people to satisfy certain wants, but will, equally certainly, increase the number of wants which the majority desire to satisfy, and only the minority can.

Josiah C. Wedgwood, The Economics of Inheritance, 1929.

4.1 Introduction

What is the relationship between inequality and poverty? Has our increasing GNP largely eliminated poverty in Canada? Or is a redistribution of income necessary to reduce the distinctions between "rich" and "poor" in our society? In this chapter, we will consider the alternative definitions of "poverty" which exist in Canada and the connection between these concepts of poverty and the concept of inequality. We examine the problem of measuring poverty and we discuss, briefly, who "the poor" are in Canada.

4.2 Defining the Poverty Line

There is no real agreement on the definition of a "poverty line" in Canada today. As Table 4-1 indicates, the four major alternative definitions use widely differing cut-off points. Using the criteria adopted by the Special Senate Committee on Poverty in 1971, a family of four which had an income in 1978 of less than $11,876 would be classed as "poor." Using the definition of poverty adopted by Statistics Canada in 1961 ("updated" in column 3)

Table 4-1

POVERTY LINES IN CANADA — 1978

Size of Family Unit	CCSD	Senate	Statistics Canada Updated	Statistics Canada — Revised		
				Canada Average	Large Cities*	Rural Areas
1	4,549	5,096	3,527	4,459	4,855	3,528
2	7,572	8,481	5,878	6,281	7.036	5,119
3	9,089	10,179	7,051	8.015	8.977	6,530
4	10,605	11,876	8,226	9,531	10,677	7,769
5	12,121	13,575 ⎫		10,656	12,004	8,682
6	13,638	15,209 ⎬ 9,403		11,696	14,269	9,528
7	15,154	16,972 ⎭		12,824	14,369	10,447

* Cities of 500,000 population or over.
CCSD — Canadian Council on Social Development
Senate — Special Senate Committee on Poverty
Source: Caskie (1979: 11-12)

such a family would be classed as poor only if its income was less than $8,226 — a difference of $3,650 or over 44 per cent!

Naturally, such widely varying definitions of the "poverty line" imply that a much larger percentage of the Canadian population will be classed as poor under the Senate committee definition of poverty than under either of the Statistics Canada definitions. These different classifications of the "poor" and "non-poor" will tend to shape our perceptions of the entire issue of poverty. Caskie (1979:26), for example, calculates that 2.8 million Canadians were "poor" in 1976 according to the "revised" Statistics Canada criterion (column 4), but by Senate Committee definition 5.4 million lived in poverty. Whether one sees poverty as a large and continuing problem of Canadian society or as a small and diminishing aspect of it will be greatly influenced by the percentage of our population which is classified as living in poverty. Our perception of the trends, as well as the extent, of poverty in Canada will also be shaped by our choice of definition. According to the CCSD and Senate criteria, poverty did not diminish in Canada during the 1970s, but using the Statistics Canada (revised) definition Podoluk (1980: 281) has concluded that the incidence of poverty fell considerably.

How do these discrepancies arise? How can it be that something as real as poor people can appear and vanish in a statistician's definition? To see why, we must examine how these poverty lines were set and how they are adjusted.

4.2.1 The Senate Committee Definition

The Special Senate Committee on Poverty used *budget standards* (as established by the Department of National Health and Welfare) for "items of basic need" for a family of four as their basic starting point. They argued that in 1969 $3,500 would provide such a family "items of basic needs," but that poverty began when less than 30 per cent of income was available for any sort of discretionary purpose. The poverty line was therefore drawn at $5,000 for a family of four in 1969 and adjusted by a points system which tried to recognize that the cost of an additional family member may be different for families of different sizes. A family of one received a weight of three; a family of two received a weight of five; a family of three received six; a family of four got seven; and each subsequent addition to the family size was assigned an added unit. (Hence the poverty line for a five-person family in 1969 was 8/7 x $5,000 = $5,714). These poverty lines were then scaled up each year by the *average percentage increase in Canadian family income.*

4.2.2 The Statistics Canada Approach

Statistics Canada first established a poverty line in 1961, and based it on the percentage of income consumers spent on basic necessities, i.e., food, clothing and shelter. Since the average Canadian family in that year spent approximately 50 per cent of its income on necessities, Statistics Canada defined as poor those families who had relatively little "discretionary income" to save or to pay for such things as medical care, the education of children, recreation, etc. More or less arbitrarily, Statistics Canada established the poverty line at that level of income at which the average family of a given size spent 70 per cent or more of its income on basic necessities. Adjustments for changes in the all-item *consumer price index* yield the "updated" Statistics Canada poverty line (column 3 of Table 4-1).

It is this method of adjustment, which accounts *only* for price inflation, that is the crucial difference between the Senate and Statistics Canada methodology. Figure 4-1 illustrates what will happen to the poverty line, over time, if it is only increased by the rate of inflation. Suppose that the poverty line was initially drawn at $5,000 per year or one-half of the average income of $10,000 per year. If there is real growth of 3 per cent per year but no inflation of prices (Panel A), in 15 years the income of the average family will be $15,579, but the poverty line will (since we have assumed zero inflation) still be $5,000 — i.e., now only one-third of the average.

More realistically, we can assume inflation is, for example, 6 per cent (Panel B). The poverty line then grows at 6 per cent per year (since it is adjusted for inflation) but average incomes grow at 9 per cent (6 per cent inflation plus 3 per cent real growth). In 15 years the poverty line will grow to $11,982, but average money income will grow to $36,425 — i.e., after 15 years the poverty line has still fallen to one-third of the average.

The fraction of the population defined as "poor" will therefore have a tendency to fall. This process occurred during the 1960s, and the Statistics Canada poverty line began to become "obsolete." Starting with 1969 data Statistics Canada began to compile the "revised" poverty line (columns

Figure 4-1

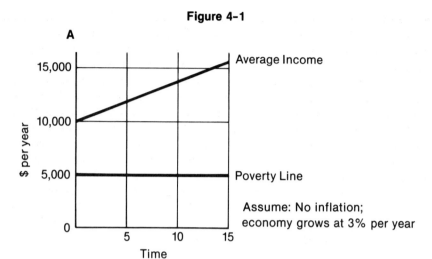

A

Average Income

Poverty Line

Assume: No inflation;
economy grows at 3% per year

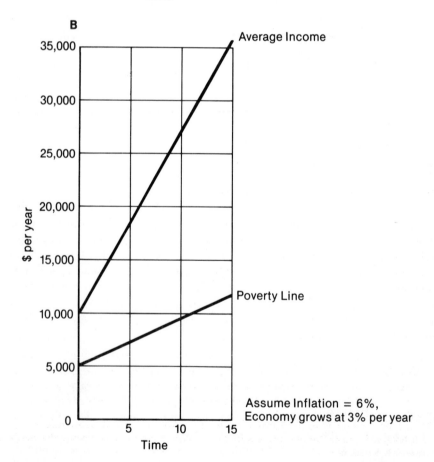

B

Average Income

Poverty Line

Assume Inflation = 6%,
Economy grows at 3% per year

4 to 6 of Table 4.1). It was argued that since living standards had improved over the decade and the average family in Canada in 1969 spent only 42 per cent of its income on basic necessities (versus 50 per cent in 1959), the poverty line should be redrawn so as to maintain a 20 per cent differential with respect to average expenditures on basic necessities (Podoluk, 1980). Since living costs for a family vary not only with the size of family but also with the size of the city in which it lives, the "revised" poverty line of Statistics Canada represents the average income at which a family of a given size, in a city of a given size range, typically spent 62 per cent or more of its income on items of basic necessity in 1969. Its publication started in 1973 and it has been adjusted for price inflation to yield the 1978 poverty line. In 1973 it was $5,983 for a family of four but by 1978 had risen to $9,531. In the meantime, the average incomes of four-person families rose from $13,961 to $24,633 — hence expressed as a fraction of average income for this size of family the Statistics Canada revised poverty line declined by roughly one-tenth (from 42.9 per cent to 38.7 per cent) over this five-year period.

4.2.3 The Canadian Council on Social Development Method

The CCSD argues that if poverty is economic deprivation, deprivation can only be considered *relative* to the average incomes of a society at a particular point in time. They therefore define the poverty line for a family of four as 50 per cent of the average income of all Canadian families. For other family sizes the poverty line is set by scaling up or down in the same way as the Senate Committee definition.

4.2.4 What is Poverty?

It has been argued that "all the numerous economic definitions of poverty contain one common element; they consider poverty a condition of having insufficient funds to maintain a (socially) acceptable standard of living" (Perlman, 1976:3).[1] The Canadian economic definitions disagree on whether this "acceptable" standard of living should be defined *relative* to the "incomes of the rest of the community" or whether it should be set at an income sufficient to meet basic needs. The CCSD argues for the strictly relativistic approach, Statistics Canada for a "needs" approach[2] while the Senate Committee definition is a hybrid. What is the rationale for these different approaches?

---

[1] The Canadian definitions of poverty lines also have in common the use of annual dollar income to define whether a family is living in poverty, thereby excluding certain types of income (e.g., capital gains or income in kind) and ignoring a family's prospect of future income or its wealth holdings.

[2] The 1969 revision recognized that revision of "needs" is required occasionally — i.e., implicitly recognized that poverty is a relative concept, but between revisions the "needs" approach is maintained.

The Statistics Canada method of establishing a poverty line has a surprising amount in common with a much earlier, pioneering effort. In 1883, Ernst Engel analysed family budgets and established a standard of living *(Volkeswohlstand)* which was that amount of income at which people spent at most 80 per cent of their income on "reasonable" satisfaction of physical needs. In constructing a poverty line by summing up the expenses involved in purchasing a minimal family budget, the Senate Committee was also following the lead of earlier researchers, one of whom wrote, "My primary poverty line represented the minimum sum on which physical efficiency could be maintained. It was a standard of barest subsistence rather than living. In calculating it the utmost economy was practiced . . . a family living upon the scale allowed for in this estimate must be governed by the regulation, 'nothing must be bought but that which is absolutely necessary for the maintenance of physical health, and what is bought must be of the plainest and most economic description'" (Rowntree, 1941: 102).[3]

The basic criticism of this "budget standard" approach is that although skilled nutritionists and expert budget planners might be able to maintain adequate nutrition within a severe budget, one cannot assume that real poor people will be able to. Cooking, as we all know, is something that many people at all income levels do not do very well. When income is more uncertain and families live closer to the margin, it may also be more difficult (even if more essential) to learn budgeting skills than in middle-class families. Finally, the monotonous virtue of the careful planning involved in these budget calculations ignores a very central part of the human make-up. As Orwell said, (in response to a 1937 newspaper article suggesting that the unemployed of England could live quite nicely if they ate more wholesomely and saved fuel by eating raw vegetables), "The ordinary human being would sooner starve than live on brown bread and raw carrots . . . . When you are unemployed, which is to say when you are underfed, harassed, bored and miserable, you don't *want* to eat dull wholesome food. You want something a bit 'tasty'. There is always some cheaply pleasant thing to tempt you" (Orwell, 1937: 86).

In comparing definitions of the poverty line the "budget" methods of calculation have an appearance of objectivity which explains much of their widespread acceptance. This appearance is, however, largely illusory. Even Rowntree's strict regimen included an allowance for tea — an item with no nutritive value. Such an item may be a social necessity but it is not a physical one. In fact, as Rowntree himself recognized, the definition of a "necessity" and of the "minimum" family budget must necessarily be relative to a particular society at a particular time.

---

[3] Some of the flavour of Rowntree's work has been carried over in the definition of poverty lines in the United States. These used as a starting point the "economy guidelines" established by the U.S. Department of Agriculture, which has been called "an eating regimen suitable for a life boat" (Perlman 1976: 9).

Deciding which are the "necessities" of life is a difficult task. Our most basic need is probably food, but the minimum daily caloric requirements of an individual depend on age, sex, body size, level of physical activity, climate and kind of housing, as well as on whether one wishes to set a standard just sufficient to prolong life or one adequate for health and resistance to disease. Level of physical activity alone can vary the needs of adult men from as low as 1,750 calories to as much as 5,000 calories per day (McKenzie, 1970: 70). Technically, it is possible to fill dietary needs at relatively low cost, if one eats only rice and lentils, but few Canadians would find this acceptable.

Once one moves beyond food, it becomes even more difficult to define a minimum standard of living since, as many suggest, "the luxuries of yesterday become the comforts of today and the necessities of tomorrow." Indoor plumbing was not, a hundred years ago, viewed as a necessity; today, a home without indoor plumbing in almost any city in Canada would be condemned as sub-standard accommodation and ordered demolished. The construction of a "minimum" budget must inevitably take into account prevailing standards in the community in which it is to be used. As Adam Smith wrote, over two centuries ago, "Custom has rendered leather shoes a necessary of life in England. The poorest creditable person of either sex would be ashamed to appear in public without them . . . . In France they are necessaries neither to men nor to women . . . . Under necessaries, therefore, I comprehend not only those things which nature, but those things which the established rules of decency have rendered necessary to the lowest rank of people" (1776: 399).

In practice, official "decency" appears to dictate that poverty begins when incomes fall below (roughly) 25 per cent to 30 per cent of the average. Table 4-2 presents data from a number of developed countries, whose official poverty lines are (statistically) drawn by quite different methodologies. In absolute dollars, these poverty lines vary enormously, by a factor of more than five. Expressed as a proportion of average income, however, they span a very much narrower range (i.e., 22 per cent to 33 per cent of the average income — with most around 25 per cent).

Public attitudes are somewhat more generous, but also remarkably consistent, on a relative basis. From 1946 to 1969 the Gallup Poll asked Americans every year, "What is the smallest amount of money a family of four needs to get along in this community?" The answer was consistently about one-half of current average family disposable income (Rainwater, 1974: 53). In money terms, average incomes changed by a factor of almost three, but the social definition of a minimum required income seems to have changed very little, *relative to the average*.

The Canadian Council on Social Development argues that if poverty is a relative concept then the definition of the poverty line should be *explicitly* relative. (They define the poverty line as 50 per cent of the average income of Canadian families.) As a result, their measure does not imply a tendency

Table 4-2

GROSS DOMESTIC PRODUCT PER CAPITA AND POVERTY NORM
(EXCLUDING RENT) SELECTED COUNTRIES FOR SELECTED YEARS

	GDP/cap. US $	Single Person poverty norm as % of GDP/cap.
United States (1965)	3,240	25.8[a]
Switzerland (1966)	2,265	30.3
Canada (1965)	2,156	23.3[b]
Denmark (1965)	2,070	24.4
Finland (1967)	1,801	24.1
France (1965)	1,626	22.4
United Kingdom (1963)	1,395	32.8
West Germany (1962)	1,321	25.4
Japan (1964)	717	30.3
Ireland (1962)	639	24.3

[a]The general assistance standard of Santa Clara County, California
[b]The general assistance standard of the Province of Ontario.
Source: Scitovsky (1976: 177)

for the percentage of the population defined to be "poor" to decrease over time *unless* the distribution of income also becomes more equal.[4] Note that a more egalitarian (but still less than perfectly equal) society can succeed in eliminating poverty, according to this definition. All that is required for the elimination of poverty is that the least well-off members of the society should not receive less than half of the income of the average member of society. A "relativistic" conception of poverty therefore implies that the issues of poverty and economic inequality are inextricably linked, not in the sense that *absolute* equality is required to eliminate poverty but in the sense that the extremes of inequality create and sustain poverty.

4.3 How Much Poverty Is There?

Traditionally, the amount of poverty has been measured either by counting the fraction of a country's population whose income lies below the poverty

---

[4]Other "relativistic" definitions of poverty have been proposed. In the United States, Fuchs (1967) proposed that the poverty line should be drawn at half the national median family income, since median family income is probably a better measure of "typical" living standards than is average family income. In Canada, Adams et al. (1971) argued that one should weight the income of a family by a system of points depending on the number of people in the family and thereby calculate the "average living standard" of Canadian families — and the poverty line should be one-half of it. These definitions differ, in technical details, but their essential message is the same — a reduction in poverty can only be achieved by moving to a more equal distribution of income. All these measures suffer, however, by being based on a single year's average (or median) income, hence if a depression cut everyone's income yet fewer people had less than half the average, they would indicate less "poverty" — a perverse result.

line (the so-called head-count method) or by calculating the ratio between the total amount by which the income of the poor falls short of the poverty line and their incomes if they were raised to the poverty line (the "poverty gap ratio" method). Simply counting the proportion of the population below the poverty line, however, pays no attention to the *amount* by which the income of the poor falls short.[5] On the other hand, measuring poverty by the size of the "poverty gap" pays no attention to the number of people who are poor. Both the "poverty gap" and the "head-count" method of measuring the extent of poverty are therefore unreliable, *regardless* of how the "poverty line" was initially drawn.

A number of alternative measures of the extent of poverty have therefore been proposed, all of which have in common an explicit consideration either of economic inequality among the poor or of economic inequality in the larger society. Sen (1979), for example, has proposed that the incidence of poverty in a society be measured by:

$p = H [1 + (1 - I)G]$ where:

H = "Head-count" — percentage of people below poverty line (however drawn);

I = "poverty gap ratio" — total shortfall of all incomes of poor from poverty line as fraction of poverty line income for all poor people.

G = Gini ratio of income distribution of poor (see Chapter 2).

This measure of the extent of poverty is therefore a combination of a head-count, the poverty-gap ratio, and the extent of inequality among the poor. Since inequality among the poor may be fairly great, (e.g., between someone just below and someone far below the poverty line) this measure indicates that the severity of the poverty problem increases as inequality among the poor increases. Other measures (e.g., that of Hagerbaumer, 1977) differ in detail but the essential point remains, that an accurate measure of poverty must be linked to a measure of inequality among the poor.

4.4 Who Are the Poor?

The *extent* of poverty may depend upon the degree of inequality of income distribution in society, but who are these people and why are they poor? Table 4-3 presents data on the distribution and the incidence of poverty in Canada in 1975. It uses the "revised" Statistics Canada definition of poverty for the same reason that it is used in most such discussions — the easy availability of data. There are two separate issues considered in Table 4-3:

---

[5]Furthermore, the paradoxical result of focusing on a "head-count" measure is that one would conclude that poverty had not increased, and might even decrease if income is transferred from a poor person to a richer one. The poor person becomes poorer, but the number of poor remains constant — unless the transfer is to someone just at the poverty line, in which case the number of poor declines.

Table 4-3

INCIDENCE AND DISTRIBUTION OF POVERTY*
— CANADA, 1975 —

Family Unit Type	% of All Poor Family Units		Incidence — Poor Family Units as % All Such Units	
No Member in Labour Force				
— Head 65 or over	33.5		53.9	
— male		14.4		42.5
— female		19.2		67.5
— Head under 65	21.8		76.3	
— male		8.5		69.6
— female		13.4		81.3
Total Non-Participants	55.3		61.9	
Labour Force Participants				
No Unemployment	27.7		8.9	
— male, head		17.9		6.9
— female, head		9.7		19.5
Some Unemployment	17.1		15.6	
— male, head		12.0		12.6
— female, head		5.1		34.8
All L.F. Participants	44.8		10.7	
GRAND TOTAL	100%		19.7%	

(sub-totals may not add, due to rounding)
*by family unit (families and unattached individuals) using 1975 Statistics Canada revised low income cut-off (i.e., 62% criterion).
Source: adapted from Smith (1979: 43-48)

the incidence of poverty (the probability with which a particular family type will be poor), and the distribution of poverty (the percentage of all poor families of that particular type). Some groups may have a low *chance* of being poor, but may be so large that even this low incidence produces a large *number* of poor people. The incidence of poverty among male-headed families with no unemployment, for example, was relatively low in 1975 (6.9 per cent), but since there were roughly 3.9 million such families they amounted to a relatively large fraction (17.9 per cent) of the poverty population. On the other hand, the quarter of a million family units headed by younger women who were out of the labour force (most of whom were single parents) had a far higher *chance* of being poor (just over 80 per cent), but totaled only about 13.4 per cent of the poverty population. As Table 4-3 indicates, the incidence of poverty varies dramatically with age, sex and labour force status. The variation and the incidence of poverty are equally dramatic when one considers separately families and unattached individuals, or when one compares different occupations, educational levels, and regions of the country. A more detailed description can be found in Caskie (1979).

4.4.1 Poverty among the Old

It is crucial to distinguish between poverty among the old and poverty within the rest of the population. Younger people may be able to escape from poverty by getting a new or a higher-paying job, but people over 65 are generally excluded from paid employment by regulation, custom and physical incapacity. They are, therefore, largely dependent on transfer income, savings, pensions or the support of relatives. To the extent that their incomes while employed were not sufficient to permit the accumulation of savings for their old age, or their employers did not provide pension plans[6], their *present* poverty is the result of the *past* operation of the labour market. Low-income workers are least able to save for retirement and also least likely to be covered by pensions. Podoluk (1980: 291) estimates that in 1976, 14.7 per cent of those earning between $5,500 and $7,500 contributed to pension plans, while 54.5 per cent of those earning over $14,000 were in such plans. Low-income workers are also less likely to be members of non-contributory plans and, due to greater employment instability, to lose pension entitlement when they change jobs. The main income source of the aged poor is, therefore, government transfer payments, and they have few realistic alternatives.

4.4.2 The Working Poor

In 1975 approximately two-thirds of poor family units of less than retirement age contained at least one member who either worked or looked for work. Indeed, 60 per cent of Canada's younger poor (i.e., under 65) derived most of their income from work (National Council of Welfare, 1977). These are the "working poor." Among this group it is primarily low wages, and not unemployment, that is the cause of poverty.

These low wages are more likely to be received by unattached individuals, by females, by people with relatively few years of education, by residents of Quebec or the Maritimes, by the self-employed and by employees in seasonal or service industries. Families with fewer earners are, of course, also less likely to be able to put together a total income package above poverty levels. Those families whose low wages are interrupted by unemployment are more *likely* to be poor but the availability of unemployment insurance lifts some such families over the poverty line and lessens the poverty gap of those who remain (A.M. Smith, 1979).

Of course, looking at current earnings may be misleading. Those who

---

[6]In 1975 only 13 per cent of the income for senior citizens came from employer pension plans (Stone, 1979: 24).

are young and have skills may (like college students) expect low incomes to be a temporary thing. Garfinkel and Haveman (1977) therefore emphasized the "earnings capacity" (see Chapter 7) of the poor in the U.S. and compared it with actual earnings. They concluded that defining poverty in terms of current income overemphasizes the temporarily low earnings of younger people, as well as the low current income of retired people (who may have savings to fall back on.) Conversely, defining poverty in terms of current income underemphasizes the "working poor." If one examines those who are "earnings capacity" poor, they are much more likely to be fully in the labour force; indeed, in order to keep their current income above the poverty line they tend to "utilize their earnings capacity more fully" (1977: 50) — i.e., work longer hours than most other people.

4.4.3 Women and Poverty

As Table 4-3 shows, the incidence of poverty is in every case higher for female-headed than for male-headed family units. Indeed, one recent study has concluded, "most Canadian women become poor at some points in their lives" (National Council of Welfare, 1979: 51). In large part this arises because women typically live longer than men and, as widows, often become totally dependent upon government transfer payments.[7] Few widows can depend on private pensions in their old age since only a minority of workers are covered by private pensions in the first instance and of those, half are in plans that give no benefits whatsoever to surviving spouses (Ibid: 31–32). Since most women are out of the paid labour force for some years as they raise a family, their entitlement to a pension from Canada Pension Plan is correspondingly less. As a consequence, the poverty of older women living alone in Canada is especially severe.

Older people and low-wage workers have long composed the bulk of Canada's poverty population, but the greatest recent change in the anatomy of Canadian poverty has been the growing importance of single-parent families. Most such families are headed by women, whose child-care responsibilities often prevent their entering the paid labour force. Employed women typically have earnings that are approximately 60 per cent of male earnings (Gunderson, 1979: 484). Averaging employed women and those who must depend on transfer payments, one finds that families headed by females had an average income, in 1975, that was only 52 per cent of the Canadian average family income (Podoluk, 1980: 287). The importance of poverty among such families has grown as their proportion of all Canadian families has increased. Excluding unattached individuals, in 1961 Podoluk calculated that 13.2 per cent of poor families were female-headed (1968: 187). By 1976 the figure was 32.5 per cent (Caskie, 1979: 38).

Absence from the paid labour force or discrimination within it (see

---

[7]Insurance payments and family savings are typically far too small to protect widows against poverty — in 1977 the average death benefits paid on life insurance policies was about $4,000.

Chapter 6.4) may prevent an escape from poverty for female-headed families, but one must beware of assuming that these families are poor because they are female-headed, rather than now being female-headed partly because they were poor previously. Using U.S. data, Schiller has argued, "a disproportionately high percentage of family break-ups occurs among the poor due to economic stress . . . family disunity may help sustain poverty, but in most cases it appears that poverty preceded, and itself helped to cause, family dissolution" (Schiller, 1976: 99). Orcutt (1976: 116) has found that unemployment of the family head is highly significant in increasing the likelihood of divorce.

Of course, we all know of wealthy couples whose marriages have broken up, just as we all know of sober drivers who have had car accidents, even though drinking increases one's chances of a car accident. Similarly, economic stress increases one's chances of a marriage breakdown, and a primary cause of economic stress is low/or uncertain family income. Broken marriages then create single-parent families, whose chances of escape from poverty are lessened by the burden of family responsibilities and by low wages for females in the labour market.

4.4.4 Implications of Low Incomes

As Rainwater (1974: 12) has put it, "Not having enough money to support a family properly means that the husband is constantly vulnerable to accusations of being inadequate or incompetent as a provider and the wife is constantly vulnerable to accusations of not being sufficiently energetic in making do. . . . These factors produce a common pattern of endemic tension and dissatisfaction within lower-class marriages." Marital instability is one result; significantly different patterns of child-rearing are another (see Chapter 6).

Relative incomes are a vital component in the process of social stratification — what Parsons (1954:69) called "the differential ranking of the human individuals who compose a given social system and their treatment as superior or inferior relative to one another in certain socially important respects." Both social rewards (prestige, authority, status) and social sanctions (such as one's treatment by the criminal justice system) are unequally distributed across social strata. In North America, economic criteria are overwhelmingly the basis for social stratification.[8]

---

[8]An enormous literature on social stratification exists (see, for example, Harold W. Pfautz, "The Current Literature on Social Stratification Critique and Bibliography," American Journal of Sociology, Vol. 58, p. 391, with a bibliography of 333 books and articles) in which it is far from uniformly established whether it is desirable to study prestige, status, class consciousness, class existence, political power, economic power, or some combination of the above. It is, however, agreed, that basic to social stratification is social inequality, and the most popular single criterion of placement of individuals is occupation, as ranked by income and education. In addition, many of the other variables used to "explain" status, prestige, etc. (such as "lifestyle," housing type, etc.) are highly related to income and wealth.

Since these criteria are "inculcated from early childhood and are deeply introjected' to form part of the basic structure of the personality itself" (Parsons, 1959:74), it is not surprising that the poor tend to have very low self-esteem and generally negative evaluations of their own capabilities (Rothman, 1978:114).

Political scientists refer to a low sense of personal efficacy among the poor, meaning that the poor feel it unlikely that they personally could influence political events and that "it doesn't make any difference anyhow." Limited personal and financial resources, plus a low sense of efficacy, mean that voter turn-out and political participation in general is much lower among the poor than among other socio-economic groups (Van-Loon/Whittington, 1976:99-122). Hence, as a popular introductory text puts it, "the 40 per cent or so of Canadians who are below or near the poverty line are almost totally excluded from the input side of the political process and have to accept the outputs with very little control over them. They are truly the silent poor" (ibid.:119).

Four general points emerge from our discussion of the incidence of poverty among single-parent families and older people. First, one must distinguish between the immediate causes of poverty (e.g., lack of a pension, single-parent status) which may be readily identifiable but which are, themselves, often the result of other more basic factors and other social processes.[9] Second, the "causes" of low (or high) income are probabilistic, not determinate. Factors such as low education or residence in the Maritimes or being an Indian are associated with a higher chance of being poor, but exceptional (or lucky) people have always been able to surmount the odds — indeed, that is what makes them exceptional. Third, probabilities are often cumulative. The woman who marries a poor husband has a somewhat higher chance of marriage break-up, a lower chance of maintaining job-relevant skills if out of the paid labour market, a lower chance of getting a high-paying job when she returns to the labour market, and a lower chance of getting adequate pension entitlement on retirement. It is the accumulation of these probabilities which determines the odds that she will be poor in her old age. Fourth, the characteristics of the labour market are central to an analysis of poverty (or inequality). The labour market contains jobs without pension entitlements (other than CPP), jobs

---

[9]It is, for example, misleading to claim that "poverty . . . is no longer a phenomenon closely related to the labour market" (ECC, 1976: 122). The poverty of the "working poor" is directly related to low wages and/or employment instability. The poverty of older people arises from their lack of pension rights or savings from their working years. Although few single parents could work full time even if offered a job, "if the men who participated in forming the families that end up on welfare were not economically marginal there would not be so many female-headed families. If economic marginality produces (1) high rates of illegitimacy and divorce and (2) a low rate of remarriage, then it is the principle cause of the welfare problem" (Rainwater, 1974: 15).

with a relatively high risk of disabling accidents, and jobs for women with pay much below that of men. The holders of these jobs have a higher chance than average of having low incomes, and their families have a higher chance of poverty.

4.5 Summary and Conclusion

(a) Sen (1979:287) has recently argued: "the measurement of poverty must be seen as an exercise of description assessing the predicament of people in terms of prevailing standards of necessities. It is primarily a *factual* rather than an ethical exercise and the facts relate to what is regarded as deprivation." In Canada four published "poverty lines" attempt to define the level of "prevailing standards," but they differ widely in the income levels they set.

(b) At any point in time in any particular society, the majority of people will probably share an idea of "minimum prevailing standards." These ideas (or as Adam Smith put it "the established rules of decency") change slowly over time and increase in proportion to increases in average incomes. Poverty is thus a relative phenomenon, with the qualification that it is relative to the long-period average of incomes and not simply "this year's" average income.[10]

(c) The Statistics Canada definitions of a "poverty line" fail to take the relative nature of poverty adequately into account, while the CCSD approach is too closely tied to a *single year's* average income. The Senate Committee definition is an untidy compromise. One can usefully check how closely one's own opinion of "minimum standards" accords with each of these official poverty lines by completing the classroom exercise below, adjusted for inflation between 1978 and now.[11]

(d) If one accepts a "poverty line" based on current income, older people, single parents and others not in the labour force form the majority of Canada's poverty population. For many of them, however, current poverty is an indirect effect of the past operation of the labour market. Most of the younger poor are "working poor" and an emphasis on "earnings capacity" would give even greater stress to their situation. Low wages are the primary cause of poverty among the working poor, followed closely by the number of earners available and unemployment.

---

[10]For example, a nation whose average income suddenly dropped drastically as the result of some calamity could well be one where a majority fell below "prevailing standards," but those standards would change if the drop in average income were long prolonged. Conversely, a sudden rise in average incomes (with income inequality unchanged) may initially reduce the fraction of the population below a "common standard of necessities" but if this increase in average incomes is long-lasting social definitions of necessities will change.

[11]It is to be noted that when one includes family allowance and child tax credit, the truck-driver in (a) is not "poor" according to the revised Statistics Canada definition.

(e) The process of income *determination* determines the incidence of poverty, but the process of income *distribution* determines the extent of poverty. If, explicitly or implicitly, we adopt a relativistic conception of the nature of poverty, then the extent of poverty in a society depends directly on the degree of economic inequality in it. The shape of the income distribution then determines *how many* people will be poor; *who* those people will be depends on the relative advantage which education, experience, sex or occupation accord to individual earnings — i.e., on the process of income determination.

Classroom Exercise:

In 1978, the "revised" Statistics Canada poverty line for a family of four in a metropolitan area of 100,000 to 499,000 population was $9,998. Assume that you are a single parent of three children, aged 3, 6, and 8 and that you have no inheritances, alimony or other outside income on which you can depend. Calculate a "typical" month's budget for your family under the following assumptions.

(a) You normally make $5.00 per hour driving a truck and work 40 hours per week. Unfortunately, your employer had to lay you off for two weeks last February and for another two weeks last November and you could not find another job during those periods.

(b) You work in an office (as a secretary) and make $140.00 per week. (i.e., $4 per hour for a 35-hour work week). You get two weeks paid vacation a year but no other fringe benefits.

Chapter 5

Of Labourers and Capitalists — The Issue of Factor Shares

The produce of the earth — all that is derived from its surface by the united application of labour, machinery and capital is divided among three classes of the community, namely, the proprietor of the land, the owner of the stock of capital necessary for its cultivation and the labourers by whose industry it is cultivated.

To determine the laws which regulate this distribution is the principal problem of political economy.

> David Ricardo, The Principles of Political Economy and Taxation, 1831.

5.1 Introduction

During Ricardo's time, his definition of the issue of income distribution made sense on two levels. The income generated by the three factors of production, land, labour and capital, was at the same time the income received by three distinct classes of the community. Hence his analysis of production by inputs was at the same time an analysis of distribution among people. In many less-developed countries today, the same rigid social stratification as in early nineteenth-century England draws clear lines between the social interests of large landowners, capitalists, and ordinary peasants and workers, but in the developed countries these lines have become blurred.

With development, of course, the relative importance of agriculture has declined, hence the role of land as a productive input is no longer as important; indeed, it is sometimes no longer separately mentioned in statistics on the "factoral" distribution of income. Labour and capital are the main inputs into the modern productive process but "labour" includes both minimum-wage, seasonal workers, and secure professionals, like doctors or business executives. Likewise, although ownership of capital is quite concentrated in Canada today (see Chapter 3), those who live on the returns from capital include both aged pensioners and multi-millionaires.

Most modern studies of income distribution in developed countries therefore emphasize the distribution of income from all sources. It is, after all, total income which enables consumption, and it is not true that all wage-earners are poor and all capital-owners are rich. Some segments of the population, like pensioners, have relatively high wealth but relatively low current income, while others with high earnings have not yet been able to acquire much wealth (see Statistics Canada, 13-547:153). On the other hand, the assets of the top 5 per cent of adults in the wealth distribution, at a normal rate of interest, are alone sufficient to put them in the top few percentiles of the income distribution, while the bottom 40 per cent of the wealth distribution, it is safe to say, receive virtually no capital income (see Table 3-4).

What is the impact of the distribution of income between labour and capital on the distribution of total income? What are the causes of this distribution of total income? What causes it to be changed (if it can be)? Section 5.2 outlines recent trends in the division between labour and capital while sections 5.3, 5.4 and 5.5 discuss alternative explanations of them. It will be seen that there is no consensus, even today, on the answer to Ricardo's 150-year-old question.

5.2 The Division of National Income

The total output of a nation is commonly defined as its Gross National Product — the total value of all final goods and services produced by the residents of that country. Since some capital equipment is used up in the process of production, one must subtract "capital consumption allowance" from GNP figures to get Net National Income, or the net output of the economy if capital stock is maintained intact. On the one hand, the uses of this output can be divided into the categories of consumption or investment. On the other hand, the receipts from its sale are divided among the various factors of production. Table 5-1 presents national accounts data on the share of each factor in net national income over the postwar years. The table is presented year by year for the 1970s since there are both significant long-run trends and short-run cyclical movements in the division of national income.

5.2.1 Trends

Perhaps the most consistent long-run change is the decline in the share of farm operators and unincorporated businesses. This trend basically mirrors the secular decline in the fractions of the labour force that are "self-employed" or engaged in agriculture. Since both these groups use their own capital, as well as their own labour, a really accurate account would assign part of their income to column (2) as due to the capital they use and part to column (1) as due to the labour they supply. Different methods of

Table 5-1

THE DIVISION OF CANADIAN NATIONAL INCOME BETWEEN FACTORS

	(1)	(2)	(3)	(4)	(5)
			NET INCOME		NET
		PROFITS &	FARM &		NATIONAL
		NET INVEST-	UNIN-	INVENTORY	INCOME AT
	WAGES &	MENT	CORPORATED	VALUATION	FACTOR
	SALARIES	INCOME	BUSINESS	ADJUSTMENT	COST
	%	%	%	%	%
1947-49	63.7	16.1	23.6	-3.4	100
1950-54	63.9	16.9	20.2	-1.1	100
1955-59	67.6	16.7	16.2	-0.5	100
1960-64	69.6	16.5	14.2	-0.3	100
1965-69	71.6	17.3	11.9	-0.6	100
1970	74.1	15.8	11.3	-0.3	100
1971	74.1	16.3	10.6	-0.9	100
1972	73.5	18.0	9.8	-1.3	100
1973	71.7	20.7	10.2	-2.5	100
1974	71.4	22.9	9.4	-3.7	100
1975	72.9	20.5	8.9	-2.3	100
1976	73.6	19.7	8.0	-1.4	100
1977	74.4	20.4	7.4	-2.1	100
1978	73.3	21.7	7.5	-2.4	100
1979	71.1	24.7	7.3	-3.1	100

(1) Wages + salaries + supplementary labour income + military pay and allowances.
(2) Corporate profits before taxes + interest and miscellaneous investment income —
dividends paid to non-residents.
(3) Accrued net income of farm operators from farm production + net income of non-farm
unincorporated businesses including rents.
Source: Finance Canada (1980:171)

assignment can give different answers. One can consider the labour earnings of the self-employed to be that income remaining after subtracting a market rate of return on capital or, alternatively, one can subtract the market value of labour supplied from total income and consider the remainder to be capital income (see Feinstein, 1968; or Kravis, 1959). Discrepancies between these two methods arise because the self-employed typically could not pay the going market rate for both all the labour and all the capital they use (i.e., they receive below-normal returns on labour or capital or both.)

The problems involved in estimating labour and capital returns among the self-employed clearly make estimates of trends in the total share of labour and capital much more difficult. Another complicating factor is the year-to-year variability in factor shares during the business cycle. As a boom gets under way, output will expand and productivity will increase as existing plant and equipment are used more intensively, but multi-year union contracts may lock many workers into fixed wages. Profits will then tend to rise faster than wages and will increase as a share of national income. Conversely, in an economic down-turn, profits fall faster than wages, and capital's share tends to decrease. It is thus usually somewhat misleading to take a single year's evidence as indicative of "labour's share" or "capital's share," as these should be averaged over the entire business cycle.

Taking all this together, Ostry and Zaidi concluded: "there has been little change in the functional distribution of income (structural shifts aside) over a relatively long period of time in this country" (1979:287).[1] To some, of course, these structural shifts are the essence of the issue. Both Haley (1968) and Feinstein (1968) found, for the U.S. and Britain respectively, that the share of labour had increased over time, at least up to the 1970s. Similarily, Atkinson (1975: 168) concluded that labour's share had shown a "long-run tendency to rise over time" in most advanced countries.

5.2.2 Personal Income

Of course, all taxpayers know that income paid is not quite the same as income received — the government steps in to take its share. (However, it's not all bad news since governments also provide transfer payments to individuals.) In addition, to the extent that companies retain profits for further reinvestment, the owners of capital may receive capital gains on the value of their stock holdings rather than spendable dividends. Spendable income after tax is what concerns most people since it is the basis of a household's current consumption. Table 5-2 presents the relationship of various measures of income.

When we referred to the income of family units in Chapter 2 it was to the personal money income before tax of all members of a family unit. Table 5-3 illustrates the increasing proportion of transfer payments in the money income of family units as estimated by Statistics Canada (an increase which, as we have seen in Chapter 3, has *not* been accompanied by a decrease in aggregate inequality.) Naturally, Table 5-3 presents only average figures for the composition of family income and there are very significant divergences. Low-income families depend far more heavily on transfer payments while investment income is a greater fraction of income for high-income groups.[2] Nevertheless, wages and salaries are the largest component of family income by far — even for the highest income categories recorded.[3]

---

[1]The post-1975 increase in capital's share can be partly attributed to an increase in the share of interest and investment income (from 6.7 per cent to 9.1 per cent).

[2]In addition, under-reporting of investment income in the Survey of Consumer Finance implies that column 3 is somewhat underestimated.

[3]In 1978, 77.9 per cent of the income of the highest category recorded, those receiving over $35,000, was wages or salaries.

Table 5-2

Gross National Product
  - Capital Consumption Allowance

= Net National Income at Factor Cost

    - retained corporate earnings
    - indirect business taxes less subsidies
    - profits accruing to government
    + interest paid by government
    + government transfer payments

= Personal Money Income before tax
  - Income tax
= Personal Disposable Money Income
    + Income in kind (e.g., from home ownership)
    + Capital Gains

= Personal Income.

Table 5-3

COMPOSITION OF TOTAL MONEY INCOME BEFORE TAX OF ALL CANADIAN FAMILY UNITS

	Wages & Salaries	Net Income From Self-Employment	Investment Income	Transfer Payments	Other Money Income	
	%	%	%	%	%	%
1951	78.9	10.3	4.4	5.2	1.2	100
1961	78.5	9.3	3.7	7.0	1.5	100
1971	80.8	5.6	4.6	6.6	2.3	100
1978	76.8	5.5	5.9	9.1	2.6	100

Sources: Podoluk (1968: 251)
Statistics Canada, 13 - 207

5.3 The "Neoclassical" Explanation

Free competition tends to give to labour what labour creates, to capitalists what capital creates and to entrepreneurs what the co-ordinating function creates.

J. B. Clark, The Distribution of Wealth, 1899.

As one of the originators of the "marginal productivity" approach to distribution, J. B. Clark argued that a "natural law" regulated the distribution of income between labour and capital.[4] This natural law was composed

---

[4]Clark, himself, was very aware of the political implications of such a theory. As he wrote, "This thesis (the "natural law of distribution") we have to prove; and more hinges on it than any introductory words can state. The right of society to exist in its present form, and the probability that it will continue so to exist, are at stake" (1899:3).

Figure 5-1 MARGINAL PRODUCTIVITY AND THE RATE OF INTEREST

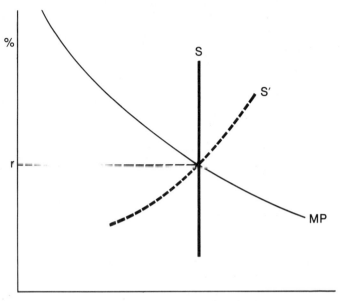

Amount of Capital Stock K

of two elements: the technological relationships governing production (i.e., the engineering relationships of input to outputs) and the relative abundance of factors. Figure 5-1 illustrates Clark's view of the determination of the rate of return to capital.

In Figure 5-1 the line MP represents the marginal product of capital (strictly speaking, capital services). Clark argued that the marginal product of capital declines as the total stock of capital increases, due to the law of diminishing marginal returns. (The *shape* of the marginal productivity schedule is governed by the state of available technological knowledge — i.e., it is seen as a purely "technical" datum.) The marginal productivity schedule (MP) represents the potential increase in total output, for a given level of supply of capital, when one additional unit of capital is added. That *marginal* return, Clark argued, determines the return all capital will receive in the marketplace. The aggregate supply of capital in a society (S) determines where an economy will be on its aggregate marginal productivity schedule, hence determining the rate of return on capital (r). In the short run, the stock of capital is fixed (at S), but in the long run the supply of savings responds positively to a higher rate of interest — hence the long-run supply schedule (S') is sloped upward to the right.

Put somewhat differently, the marginal productivity schedule can be seen as the aggregate demand curve for capital at any given interest rate —

so the rate of return on capital (r) is set by the forces of supply and demand. Demand (MP) is seen as determined solely by technical relations of production. Supply (S) is seen as determined by the past and current savings, i.e., the abstinence from current consumption, of individual households.[5] The rate of return on capital (r) then becomes the "return for waiting." Total payments to owners of capital are then equal to the rate of return times the stock of capital (i.e., = r x K). Payments to labour are similarly determined by marginal productivity, hence Clark's "natural law" argues that the shares of national income received by labour and capital are determined purely by relative factor abundance and socially neutral technological relationships.

A special case of this approach is provided by the Cobb-Douglas production function. Cobb and Douglas (1943) argued that total output can be predicted by equation F5:1.

$$\text{F5:1} \qquad \text{Total Output} = cL^{\alpha}K^{B}$$

L = total labour services
K = total capital services
$\alpha + B = 1$

If the wage (w) is equated to the marginal product of labour and the rate of return (r) is equated to the marginal product of capital (as will tend to happen in competitive markets) then it can be shown that *regardless of the labour/capital ratio* the total shares of labour and capital will remain constant (i.e., $wL/rK = \alpha/B$ for any K/L). (See, for example, Bronfenbrenner, 1968.) This "production function" relationship therefore "explained" the presumed constancy of factor shares in developed economies (more complex production functions can be used to explain a long-run movement in factor shares.)

Elements of this early viewpoint can still be found in introductory textbooks,[6] but one of the theoretical advances of the 1970s has been the widespread recognition that Figure 5-1 is founded on a logical fallacy. That is, Figure 5-1 is founded on a logical fallacy if there is more than one type of capital good in existence (the only reasonable assumption), since "Capital" must be some aggregate of all the various specific capital goods in the economy. But how can one add together the services of drill presses, lathes, buildings and computers? These can be added together to produce "Capital" only if they are measured in a common unit — but dollars will not do. If one adds the *prices* of capital goods up, one is forgetting that these prices will depend on the value of the future stream of returns which each capital good is expected to generate. But the present value of these future returns depends[7] on the rate of interest. Hence the "amount" of the capital stock

---

[5]In a fully integrated model, these savings decisions may be explained in a "life-cycle" framework (see Chapter 10.2).

[6]Compare, for example, the diagrams in Clark (1899:201) and Lipsey (1979:370).

[7]See Chapter 7 for a discussion of present values.

depends on the rate of interest, but the "amount" of the capital stock is supposed to *determine* the rate of interest.

Bliss (1975:162) therefore investigated the conditions under which capital goods can be aggregated into "Capital" (or labour types into "Labour") in a competitive general equilibrium model, and concluded that they are so special that "we can safely dismiss them from serious consideration" (see also Koopmans, 1977). He argues, however, that one can speak meaningfully of the marginal products of particular *types* of capital equipment and that at any point in time each capital good will generate a stream of returns over time to its owner. One cannot, however, speak in general terms of "the" rate of return on "Capital" in aggregate or "the production function" relating "Labour" to "Capital" (Bliss, 1975: 144-195, 238-244) — nor does one need to, since all the results of competitive general equilibrium theory can be obtained without specific reference to the aggregates of "Labour" or "Capital" (for a recent example see Varian, 1978).

Only for convenience (e.g., in presenting a diagram) does competitive general equilibrium analysis restrict itself to the case of two goods or two inputs,[8] since discussion of "n" goods or "m" types of labour is much more realistic. In this modern view, the distinction between "Labour's" share and "Capital's" share is then meaningless. An individual's income in any period is the sum of the returns to his or her *particular capital assets* plus his or her labour earnings. There is no particular significance attached to the "factoral" distribution of income and no expectation that it can be easily explained (see, for example, Lipsey 1979:396).

5.4 The Post-Keynesian Approach

The share of wages in the value of output varies, from one country to another and one period to another, with the strength and militancy of trade unions and the help they get from social arrangements.

J. Robinson and J. Eatwell, *An Introduction to Modern Economics, 1973.*

For the "Cambridge school" of economists the proof that one cannot derive "technically" a division of national income between labour and capital was simply an indication that the division of income between labourers and capitalists is a *social* and not a technical relation. This approach starts from the money-wage bargain made between workers and capitalists and argues that capitalists typically set prices by a "mark-up" over their costs. Total profits are then the value of sales minus costs and are determined by volume of sales and the rate of mark-up. Total labour costs are determined

---

[8]For a discussion of marginal analysis as a special case of general equilibrium analysis see Bliss (1975: 95-118).

by labour's aggressiveness in bargaining for money wages and the level of employment. The level of employment is, in turn determined by the level of aggregate demand.

This is not a theoretical system that automatically tends to equilibrium, nor is it a system designed for a stationary economy. The Cambridge authors regard the possibility that their model can predict a disequilibrium situation to be a valuable addition to its realism, although under certain conditions steady-state growth is possible. Total demand in the economy is set, in the model, by workers' consumption plus the investment decisions of capitalists. The Cambridge school argues that capitalists save out of profits, and if the savings propensities of capitalists generate the amount of investment the economy needs to stay on its long-run growth path, then and only then will the economy be in equilibrium steady-state growth. Asimakopoulos (1977:341) however, argues that "capitalist development is unlikely to be 'smooth' " since nothing in the model *guarantees* that the appropriate level of investment will be undertaken.

In general, the Cambridge school argues that total income (Y) can be split into wages (W) and profits (P).

F 5:2 $$Y = W + P$$

Investment (I) must equal saving (S) if the economy is to be in equilibrium. For simplicity, assume that only capitalists save, at a rate $\propto$ out of the profits they receive.[9] We then have:

F 5:3 $$\propto P = I$$

hence:

F 5:4 $$P/Y = (I/\propto) \times (1/Y)$$

We can then see why the Cambridge school argues "workers spend what they get and capitalists get what they spend." The more capitalists spend, the lower is $\propto$, hence the higher is P in equation F5:4! There is thus no abstinence, no "reward for waiting" and no natural law involved in the Cambridge model. The division of national income is dependent on the pressure of workers in bargaining their wages and on the savings and investment decisions of capitalists — hence it is subject to change by political or trade-union action and by the unpredictable investment decisions of capitalists.

5.5 The Marxist Tradition

The value of a commodity is determined by the total quantity of labour contained in it. But part of that quantity of labour is realized in a value, for which an equivalent has been paid in the form of wages; part of it is realized

---

[9]Pasinetti (1974:127) shows this assumption is simplifying but not essential.

in a value for which no equivalent has been paid. . . . The surplus value, or that part of the total value of the commodity in which the surplus labour or unpaid labour of the working man is realized, I call Profit.

Karl Marx, Value, Price and Profit, 1899.

The Marxist approach to the divison of national income is but one aspect of a many-faceted intellectual movement, which embraces historical, socio-logical, philosophical and political aspects, as well as the purely economic. The historical perspective of Marxism sees existing Western social insti-tutions as but one stage in the long evolution of human history, a stage which, like European feudalism or the city states of Greece, is fundamen-tally transitory. The fundamental problem of Marxist social science is then to understand the determinants of social change, the "laws of motion" which underlie human society and human history. As a school of sociology, Marxism defines social classes in terms of their relation to the means of production,[10] and argues that those who own the means of production have fundamentally conflicting interests with those who do not.

As a philosophical viewpoint, Marxists use the method of dialectical materialism. They argue that society can never be in static equilibrium; rather, throughout history each form of human society has contained within itself the conflicts, i.e., the class conflicts, whose resolution generates a new stage of historical evolution and a new set of class conflicts. The political analysis of Marxism argues that the state can never be neutral in these conflicts. Indeed, since the social institution of property can only survive with the protection of the state, the state generally serves the interests of dominant social classes. Marx argued: "the economic structure of society is the real basis on which the juridical and political superstructure is raised, and to which definite social forms of thought correspond; the mode of production determines the character of the social, political and intellectual life generally" (Marx, 1887, 1:82). Here, however, we only have space for the narrowly economic aspects of Marxism — in particular, the Marxist discussion of the divison of national income and the empirical measures of it which exist.[11]

---

[10]Under feudalism, the primary means of production was land; in industrial societies it is physical capital.

[11]The term "Marxist" is capable of many meanings. In practice it is used very loosely by some to mean "undesirably left-wing" and very strictly by others to distinguish between those who are "true" Marxists and all others. One must distinguish between a Marxist analysis of modern societies and a Marxist political program — neither necessarily implies the other. Here we refer to Marxist economic analysis and define it as "analysis of the historical process of capitalism based on the labour theory of value." It should be noted that many Marxists would object to the idea of considering "economic" Marxism independently from Marxism's historical and sociological perspectives.

Since Marxists aim at explaining the transition of capitalism, and view the defining characteristic of capitalism as the private ownership of capital, and since they see class conflict as the dynamic which engenders social change, it is natural that Marxists see the division of national income between labour and capital as the *primary* aspect of economic inequality in capitalist societies. (The distribution of income among families (Chapter 2) is of subsidiary theoretical importance.) Speaking loosely, this is the distribution of income into factor shares, but more exact Marxists refer to the "rate of exploitation," and the organic composition of capital — concepts which are defined in terms of the labour theory of value.

The labour theory of value states that the value of any commodity is determined by the socially necessary labour-time required for its production. Economic activity is the process by which man creates objects of use from his natural environment, objects which require the input of human labour to be of value. At any point in time, the socially necessary labour required to produce a commodity is determined by the state of scientific knowledge and the cost of maintenance of human labour power. Labour is involved in production both directly (referred to as variable capital "V") and indirectly through the use of capital equipment. In the labour theory of value, capital equipment (constant capital) is simply "congealed labour," the product of man's past exertions. Through wear and tear on machinery, a certain amount (c) of constant capital is physically used up in the production process. Total labour involved in production is therefore equal to $c + V$, but in capitalist societies commodities exchange for more than the labour cost of their production — i.e., the exchange value of a commodity is given by:

F5:5 $$\text{value} = c + s + V.$$

Since capitalists own not only the capital stock but also the product[12] they receive the surplus value (s). In other words, a worker produces a certain amount of value in a working day, but receives as pay only V, which covers the cost of his subsistence (i.e., it is sufficient to "reproduce" labour for the next working period). Part of the working day is then devoted to producing enough output to cover wages, part to covering capital used up in production and part is surplus and is appropriated by the capitalist. The ratio between the time during which the worker produces "for himself" and the time during which he produces for the capitalist is s/V, i.e., the rate of surplus value which is "an exact expression of the degree of exploitation of labour power by capital, or of the labourer by the capitalist" (Marx, 1887:

---

[12]The Marxist idea of alienation stems from the idea that man is fundamentally a creative being, projecting himself upon the natural environment through his labour, but the division of labour in capitalist production and the worker's lack of ownership of the product of his labours means that he is estranged from it, hence alienated (see Marx, 1844:287-301).

1:218). (Recently, Wolff has estimated that the rate of surplus value in the U.S. has risen gradually over the period 1947-1967 from 1.009 to 1.122 (1979:334).[13]

The existence of surplus in the production process is a necessary condition if economic growth is to occur. Capitalists receive s, but consume only part of it and reinvest the rest. Capital is therefore the source of "self-expanding value" since this investment produces in its turn more surplus and more investment. As capitalist growth continues, increasing investment means an increase in the organic composition of capital ($c/c + V$), which in the Marxist view creates a tendency to a falling rate of profit, as profitable investment opportunities are used up. The quest for new investment opportunities makes capitalism a dynamic and expansionary social order. Backward nations are integrated into the world market as accumulating surpluses seek new opportunities for profit, and expanding production seeks new markets.[14] Unless balanced by changes in the rate of exploitation, however, the increase in the organic composition of capital will periodically produce a lack of investment opportunities, a lack of sufficient aggregate demand to absorb production and a "realization crisis" where goods remain unsold and a depression occurs.[15] This cyclical instability of capitalism is, of course, seen as a key element in the development of a proletarian movement and of political action which will spell the demise of the private ownership of capital stock.

When Marx said, "The capitalist mode of production abolishes private property and private labour" (Marx, 1887, III:266), he meant that the growth of monopoly and the concentration of capital deprives small businessmen and independent farmers and artisans of the private property which used to be the source of their independence. Increasingly, the self-employed are converted to paid employment, owning (and selling) only their labour power. Marxists therefore emphasize the concentration of capital — a concept quite different from the inequality of wealth discussed in Chapter 3.3. "Capital" for Marxists refers to constant capital, "the raw material, auxiliary material, and the instruments of labour" (1887, 1:209). Unlike "wealth," it includes neither the consumer durables required to reproduce labour power nor the price of unimproved land whose rents are merely a return to their scarcity — it is thus a narrower concept than either the "wealth" or "riches" we referred to in Chapter 3. A measurement of "capital" in the Marxist sense would include corporate financial instru-

---

[13]The exchange value of commodities is not, in general, equal to their price in the market. The transformation of labour values into equilibrium market prices is a topic which is beyond the scope of this chapter, but a full discussion may be found in Morishima (1973).

[14]Hence, the Marxist theory of imperialism — see Lenin (1917).

[15]Obviously, this is a thumbnail sketch of Marxist economics — for a fuller picture, see Sweezy (1942) or Mandel (1969).

ments (i.e., debt, equity) and that fraction of other financial assets used to finance capitalist production. Since these assets are the ones which the Survey of Consumer Finance underestimates most seriously (Davies, 1979), precise statements on the inequality of their ownership must be interpreted with caution. The 1970 SCF did, however, find that less than 10 per cent of Canadian family units had any appreciable direct holdings of these assets (Statistics Canada 13-547).

The differentiation of earnings is accorded a relatively minor place by Marxist writers. For Marxists, the primary contradiction of capitalism is the conflict between labour and capital. Marx himself explicitly recognized that not all labour is identical, but argued that "skilled labour counts only as simple labour intensified, or rather, as multiplied simple labour" (1887, 1:84). He saw the value of skills as the value of the human labour used to produce them — a concept which is not so very far from Smith's initial view of human capital (see Chapter 7), although the value and the price of skilled labour may diverge in the marketplace. Some of the radical authors cited in Chapter 8 are attempting to integrate their insights on labour markets into a Marxist historical perspective, but the integration with Marxist economics is less clear.

Two important failures of Marxist analysis are its forecast of a falling rate of profit, and progressive immiserization of the working class. Wolff (1979: 340) has concluded, "Marx's law of the tendency of the rate of profit to fall is theoretically unsound and there is no support for it during my period of investigation." Real living standards have increased substantially since Marx wrote. (Marx himself carefully defined "subsistence" as "in every country determined by a traditional standard of life." (1899: 97))[16]

Despite its relatively underdeveloped state, Marxism offers an extremely broad perspective on the issue of inequality in modern societies. Debate between Marxists and neoclassical economists regarding inequality often degenerates, however, into a dialogue of the deaf: the two schools of thought ask different questions, take different assumptions for granted, use different definitions and, as a result, provide different measurements of inequality — measures which are only understandable within their particular theoretical context.

For a neoclassical economist, the issue is to predict changes in the income distribution which arise as a result of individual or government decisions within our existing social and institutional framework. For Marxists, change in that framework is the central issue. Where a neoclassical economist will see the state as essentially neutral, responsive to the

---

[16]These failures of Marxism must, however, be compared with the failures of alternative viewpoints. A naive competitive general equilibrium analysis predicts that markets will clear and economies will be in stable equilibrium. Unemployment and cyclical instability therefore require "higher-level" rationalization.

pressures of the majority, a Marxist will argue that the state can never be neutral in distributional issues and that in capitalist societies it generally acts in the interest of the minority who control capital. Where a neoclassical perspective sees interest payments and dividends as returns to a factor of production, which is itself created by individual saving/abstention, a Marxist perspective sees these payments as surplus value, created by the use of capital (congealed labour) and appropriated by capitalists. Where neoclassical economists view the economy as generally being either at or tending to equilibrium, and social and political institutions as basically constant or changing due to their own internal logic, Marxists see the economy as developing unevenly, as inherently unstable, with an intimate connection with social and political forces. Most importantly, Marxists see the possibilities for reform which will limit the domain of inequality as fundamentally limited within existing social and political institutions, hence argue for their radical transformation. Neoclassical economists, however, assert that radical change in social and political institutions is probably unnecessary for the achievement of economic equality.

5.6 Conclusion

There are at least three very different answers to the "principal problem of political economy" which Ricardo identified a century and a half ago. Each answer is more of a movement in the history of ideas than a single concise statement, but the differences between each school of thought are so profound that there is little likelihood that a consensus will emerge for many years to come, if ever. An assessment of the relative merits of each approach would require at least a book on its own. However, although it is beyond the scope of this volume to attempt a grand survey, that simply means that the issues involved are of great importance and considerable complexity, and they should be debated and considered by all serious students of economics.

Does it make no sense to speak of "labour" and "capital"? Is profit equivalent to exploitation? Does economic stability depend on the "animal spirits" of investors? These issues go to the heart of economic analysis and can only be clarified by continual debate.

Since theories which "explain" the inequality of earnings are more tightly focused, in Chapters 6 to 9 following, we adopt a much more critical stance. Earnings, as we saw from Table 5-2, constitute most of the money income of Canadian families; hence theories which "explain" the distribution of earnings deserve especially intensive scrutiny. For the vast majority, it is differences in earnings which determine where they will place in Canada's income distribution.

Chapter 6

Of Chance, Ability, and Sex

6.1 Introduction

Since labour earnings make up most of the income of most of the population, the next three chapters comprise a critical appraisal of theories of the determinants of individual earnings, and the connection between those theories and the aggregate distribution of income. The role played by individual choice in earnings determination is treated very differently by the authors cited in Chapter 7 and those cited in Chapter 8. In large measure those differences centre around different conceptions of the nature of education, of work experience and, above all, of the realistic options individuals face. In this chapter, however, we discuss the role played in earnings determination by three variables which are *not* subject to individual choice — chance, genetically-inherited ability, and sex.

6.2 Inequality — A Matter of Chance?

One of the recurring regularities of aggregate income distribution statistics is that they reveal a distribution that is, approximately, often "log-normal"; that is, if in Figure 2-2 we had graphed the *logarithm* of income along the horizontal axis we would have observed a curve which almost fits the familiar bell curve of statistics textbooks.[1] The log-normal distribution, as it turns out, has some interesting mathematical properties. In particular, if income is determined entirely by chance (an almost nihilistic view) in the sense that one's income this year is a random fraction of one's income from

---

[1]One must say "almost fits," since the distribution of the logarithm of income is usually, in fact, more peaked (lepto-kurtic) and has a fatter upper tail than the standard log-normal. A log-normal distribution can be summarized in two parameters — the mean and the variance. For this reason, the variance of the logarithm of income is occasionally used as a measure of income inequality, although it does not always satisfy the "principle of transfers" as noted in Chapter 2.

last year,[2] it can be shown that the distribution of income will be, in aggregate, log-normal.[3]

Recently, Thurow (1975), and Wold and Whittle (1957) conjectured that this sort of random process could be a model of the wealth distribution as well. Champernowne (1953) and Solow (1951) have proposed similar models of the income distribution, but the basic flaw remains — a "chance" model of income distribution does not really *explain* anything and does not fit the underlying data all that well.[4] How much difference is there, after all, in saying that income distribution is due to fate, or saying that income distribution is due to the operation of unknown random processes? In addition, as Sahota (1978: 7) has said, "the theory provides a stamp of scientific respectability for the age old myth that the goddess of fortune is blind, poverty hits at random, none is destined to abjection from birth, and the sons of poor families have the same chance for success as anyone else," despite a great deal of evidence to the contrary. Finally, there is the problem that random movement can generate a stable distribution of income only after an implausibly long period of time has elapsed (Shorrocks, 1976), and that when one examines the stable distribution which would be generated if income movement were a random process, this distribution is usually quite unlike the actual distribution of earnings (Osberg, 1977). There is clearly much more to the income distribution process than chance.

---

[2] We postpone discussion of possible individual choice between occupations with different risks to Chapter 7.2.4.

[3] Gibrat (1931) called this the "law of proportionate effect." It can be expressed as

F6:1
$$Y_t = P_{t-1} Y_{t-1}$$
where Y_t = income in period t
P_t = a random variable

By expansion, this becomes:

F6:2
$$Y_t = (P_{t-1}) (P_{t-2}) (P_{t-3}) (P_{t-4}) \ldots \ldots Y_o$$
where Y_o = income in initial period

In terms of logarithms:

F6:3
$$\ln Y_t = \sum_{i=1}^{t} \ln (P_{t-1}) + \ln Y_o$$

If Y_t is an independent random variable, the central limit theorem will apply and one obtains:

F6:4
$$\ln Y_t \sim N (\mu, \sigma^2)$$

This implies that the inequality of income increases as t increases. Rutherford (1955) argued that this might be true within each age cohort, although the size of an age cohort decreases with time as its members die off.

[4] The conclusion of Jencks (1972) that chance was an important factor in earnings determination was based on the low percentage of variance in earnings explained by his regressions, which may mean that chance is responsible or may mean that the regressions have not been correctly specified.

6.3 Inequality — A Matter of Unequal Ability?

One of the most prevalent popular explanations of economic inequality (and especially of the inequality of earnings) is that it is due to inequalities in ability.[5] But what do we mean by ability? If we use the term to mean "the ability to earn money" then we have a prime example of a non-refutable, circular argument, since we are saying in effect, "more able people earn more money, but the only way we can tell if they are more able is if they earn more money." A theory which attempts to explain the distribution of earnings with reference to ability therefore faces a number of major hurdles:

(a) There must be some way of testing this presumed ability which is independent of current earnings.

(b) One must have some evidence of how this ability is distributed among the population if it is to explain the distribution of earnings among the same population.[6]

(c) Even if ability determines earnings within a labour market, the distribution of ability can only determine the distribution of earnings if everyone competes in the same labour market. Where "non-competing groups" exist, individuals' earnings will be determined both by their own ability *and* by the labour-market they are assigned to (see Staehle, 1943). A theory of the overall distribution of income is therefore incomplete unless it can also explain the extent of the discrimination which separates labour markets.

(d) As Sattinger (1975) has shown, people with different levels of ability will usually have a comparative advantage in performing different sorts of tasks, and it will in general pay employers to assign workers to the task for which they are best suited. But what determines the productivity of different tasks? One needs a theory of tasks (i.e., of the demand for ability), as well as discussion of the supply of ability, before one can explain how the distribution of ability determines the distribution of earnings.

(e) Many sorts of ability can produce income. The ability to sing, to put a puck in a net, to convince customers, to calculate the stresses in a bridge — these can all produce income. The overall distribution of earnings is a summation of the earnings distributions within a large

---

[5] The assignment of ability has been seen by some as a chance process, a "genetic lottery" (see Gibrat, 1931: 194).

[6] It is often presumed, for example, that intelligence is normally distributed in the general population, since IQ scores are. But it is usually forgotten that IQ tests are scaled so as to produce a normal distribution (see Ryan, 1972). Stamp (1937) and Davies (1941) contended that mental capacity was not "normally" distributed but was highly skewed. When one does not know the true shape of the distribution of intelligence one can hardly say it determines the shape of the distribution of earnings.

number of occupations, such as singer, hockey player, salesman and engineer. The shape of the distribution will depend not only on how high and how unequal salaries are within each occupation, but also on how many there are in each occupation — i.e., the extent of inequality depends not only on the differences between the earnings of rock stars or NHL players and those of beverage-room bands or minor-leaguers, but *also* on how many there are of each occupation relative to engineers and salesmen. A theory of the demand side of the economy is required to predict the number in each occupation, as well as the inequality of rewards in it.[7]

One can, of course, see these difficulties as challenges. In the last decade, rich new data sets have become available, and the progress of computer technology has made easy a level of analysis that was previously impossible. By following a "panel" of individuals from youth, and recording test scores while young and occupation and earnings when older, economists and sociologists have begun to identify which measured abilities seem to matter in the earnings-determination process, and how much. One must caution, however that these are studies of *individual* earnings determination. Whether one can extrapolate from why an individual gets ahead to why society is unequal is a subject we discuss in Chapter 9.1, and to anticipate, our conclusion is that one can only do so under very special conditions.[8]

As well, in order to generalize from a small sample to society as a whole about the determinants of individual earnings, one has to have data which are representative of society as a whole.[9] No one set of panel data is fully representative of the general population, but Jencks (1979) has attempted to compare and condense the findings of the 11 major panel studies done in the U.S. to date. (No long-run panel study has yet been done in Canada.) Two major questions have often been asked by researchers: (1) How important is genetic inheritance vis-à-vis socio-economic background in the production of ability? (2) What is the relative importance of ability, social background and acquired skills (such as education) in determining individual earnings?

---

[7]If all abilities are highly correlated then a person who is good at one thing is good at most other things — hence one might as well talk of "ability." Or, if almost everyone is in one occupation, the number of abilities which exist hardly matters. Neither is reasonable. See Mandelbrot (1962), Roy (1950) or Osberg (1975: 17-29).

[8]An "efficiency units" model, for example, (such as Taubman, 1976) assumes that the market will always pay relative wages equal to relative "capacity," i.e., there is no comparative advantage for particular abilities in particular tasks, and perfect substitutability of labour types exists.

[9]Taubman (1976, 1974) for example, uses data on a sample of World War II air force volunteers who were extensively tested then, and followed up in 1955 and 1969. Since they were initially selected on the basis that they were male, with above average IQ and schooling they would be expected to have above average earnings. The segmentation perspective argues (see Chapter 8) that one cannot generalize from their experience to that of the disadvantaged.

6.3.1 Nature Versus Nurture

The issue of "nature versus nurture" in the creation of human abilities has an extremely long history. In recent years people such as Jensen (1969, 1970) and Shockley (1970) have argued that genetic inheritance is the primary cause of differences in intelligence (as indicated by IQ scores) and that these differences in intelligence are the cause of diffences in earnings. If both of these statements were true then it might be thought that the existing earnings distribution was a "natural" one or that government policy should emphasize selective breeding (eugenics) to change inequality (Shockley, 1970).[10] Most social scientists, however, argue that the dif- ferences between individuals' environments are much greater than the differences between their genetic inheritances. Lydall, for example, con- cludes in his encyclopedic study that the most important factor likely to influence a new-born child's earnings is "the socio-economic class into which it is born and in which it grows up" (1968: 135).

How can we disentangle the legacy of nature from the effects of nurture? Genetic inheritance gives us the chromosomes that determine whether we will be black or white, male or female, but from the moment of conception humans differ enormously in the nurture they receive from their environment. Smoking, alcohol and drug use, nutrition, and exercise by pregnant mothers have all been shown to affect the size and healthiness of the child they bear. Women differ widely in their awareness of these factors and their ability to afford adequate rest and nutrition. As a result, there are significant differences between social classes in the incidence of premature delivery and of abnormally low birth weight babies. As a Vancouver study reported, "Low birth weight has long been recognized as one of the major causes of deaths and handicaps in infants" (Ross and Rutter, 1978:1). Vernon (1979: 100) has described as a vicious cycle "the widespread syndrome of poverty, maternal ill-health and pregnancy and delivery abnormalities associated with poor growth and intellectual and emotional disorders in the children."[11]

---

[10]That a "natural" distribution should be accepted as desirable or inevitable is far from obvious. It is natural, for example, to have spring floods but desirable and possible to build dikes to prevent them.

[11]Mental retardation is, for example, ten times more likely in low birth weight babies (i.e., those less than 2.5 kg.) than in normal babies (Perkins, 1974), and a higher incidence of motor disorders also occurs. Butler and Bonham (1963: 139) report that in the U.K. the incidence of abnormally low birth weight was 3.6 per cent in the highest social class and 8.2 per cent in the lowest. These differences are not inevitable. The Vancouver project was successful in reducing the incidence of low birth weight in a high risk sample to 2.8 per cent (compared to a Vancouver average of 7.2 per cent) by a combination of counselling and nutritional supple- ments (see Bradley et al., 1978). Brown (1978) reports similar results for the Montreal Diet Dispensary's work in low-income areas of Montreal.

6.3.2 Pre-school

When educators estimate that "about 50 per cent of cognitive development of children occurs by the age of three or four" (Sahota, 1978:20; see also van der Eyken, 1977: 70), it is clear that a person's pre-school environment is very important to their eventual life-chances. Almost all of this early environment is created by one's parents and it is in these early years that basic personality traits such as self-confidence and achievement motivation are largely shaped. Time spent in parent-child interaction has been identi-fied as a key variable, one which is a significant determinant of later IQ scores (Leibowitz, 1974). Hill and Stafford have estimated that high socio-economic status mothers spend, on average, 2.25 times more hours with their pre-school children than low-status mothers (1977: 533). As a result, as Leibowitz (1977) has demonstrated, the vocabulary of pre-schoolers is positively related to their mother's education, household assets and activities with the child. In "human capital" terminology this is seen in terms of higher income families being able to make greater investments in "child quality" (see Chapter 7.4), but social classes differ in much more profound ways than simply the time they spend with their children.

Hess (1970), for example, reports that in a study where mothers were asked to teach their pre-school children a simple task, significant differences in teaching strategies emerged, along class lines. Economically poorer mothers were, in brief, poorer teachers, more likely to become frustrated and simply to direct their children. These differences in maternal control techniques arise, Hess argues, out of quite understandable adaptations of the mothers to their own life situations (i.e., endemic economic stress and general powerlessness), but produce in their children a frustration with learning situations and an expectation of failure. Conversely, middle-class mothers who verbalize their instructions more effectively and who appeal to specific arguments rather than direct commands appear better able to set up effective learning situations. The success a child achieves in such a situation is a strong positive reinforcement for attentiveness and effort in a future learning situation.[12]

Social classes differ in their language usages, in their emphasis on control versus autonomy in child-rearing, in the value they place on inhibi-tion/reflection versus impulsiveness/expression, and in their possession and use of books, newspapers and other informational media. Many of these differences (such as discipline strategies or language usages) are imitated by children and passed on quite unconsciously by parents, while some differences (such as encouraging reading or controlling television) are

---

[12]Phelps-Brown (1977: 220) cites similar British evidence on class differences in child-rearing patterns. Physical development also differs by social class. In a study of 10,901 Halifax school children in 1968-69 Welch et al. found that "socio-economic factors strongly influence the stature (height and weight) of children in the area studied" (1971: 373).

conscious parental choices. Whatever the cause, however, when children arrive at school, "middle class children are advantaged not merely in such surface characteristics as better clothing or a different speech accent; they are also much more fluent and grammatical in expressing ideas, they have had a lot of experience at home in school-type tasks, and they are generally more cooperative with teachers and accepting of school aims; they will, therefore, settle down to learning more readily" (Vernon, 1979: 124).

6.3.3 The School System

Early social reformers saw education as the great equalizer, but do all children receive equal opportunities once they are in the school system? First, of course, one must ask which school system do they enter, public or private? Second, one must examine the school board and school they go to. Third, one must look at which class within their school they are assigned to. Fourth, one must examine whether teachers treat children from different backgrounds within the same class in an unequal manner.

In Canada, attendance at private schools is highly associated with economic success. In 1951, 34.2 per cent of the corporate elite of directors of major Canadian corporations had attended private schools, and by 1972 this percentage had increased to 39.8 per cent (Clement, 1975: 244, 267). Since only approximately 2 per cent of elementary and secondary school students in Canada were enrolled in private schools in 1970-71, it is clear that the probability of economic success is dramatically raised by attendance at such schools. It is equally clear that only a small minority of parents can afford the fees involved.

Those who attended the public school system are generally assigned to a school board and a school on the basis of the area of their parents' residence. Since school boards are partially funded from property taxes, the resources available to the school are dependent on the prosperity of the region which supports them.[13] As a result, the Economic Council of Canada estimated that in 1966, Alberta spent $450 per year per student on elementary and secondary education while Newfoundland spent $180 and the other three Maritime provinces were all in the range of $250 to $260 (the Canadian average was $390). Student-teacher ratios and the qualifications of teachers were also significantly worse in poor provinces (ECC, 1969). Even within relatively wealthy provinces, Humphries (1971) found significant differences between rural and urban Ontario school boards in resources, curriculum and teacher quality. Current inequality in earnings may therefore well be at least partially dependent on these past inequalities in educational inputs.

---

[13]Most Canadian provinces have some form of provincial involvement in school funding and Canadian cities have generally been amalgamated into metropolitan districts, hence the inequality in school funding in Canada is probably less than in the patchwork quilt of school board districts typical of the U.S.

Perhaps even more important is the "tracking" that goes on within school boards and within schools. Buttrick (1974) reports that Toronto high schools in high-income areas retain 96 per cent of entering students until grade 12 (54 per cent go on to university), while high schools in low-income areas retain only 60 per cent until grade 12 (only 24 per cent go on to university). Tracking within schools is ostensibly done in the interests of the child, based on objective criteria, but it is hard to believe that class attitudes do not colour the picture when we examine the probability of being placed in a slow-learner stream. Martell (1974) reports results from a 1971 survey of Toronto students indicating that 0.2 per cent of the children of accountants, engineers and lawyers were placed in slow-learner classes, compared to 4.1 per cent of the children of labourers, taxi drivers, etc., and 13.4 per cent of the children of those on welfare or mother's allowance (1974:59). A child's probability of placement in such a stream is 20 times greater if his or her father is a labourer and 67 times greater if his or her parents are on welfare — *far* higher than could be expected on purely "objective" grounds. Not only are middle-class children more likely to exhibit behaviour patterns that are favourably judged by middle-class school administrators, but middle-class parents also tend to be more aware of the adverse consequences for their child of slow-learner placement and more able to do something about it.

The differential treatment of children within classrooms is a contentious issue, with some (e.g., Vernon, 1979) arguing that, controlling for achievement, a child's socio-economic background does not affect teacher behaviour. Rist (1970: 413), however, cites some 13 studies which indicate "that the teacher's expectations of a pupil's academic performance may, in fact, have a strong influence on the actual performance of that pupil" — i.e., teacher expectations become a self-fulfilling prophecy. His study describes the process of initial grouping of children in kindergarten into fast and slow learners, on the basis largely of language, clothing and manners, which in effect split the class he studied by socio-economic background. This initial grouping and the more favourable attention paid to the fast learners soon produced differential achievement, different responses in the classroom and different records of inattention and indiscipline which formed an "objective" basis for streaming in later grades. Since students' formal dossiers and informal reputations went with them from grade to grade, it was very difficult for lower-class children to escape the results of their initial labelling.

Treatment within school interacts with the expectations of parents and peers outside school. Forcese (1975: 68, 70) comments, "Research in Canada has confirmed that (educational) aspirations are principally a function of the social class level of one's family, and rural versus urban residence — not altogether unrelated factors . . . . Lower-class children are in a very real sense socialized to aim much lower than their middle-class counterparts." It is unlikely one will achieve what one has been taught not to aim at. Forcese sees the school system as an essentially middle-class institution in which middle-class children feel comfortable and tend to do adequately well, while working-class children are, in the majority, screened out.

6.3.4 Social Inheritance

Although lower aspirations, a higher drop-out rate in high school and financial constraints mean that a minority of working-class children go on to attend university, clearly some do. Clearly, the majority of working-class children are born healthy, have attentive parents, are not assigned to slow-learner classes and do graduate from high school — but a much larger majority of middle-class children receive these benefits. Children from middle-class and upper-class backgrounds therefore have a systematically higher *probability* of educational and economic success, since the cycle of advantage is cumulative. No single factor in the different class background of working-class children prevents, absolutely, the achievement of high incomes, but the accretion of disadvantages makes it more unlikely. Jencks concludes his summary of 11 panel studies on American men by arguing, "All aspects of family background explained about 48 per cent of the variance in mature men's occupational statuses [and] the most important single-measured background characteristic affecting a son's occupational status is his father's occupational status" (1979: 214).[14]

Brittain (1977: 19) concluded in a U.S. study that family background characteristics explained 57 per cent of the variance in a composite measure of economic status, while just six *measurable* family background variables explained 44 per cent of individual variations in economic status — i.e., there is a very strong tendency for children to inherit the economic status of their parents. His finding (1977: 138) that much of this socio-economic inheritance is mediated through the school system is very similar to that of Husen's 26-year study of 1,500 Swedish children (see 1969: 158). Brittain puts his own findings in very concrete terms when he notes that a man born into the top 5 per cent of families had a 63 per cent chance of a 1976 family income of over $25,000, while a man born into the bottom 10 per cent had a 1 per cent chance of that level of income (1977: 72).

6.3.5 Genetic Inheritance

The "nurture" received by children therefore differs very substantially, both within and outside the family. "Nature" also gives us different genetic

---

[14]Detailed occupational social-status measures are constructed from measures of average occupational education and earnings (see Coleman, 1978). Transitory variation in earnings and the enduring discrepancies between different members of the same occupation mean that family background explains considerably less of the variance in individual annual earnings (see Jencks, 1979: 217).

endowments, but assessing their relative importance in educational or economic success requires a measurement of genetic inheritance which is *independent* of social inheritance. In practice, this is impossible. The physical and mental development of children under two years of age has been tested, but such early IQ test scores have zero correlation with later childhood or adult IQ (Vernon, 1979: 81). The IQ scores of older children are more stable, but do these scores measure one's heredity or one's environment?

"Twin studies" have attempted to resolve the nature/nurture issue by comparing the achievements of twins whose genetic endowment is identical (i.e., identical, monozygotic twins). The methodology of much of the early work in this area was to take a sample of identical twins, some of whom had shared the same family environment and some of whom had not (i.e., were separated and reared in different families). The heritability of ability was then assessed by analysis of the variance of IQ. The extent of correlation of the IQs of identical twins reared in different environments was asserted to be an indicator of the heritability of ability in the general population.

In studying separated identical twins, however, one does well to ask why they were separated in the first place. Kamin (1974) produces evidence that the most common reason for separation in early studies was economic (i.e., the family could not support both), and the most common practice was for a friend or relation to take one of the twins (i.e., their social environments tended to be quite similar.) In neither social origin nor environment were these twins representative of the general population. Unfortunately, the principal researcher in this area, Cyril Burt, believed very strongly in the importance of genetic influences — to the point of adjusting, and in some cases, falsifying, his data (Hearnshaw, 1979; Kamin, 1974). Since data on separated identical twins are extremely hard to come by, many subsequent researchers relied heavily on Burt's work (e.g., Jensen, 1969), and revelation of this fraud has deprived their work of any credibility. Kamin (1974) has analysed the work of Burt and others in this field and concluded that *if* one were to rely *solely* on twin studies, "there is no reason to reject the hypothesis that IQ is simply not heritable" (1974: 67). Others (e.g., Vernon, 1979) argue that genetics does influence IQ, but to a degree that "cannot, as yet, be quantified."

The connection between IQ and economic success is, of course, far from obvious, since so many other abilities and other variables also affect earnings. Jencks, for example, reports that higher IQ correlates with higher earnings among American men, but much of this is mediated through the school system — i.e., higher IQ correlates with more years of education, which correlates with higher earnings (see Chapters 7 and 8). Holding constant demographic background and amount of schooling, achievement on tests of academic ability has minimal correlation with earnings for American men under the age of 30. Among older men, a 15 point difference in IQ scores is associated with a *maximum* 14 per cent difference in earnings. Lillard (1977) argues that males with higher IQs do tend to do better financially later on in life, and that there is a significant interaction effect between ability and education in the speed at which earnings rise with age. However for men with a similar level of education the differences associated solely with measured IQ are relatively small — i.e., "the effects of test performance on earnings are not very large relative to the overall earnings gap between the rich and the poor in general" (Jencks 1979: 121).

6.3.6 Recent Twin Studies

Taubman (1976) attempted to examine the influence of a common genetic endowment on earnings by contacting a sample of 2,000 twins (both fraternal and identical) who were about 50-years old in 1974. He argued that if genetically inherited ability is important, then genetically identical twins should have earnings which are more similar than fraternal twins. Partitioning the variance of earnings into genetic, environmental and family influences produced his estimate that 18 to 41 per cent of the variance in the log of earnings was due to genetics (1976: 867).[15] Twins are, however, a "rather peculiar sample" (Vernon, 1979: 178), whose average IQ is somewhat less than that of the population in general, whose parents tend to treat them more similarly than most siblings are treated, who have to share parental attention with their twin, and who may interact more with each other than siblings normally do. Assortative mating means that the genetic endowment of their parents is probably correlated rather than random, while sample attrition means that Taubman's respondents tended to be of higher socio-economic status than the population at large. Twin studies therefore "involve as much social science theorizing as genetic theorizing" (Goldberger, 1979: 336).

Since Taubman was forced to make a number of strong assumptions, Goldberger simply substituted a different set of assumptions, using the same evidence, to yield the result that 0 per cent of the variance in socio-economic achievement was attributable to genetic differences (1979: 341). His point is not that genetics in fact has zero influence, but that his assumptions can fit the data equally well. The basic problem in this and other studies of human genetic inheritance, is that assessing heritability requires the placing of identical genetic material in environments that are randomly selected on a large enough scale so that one can say with statistical confidence that differences in environment are uncorrelated with genetic

---

[15]Since the estimating equations are under-identified, only an estimated range is possible and this estimate is highly qualified. Goldberger (1978) criticized the econometric specifications very severely. Even if this is a true estimate for this sample, it is highly unclear how, without consideration of demand factors, conclusions from an advantaged group of white males can be generalized to the population as a whole.

differences and will average out. This is possible, if difficult, in controlled experiments in agricultural research stations, but impossible in real human societies. Perhaps the safest conclusion is that for humans, "precise heritability studies are out of the question" (Crow, 1970: 157). Goldberger (1979) argues that there is little hope for narrowing the range between estimates of 0 per cent and estimates of 41 per cent for the variance in earnings explained by genetic endowment.

Goldberger's more important point, however, is to ask why we should care about how much of the variance in earnings is due to genetic factors. As he points out, "some genetically based handicaps are remedied at low cost, some environmentally based handicaps are remedied at great cost if at all" (1979: 345). Genetic inheritance may, for example, produce poor eyesight or hearing which impedes learning and productive work, hence genetic factors may imply low earnings, but eyeglasses or hearing aids are relatively cheap solutions. Conversely, some of the "environmental" handicaps of a deprived family background are extremely difficult to eliminate. There is simply no reason for accepting genetic influences on the income distribution as more inevitable or unalterable than environmental influences. Public policies to decrease inequality may be designed to mitigate genetically inherited *or* environmentally-acquired individual differences, *or* may be aimed at changing the environment within which individuals function — any or all may be effective.

6.4 Differences in Earnings between the Sexes

Although the degree of genetic inheritance of IQ may be unclear and the significance of IQ for earnings even more hazy, genetic inheritance does determine race and sex, and there are very significant differences between races and between men and women in earnings. In the U.S., for example, black men received 64 per cent of the earnings of white men, and black women earned 86 per cent of the earnings of white women in 1970 (Freeman, 1973). In part these differences are due to the different occupations and industries in which black employment is concentrated and, to some degree, to lower average levels of education. Even highly-educated blacks have, however, historically received far less benefit from their education than equally qualified whites. College-educated whites tend to earn more to start and to earn more later as promotions increase their responsibilities, while blacks have in the past remained in lower-level jobs (see Arrow, 1972 for a classic discussion).[16]

---

[16]Recent evidence, however, indicates that the picture may be changing as a result of the anti-discrimination measures of the 1960s. Hoffman (1979), Welch (1973) and Link et al. (1980) argue that an improved quality of black education and greater pay-offs to education are narrowing the earnings gap, at least for younger blacks. Akin and Garfinkel (1980), note that gaps still remain, while Lazear (1979) argues that any narrowing is illusory if blacks receive less training on the job and fewer future chances for promotion.

The smaller size of Canada's non-white population has meant that less economic analysis of racial discrimination has been done in Canada. In part, this neglect may also be because the racial dimension to Canada's economic structure is regionally differentiated. Analysis of the issues involved for West Indian and Asian communities in Toronto and Montreal (where racial issues are often mixed with the problems of newly-immigrated communities) requires, for example, quite a different approach than that appropriate for the black community of Nova Scotia, which dates from the late 1700s (see Wien, 1977), or the native Indian population. In this section we consider only the issue of sex-based differences in earnings, and theories which explain sexual discrimination — not because racial discrimination in Canada is unimportant to the people who suffer from it, but because a much larger fraction of the Canadian population faces personally the issue of sexual differences in earnings.

6.4.1 Male and Female Earnings

The overall differential between male and female earnings in Canada has been alluded to in Chapter 4. Average female earnings in Canada, as in other developed countries, tend to be between 50 per cent and 60 per cent of male earnings (Lydall, 1968; Gundersen, 1980). Comparing all wage-earners, in 1971 average female earnings were 47 per cent of average male earnings, but since a higher percentage of women than men work part-time, one should compare the annual earnings of full-year workers. Female full-year workers earned, on average, 60 per cent of male full-year workers (Ostry, 1979: 340). How much of this differential is due to experience, education and occupation or other factors related to productivity? How much is due to discrimination?

By way of illustration of some of the issues and difficulties involved in assessing male/female earnings differentials, we present Table 6-1. This table has its own intrinsic interest to economics students (although one must remember that these are 1970 dollars), but it also has its puzzles. What brand of economist is it who has grade 8 education or less? Clearly caution is required in interpreting differences within similarly labelled occupations, since very different types of work may be lumped together under the same occupational heading. At every age and education level for which there are estimates, however, male earnings exceed female earnings, a finding which holds within the *vast* majority of occupations, age/education groups, and local labour markets.[17] Comparison is not always possible since some cells of Table 6-1 are blank — i.e., there are not enough women in that category to make a valid comparison. (If we had examined secretarial wages, we would have found too few men for valid comparison.)

---

[17]This table is one of 147 occupations looked at by the Department of Labour (1975); in 94.2 per cent of within-table comparisons men earned more (1975: 84).

Table 6-1

ECONOMISTS* (SELF-DESCRIBED)

Sex/differential	Education	Age 25-34 $	Age 35-44 $	Age 45-54 $	Age 55-64 $
Women	Grade 8 or less	—	—	—	—
Men		8,632	9,457	8,888	8,586
Differential M-W		—	—	—	—
Women	Grade 9-13	6,502	6,675	6,626	4,935
Men		9,868	12,002	11,529	10,626
Differential M-W		3,366	5,327	4,903	5,691
Women	Some university	7,185	10,277	11,454	—
Men		10,780	12,593	12,932	12,621
Differential M-W		3,595	2,316	1,478	—
Women	Bachelor degree	9,064	•	•	•
Men		11,021	14,405	15,741	16,597
Differential M-W		1,957	—	—	—
Women	First professional degree	—	—	•	—
Men		12,184	15,489	15,405	17,880
Differential M-W		—	—	—	—
Women	Master or doctorate	9,758	15,289	15,589	•
Men		12,724	17,510	20,028	21,154
Differential M-W		2,966	2,221	4,439	—

*full-year, full-time workers only.
Source: 1971 Census data, reported in Department of Labour (1975: 110).

One must therefore distinguish between discrimination in pay, discrimination in access to jobs and discrimination "before the market." Discrimination "before the market" refers to the differences in upbringing of boys and girls which encourage them in different values, which direct them to different educational programs and which support them to different degrees within those programs. As Phelps-Brown puts it, "Though half the intelligence of every country is in women's heads, that half does not develop the same qualifications for paid employment as the men's half" (1977: 148). In the terminology of Chapter 7, there is not as much investment in the "human capital" of women, hence part of their lower average wages is due to their possession of fewer educational and occupational qualifications.

6.4.2 Canadian Estimates of Male/Female Discrimination

Gundersen (1979) attempted to estimate the extent of discrimination in pay, while controlling for productivity-related characteristics. Using 1971 census data he estimated a regression equation to predict the earnings of men and women. On average, full-year female workers earned approximately 60 per cent of male earnings, but Gundersen's estimates were that if they had had the same education, experience, and training, and the same occupational, industrial and other characteristics as men, their annual earnings would have been 76 per cent of male earnings on average — leaving a 24 per cent gap due to women receiving different returns for their qualifications (i.e., pay discrimination).[18]

Robb (1978) argued that one should *not* control for industry and occupation, since one form discrimination might take would be to deny women access to high-paying industries and occupations. Denial of access to some jobs means an increase in the supply of female labour to other jobs. "Sex ghettoes" of employment may become overcrowded, hence have depressed wages. Robb's evidence from Ontario in 1971, was that if one examined all men and all women, 75 per cent of the gross differential in wages was due to discrimination. Women, however, often have less job experience because they have left the paid labour market for a time, in order to raise families. If we compare men with single women over 30, (who have probably remained full-time in the paid labour force) Robb's estimate of the discrimination factor falls to 36.9 per cent. To use again the terminology which we will develop in Chapter 7, women who withdraw from the paid labour force to care for children may suffer a "depreciation" in their "human capital" as job skills deteriorate (Mincer and Polachek, 1974). Women who anticipate absences from paid labour may also consciously choose occupations which do not demand a continuous job attachment — i.e., generally have little on-the-job training or career advancement.

In contrast to a model of voluntary choice, many feminist writers (e.g., Blau, 1972; Kessler-Harris, 1975) emphasize that sexual stereotyping in family life and in schools produces a social definition of "women's work" in the labour market.[19] One can thus approach the issue of male/female pay differentials from two very different directions — one emphasizing voluntary choice and the economic rationality of role differentiation within the family and the other emphasizing the socially-created biases and expectations which exclude women from some roles and men from others. Sometimes these approaches seem to differ more in rhetoric and intonation than in substantive predictions, but in the analysis of employer discrimination they come to quite different conclusions.

---

[18]Holmes (1976) estimated that potential female lifetime earnings were on average 41 per cent of those of men (which is questionable since this study used age instead of experience to estimate earnings functions for all women, regardless of work histories), and that 75 per cent of the differential (or 44 per cent = .75 × 59 per cent of the male wage) was due to pay discrimination.

[19]The literature on male/female earnings differentials is far too large to summarize. Gundersen (1980: 360-370) gives a good list of references.

6.4.3 Employer Discrimination — One Approach

One can distinguish, for some purposes, between prejudice against women (i.e., believing they cannot do as good a job as men) and discrimination against women (preferring men over women even knowing they can both do an equally good job, on average). Concentrating on discrimination, Becker's classic study of 1957 argued that discrimination in a particular labour market might be due to employers' tastes — in this case an aversion to hiring women. In Panel A of Figure 6-1 one might place employers in the order of their degree of aversion to hiring women. In Figure 6-1 the vertical axis represents female wages as a fraction of male wages and the horizontal axis measures number of women (who are of the same productivity as men). Employers who are indifferent between hiring men and women (non-discriminatory) will be willing to hire women when they get the same wages:

$$\frac{Wf}{Wm} = 1$$

An employer with mildly discriminatory tastes would prefer men if wages were equal but if female wages were, for example, 90 per cent of male wages he would hire the cheaper female labour. An employer who is strongly averse to female workers would be at the extreme right of schedule D and would only hire female labour if women received, say 30 per cent of the male wage.

The wage ratio between men and women would, in this market, be determined by the demands of the various employers and the supply of female labour. If S_1 were the supply curve of female labour, the equilibrium wage ratio between males and females would be W_1. Relatively non-discriminatory employers would hire only women (F_1 in total), paying them the going market rate which is W_1 per cent of the male wage, while more discriminatory employers would hire only men, paying the full male wage.

In Panel B, however, we can see the impact of these discriminatory decisions on firm costs (quantity produced is measured on the horizontal axis). AC_F represents the average cost curve of a firm which hires women and AC_M represents the cost curve of a firm hiring men. Firms paying the full male wage rate will have a cost disadvantage. If the product market is a competitive one, relatively low cost (female labour force) firms will expand, hence their demand for labour will increase (represented by the demand schedule D^* in Figure 6-1). This increase in the demand for female labour will, if nothing else changes, bid up its price, moving the equilibrium female/male wage ratio closer to 1/1. This neoclassical argument then predicts that discriminatory wage differentials will be eroded over time *if* the market is competitive (i.e., there will be more, longer-lasting discrimination in non-competitive sectors). Since discriminatory tastes are an irrational preference, the logic of competition eventually will force discriminating employers from the market place. Of course, if the supply schedule S_1 of female labour shifts to S_2 and more women enter the paid

Figure 6-1   EMPLOYER DISCRIMINATION IN LABOUR MARKETS

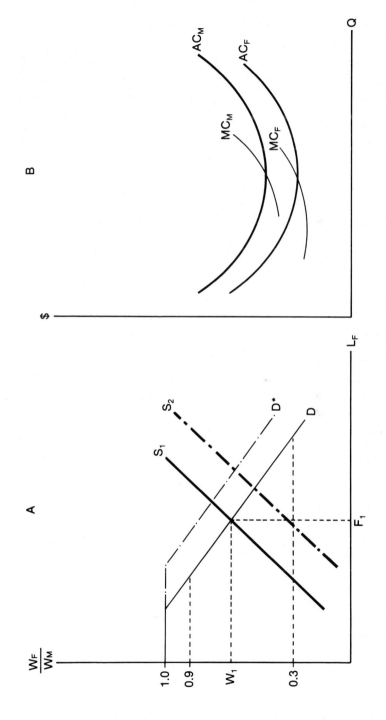

labour market (perhaps as a result of changing attitudes among women about paid work versus housework), the equilibrium wage ratio may not increase and could even fall, in the short run. Unless the supply schedule keeps on shifting, however, at a faster rate than non-discriminatory employers expand hiring, the male/female wage ratio will move toward 1/1. This perspective therefore argues that the basic logic of capitalism is to eliminate employer discrimination, and that if one wants to combat discrimination the most effective government policy is probably to encourage competition in the market place.

6.4.4 Employer Discrimination — Another View

In Chapter 8.2.3 we discuss the "institutional" perspective on discrimination which argues that most productive skills are created through on-the-job training and that wage rates are fixed by institutional rather than market forces. This implies that there is little cost to an employer in exercising a preference over the type of labour he desires to hire. If product markets are in addition viewed as generally oligopolistic and fairly non-competitive in price terms (with most competition taking the form of product innovation and/or marketing), differences in production costs would in any event have a much smaller impact on the market share of discriminating and non-discriminating employers. It follows that there would be little tendency for discriminatory wage differentials to be eroded over time by market forces.

In addition, many writers (e.g., Kessler-Harris, 1975) argue that it is not an accident that most employed women are in occupations of subordinate authority that have an overtone of "nurturing" (e.g., nurse, secretary, waitress). Such "sex ghettos" accord well with traditional viewpoints on "femininity," and often have strictly limited promotion possibilities, low pay and poor fringe benefits, partly because they are crowded with women who have few other options, and partly because "women's work" is systematically undervalued in a male-dominated society (Bergmann, 1971, Weisskoff, 1972). In this view, occupational and job segregation are the primary mechanisms of discrimination, both "before the market," in the socialization and training of workers, and "in the market" where employers really do not believe that women and men are of equal productivity.

Since sexual stereotyping is seen as the major cause of discrimination, and it is seen as having little tendency to be eroded by market forces, the policy measures advocated are largely administrative. Anti-discrimination legislation, for example, prevents employers from specifying that they desire male or female workers, and gives employees the right to sue for damages if discrimination is suspected.

Somewhat stronger are mandated affirmative action plans which compel employers to make extra efforts to hire and promote members of discriminated-against groups. Stronger still are hiring and promotion quotas. All these measures are legislative "interferences" in the labour market, seen as necessary since the labour market is seen as having little tendency to produce "equal opportunity" for males and females on its own.

These two perspectives on discrimination would both agree that women face a problem of constrained choices in the labour market. The first emphasizes the choices which women make on the supply side of labour markets and the long-run operation of competitive markets. The second argues that the constraints women face are the real issue, and one can explain these if one focuses on the demand side of highly imperfect labour markets. Their authors would agree on the undesirability of discrimination but disagree fundamentally on what to do about it.

Chapter 7

Human Capital and the Neoclassical Perspective

When any expensive machine is erected, the extraordinary work to be performed by it before it is worn out, it must be expected, will replace the capital laid out upon it, with at least the ordinary profits. A man educated at the expense of much labour and time to any of those employments which require extraordinary dexterity and skill, may be compared to one of those expensive machines. The work which he learns to perform, it must be expected, over and above the usual wages of common labour, will replace to him the whole expense of his education, with at least the ordinary profit of an equally valuable capital. It must do this too in a reasonable time, regard being had to the very uncertain duration of human life, in the same manner as the more certain duration of the machine.

The difference between the wages of skilled labour and those of common labour is founded upon this principle.

Adam Smith, The Wealth of Nations, 1776.

7.1 Introduction

These words of Adam Smith have been much repeated in the more than two centuries since they were penned. Today, this small paragraph has expanded into a vast and growing "human capital" literature which represents the largest and most influential economic approach to the differences of individual earnings. In this chapter we outline the approach of the human-capital school to the study of economic inequality. The theory comes in two parts — that which concerns the determination of individual earnings (section 7.2) and that which concerns the determination of the distribution of earnings (section 7.3). As we shall see, the link between these parts can be questioned. The implications of this debate extend beyond economics, in that such sociological approaches as status-attainment models can come fairly close to a human-capital methodology. Of course, one must stress that these models concern the distribution of earnings among individuals, and not the distribution of income among families, or economic inequality more broadly defined. Wages and salaries are the primary income source for the vast majority of people (see 5.2), but a full theory has to consider as well, income from wealth — i.e., the share of total GNP going to owners of property and the distribution of that ownership. Chapter 10 discusses the determinants of property ownership. In this chapter, section 7.4 considers the family, in terms both of total earnings and the "production" of inequality across generations. Section 7.5 presents a summary and conclusions.

7.2 The Determination of Individual Earnings

7.2.1 Human-Capital Investment

The crucial notion underlying the human-capital model is that of the voluntary deferral of returns — i.e., investment. Becker has defined human-capital investments as "activities that influence future monetary and psychic income by increasing the resources in people" (1964: 1).[1] Such a deferral of returns is involved if, for example, an individual were to choose between the two occupations pictured in Figure 7-1. Choosing occupation A implies that up to age 24, one would receive lower income — e.g., $6,000 less at age 20. After age 24, those who choose occupation A begin to benefit from the choice — e.g., by $10,000 per year at age 50. The cost of the "investment" involved in choosing occupation A over occupation B is the lower income one receives up to age 24; the benefits involved are the higher income one receives after age 24. The crucial "human capital" question is, when are the costs worth the benefits?

To answer this, one must look at how much it costs an individual to wait until the age of 24 for a higher income, as well as how much higher that income eventually is. If tuition must be paid or books bought, it is quite possible that choosing occupation A might involve a period of training in which income was less than expenditures (i.e., negative) and these initial deficits must be financed in some way. Borrowing capital involves an interest charge. Indeed, even if one did not actually have to borrow, one must still pay attention to the rate of interest since the money used to finance training could have been invested somewhere else. This time-cost of money is central to the idea of discounting. If R is the interest rate per annum, one dollar today will compound to $1 \times (1 + R)$ in a year's time. Conversely, however, it would only take $1/(1 + R)$ today on which interest was compounded at R percent to equal $1 in one year. The *present* value of $1

---

[1] The concept of "human capital" is far broader than merely the impact of training on earnings. For a discussion of the "music capital" involved in listening to serious music or the "euphoric capital" involved in drug addiction, see Stigler and Becker (1977); for a discussion of human interaction in general see Becker (1974).

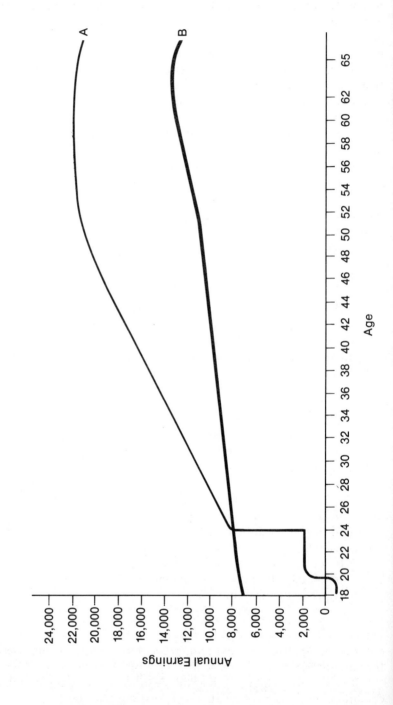

Figure 7-1 HYPOTHETICAL AGE/EARNINGS PROFILES FOR TWO OCCUPATIONS

received a year from now is $\$1/(1 + R)$, and the present value of $1 received in two years is even less. In general, the higher the rate of interest the greater is the cost of waiting and the farther a benefit is in the future, the less it is worth today. Discounting takes this into account, and enables one to calculate the equivalent, in current income, of future returns in alternative occupations. Mathematically, if V_i denotes a sum of money to be received in i years, that sum of money now has a present value equal to $V_i/(1 + R)^i$.

If E_i^A is the earnings of an individual i years from now if they choose occupation A and E_i^B is their earnings in i years if they choose occupation B, the differential in earnings between the two occupations in any year is $E_i^A - E_i^B$. In Figure 7-1 this is the vertical distance between the curves, and at age 20 it is equal to -$6,000, while at age 50 it is equal to +$10,000. An individual who is deciding between careers is assumed, in the human-capital model, to be aware of the differences in earnings between occupations at different points in the future. An individual is also assumed to calculate the present value of the differential between earnings in each occupation, for each year (i.e., to calculate $(E_i^A - E_i^B)/(1 + R)^i$). Up to age 24, this will produce a negative number since the earnings in occupation B are actually higher than those in occupation A (i.e., there is a cost to choosing A). After age 24 the difference is positive, when the benefits of choosing A start to be received. A rational choice clearly involves looking at the costs and benefits over one's entire working life, i.e., adding the cost and benefits to give the net present value of the benefit of choosing occupation A.

F 7:1

$$NPV = \frac{E_1^A - E_1^B}{(1 + R)} + \frac{E_2^A - E_2^B}{(1 + R)^2} + \frac{E_3^A - E_3^B}{(1 + R)^3} + \frac{E_4^A - E_4^B}{(1 + R)^4} + \cdots + \frac{E_n^A - E_n^B}{(1 + r)^n}$$

7.2.2. Equilibrium

In this example, if the net present value of choosing occupation A over occupation B was positive when the interest rate was 5 per cent, and if one could borrow for 5 per cent or less, someone who wished to maximize earnings would enter occupation A. The human-capital model argues that we all make such calculations, implicitly or explicitly. One might then ask, if *everyone* could borrow money at 5 per cent, wouldn't *everyone* try to enter occupation A? Wouldn't this be a disequilibrium situation? The answer is yes — but that equilibrium might occur in either of two ways: (a) interest rates might rise to the point that the advantage of occupation A, on a present value basis, would disappear, *or* (b) the higher net advantage of entering occupation A would prompt an increase in the supply of labour to that occupation and a decrease in supply of labour to occupation B.

If wages are flexible, such a change in the relative supply and demand conditions in the two occupations means that the wages in A tend to fall and the wages in B tend to rise, thereby decreasing the differential between the wages in A and in B. This differential will continue to narrow as long as the supply of labour to occupation A is increasing and the supply of labour to occupation A would continue to increase as long as there were net benefits, at the market rate of interest, to choosing A over B. The labour market will therefore be in equilibrium only when there are no net benefits to be obtained by choosing occupation A over occupation B — i.e., when the present value of all occupational earnings streams are equal.

Naturally, many assumptions are required for this strong result. One must assume that: (a) individuals are well informed of the future prospects of different occupations; (b) that they are of equal ability; (c) that they have the same taste for money income vis-à-vis leisure and the non-monetary aspects of jobs; (d) that they have access to capital at equal rates of interest; (e) that they compete in labour markets where wages are flexible, and (f) that occupational entry and the supply of training are unrestricted. Note, however, that even if all of these conditions hold, the human-capital model does *not* predict that in equilibrium all individuals will have equal annual earnings. Indeed it predicts that inequality of annual earnings will exist. In our example, an inequality of $6,000 will exist between the annual earnings of 20-year-olds and an inequality of $10,000 between the annual earnings of 50-year-olds. Since people of different ages are at different points in their earnings streams, the range in annual earnings of the entire population will be much larger. If, in our example, we considered people of all ages in occupations A and B we would observe that the range was from a high of plus $20,000 to a low of minus $1,000. If the labour market of this example is in equilibrium, however, the net present values of the two earnings streams will be *equal* at the market rate of interest.

From the human-capital perspective, therefore, it is inequality in the discounted value of lifetime income which best indicates "true" economic inequality (see section 3.4), since individuals with the same value of lifetime income may, in any given year, have unequal incomes. If assumptions (a) to (f) above hold, a competitive labour market will be in equilibrium when all occupations have equal net present value. As a result, occupations which involve a long period of training must have higher wages on average in order to compensate for the low income of training years. Of course, such a theory can only explain the demand for training by individuals who are induced (by variations in wages) to enter different occupations. Where the supply of training is restricted (i.e., assumption (f) does not hold), training will acquire a scarcity value and wages in that occupation will rise above that which is strictly required to entice entrants. Occupations will then differ in net lifetime present value as a result of a "market imperfection" in the supply of training. As Blaug (1976) has pointed out, in most countries there is not much of a market mechanism for the supply of training, since governments largely fund education and determine its priorities.

The United States, with its many privately funded universities and training institutes, probably comes closer than most nations to possessing a market mechanism for the supply of training and it is there that the human-capital school has its greatest influence. Scores of studies (Blaug, 1976 and Mincer, 1970 provide partial lists) have found that, in general, those who are more highly educated and have more work experience have higher earnings (see 7.3.2 below).

In 1978, however, the average salary of American college professors was somewhat less than the average earnings of coal miners or automobile workers (Blumberg, 1979), despite the long years of formal education required to become an academic. Is this because coal miners and auto workers are highly unionized whereas American professors are not? Or is it because in such aspects as social status, risk of injury on the job, freedom from direct supervision, job monotony and pleasant working conditions, it is much more pleasant to be a professor than to be a coal miner or an auto worker? Is this the reason why Lacroix and Lemelin (1980:468) found that in Canada the rate of return to a master's degree is 9.8 per cent but the rate of return to a Ph. D. is 0.9 per cent? The lower wages of academics could be seen as due to a combination of a lack of union power (another market imperfection) or to the existence of "compensating differentials" in pay which enable more pleasant occupations to attract labour even at a lower wage.

7.2.3 Compensating Differentials

The idea of compensating differentials goes back, again, to Adam Smith who argued that "the whole of the advantages and disadvantages of the different employments of labour and stock must, in the same neighbourhood, be either perfectly equal or tending to equality." Wages are, of course, only part of a job's attractiveness or unattractiveness — a point recognized explicitly by Becker in his definition of "human capital" by his emphasis on "monetary and psychic income." Figure 7-1 really represents, then, the special case where occupations A and B are similar enough on balance in non-monetary characteristics that an individual will choose only on the basis of money income. More normally, occupations will differ substantially in non-monetary aspects and people will choose career paths on the basis of "the whole of the advantages and disadvantages," both monetary and psychic. There would therefore be nothing irrational, for example, about a person choosing to be a jazz musician for $6,000 a year for the rest of his or her life rather than an accountant for $20,000 or more, *if* that person loved music and hated accounting.

Clearly, "compensating differentials" are a powerful idea. If Adam Smith's statement were true and the whole of the advantages and disadvantages of employment were in fact equal, then the inequality of money incomes which we observe would be highly misleading, since "compensating differentials" would mean that "total" incomes (money income plus psychic income) were really equal. If this were true, then a government policy to increase the money income of the poor (defined in money terms) would *increase* inequality, by raising their "total" income *above* that of everyone else. If one really believed in the theory of compensating differentials one would, for example, argue that a Newfoundland outport fisherman with a money income of $8,000 and a Calgary oil-field worker earning $35,000 are equally well-off, since the Newfoundlander has some non-cash income and lives in a more tightly-knit community, without worries of pollution or crime.

But do non-monetary aspects of jobs *accentuate* or *reduce* the inequality of pay? Is a doctor burdened with responsibilities and pressures and an orderly carefree and easygoing? Or does the doctor love the power and status of his profession and the orderly hate cleaning bed-pans? Clearly there has to be some way to *test* the existence of "compensating differentials" or they may simply become a way of "explaining" everything that has no other explanation.

One problem with tests of the idea of compensating differentials is represented in Figure 7-2, where the horizontal axis measures the number of workers in job A which involves "outside work," and the line W represents the money wage available in "all other jobs" which demand similar qualifications. The supply curve for job A is represented by SS_A, which slopes upward to the right. Some people *prefer* outside work and would accept a lower money wage in A in preference to working elsewhere while others dislike it and would demand a wage premium. What will the "compensating differential" be? It depends on whether demand for this job is high (D') or low (D''). In the former case a wage premium must be paid in job A since the marginal person hired for the job dislikes it; in the latter case the wage in A is less than that paid elsewhere since the marginal person actually prefers the job. The tastes of the marginal person can rarely be predicted unambiguously and the characteristics of actual jobs are hard to quantify in all but a few dimensions, so tests of the theory of "compensating differentials" are, to date "inconclusive with respect to every job characteristic except the risk of death" (R. Smith, 1979: 347).

The risk of death on the job can be quantified (from accident statistics) and can unambiguously be said to be disliked. Viscusi (1978) found that hazardous jobs do tend to have a small wage premium and, as expected, that they tend to be filled by workers with fewer assets — i.e., the poor tend to do more hazardous jobs (at a somewhat higher wage) while the more wealthy can "afford" to "purchase" more job safety. Otherwise, however, there is no strong evidence to support the theory of compensating differentials as a general explanation of unequal money wages.[2] One ought to

---

[2]The Lucas (1977) study is, for example, saturated with data problems.

Figure 7-2 COMPENSATING WAGE DIFFERENTIALS FOR "OUTSIDE WORK"

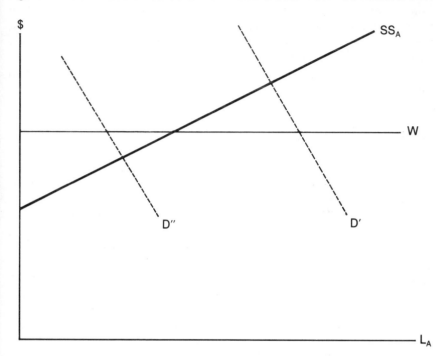

mention that the "dual labour market" theory to be discussed in Chapter 8 predicts that disagreeable jobs will be paid less (not more) than average.

7.2.4 Uncertain Rewards — Risk and Inequality

Jobs, careers and occupations differ in the uncertainty of their rewards, as well as in other characteristics — a fact on which Friedman (1953) based a theory of the extent of inequality in general. Friedman argued that if each individual had a choice of occupations which had different degrees of riskiness in their returns (e.g., movie actor versus policeman), then people who liked risk would tend to choose occupations with a chance of a few high rewards as well as the chance of many low rewards, while "risk-averters" would choose occupations whose possible returns were all very similar. If everyone had the same options but each person chose separately and their choices did not affect one another, then societies where many people were risk-lovers would, he argued, have more unequal income distributions (because more people would be in the risky occupation) while societies with a "risk-averting" population would be more equal.

This is an important prediction since, as Friedman put it, "inequalities resulting from deliberate decisions to participate in a lottery clearly raise very different normative issues than do inequalities imposed on individuals from the outside" (1953: 290). He went on, in another work, to argue that "much of the inequality produced by payment in accordance with product reflects "equalizing" differences or the satisfaction of man's taste for uncertainty" (1962: 148). If inequality is conjectured to arise from deliberate participation in a lottery, on equal terms with all others, one's perception of inequality clearly changes. Money incomes may be unequal but "life-chances" were assumed equal — does inequality "really" exist? If people have different likings for job lotteries, should the state restrict their choice of lotteries by equalizing money income?

Even aside from the issue of whether people actually get to make such choices, Kanbur (1979) has recently shown that Friedman's predictions were based on highly restrictive assumptions — i.e., they depend entirely on a partial equilibrium approach. In a general equilibrium framework, the average return in risky occupations will be forced down when more people enter those occupations. Average incomes in a society with more risk-lovers will then tend to be lower, and overall its degree of inequality *cannot be predicted a priori.* As Pissarides (1974: 1,264) has also concluded, "there is no simple relationship between the degree of risk aversion (in a society) and the extent of income and wealth inequalities." One cannot predict, from theory, that societies where people are more risk-taking will be more unequal — they could be *less* unequal — hence Friedman's position is more a personal point of view than a general proposition of economic theory.

7.2.5 Inequality of Opportunity

Writers in the human-capital tradition usually tend to see the unfettered market as the best mechanism available for the achievement of individual freedom and self determination, but individuals may differ in their access to the funds required for investment in the human-capital market. The education of some students is paid for by their parents, others must borrow and still others find it impossible to finance further training. To a human-capital economist, it seems natural to conceptualize these inequalities of opportunity as differences in the cost of acquiring human capital — and many of their policy recommendations for equalizing opportunity amount to equalizing the costs of human-capital investments.

Inequality of opportunity can be represented in Figure 7-3 by the existence of different supply schedules of funds for different individuals.[3] Individuals who face S_1 can acquire financing for training only at a high initial interest cost and find, relatively early, that it is impossible to borrow further (i.e., they face an infinite interest rate beyond Y_1). Individuals who

---

[3] Along the vertical axis of Figure 7-3 we measure the marginal return to investment in human capital — i.e., the internal rate of return on the last year of training undertaken. The horizontal axis measures years of training.

Figure 7-3

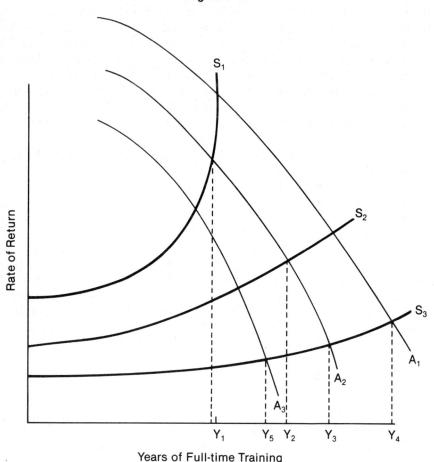

Years of Full-time Training

face supply schedule S_2 can finance further years of training, but at steadily increasing marginal costs, perhaps because they have to turn to progressively more expensive sources (from family funds and low-cost government loans, for example, to bank loans). Those fortunate individuals facing supply curve S_3 can obtain low-cost funding (e.g., from their families) for as many years of training as desired, with only gradually increasing costs.

Persons who wished to maximize their wealth would invest in training until their marginal costs equalled the marginal return from training. If A_2 represents the marginal rate of return from each year of training for a person of average ability, it is reasonable to expect A_2 to be downward sloping. Initial years of education teach such invaluable skills as literacy and numeracy, which have very high returns. Later years of education and training may yield smaller increments in useful knowledge[4], hence have a lower marginal rate of return. A rational person of average ability who was from a poor background (faced supply curve S_1) would then acquire Y_1 years of training, as marginal cost equals marginal return at that level of training. A rational person of average ability from a middle-class background (i.e., curve S_2) would acquire Y_2 years of training while someone from a well-off background (curve S_3) would acquire Y_3 years of training — i.e., controlling for ability, people from more advantaged backgrounds would acquire more training as youngsters, and hence would have higher earnings as adults.

A rational person will acquire training to the point where the marginal return equals the marginal costs, *if* that person actually makes the decisions involved. If someone else makes the decision, the answer is less clear, and early writers (e.g., Pigou, 1932: 493) were concerned that parents made "human capital" decisions for their children, but did not have to bear the consequences of those decisions. As Chapter 6 discussed, the pre-school and early childhood years are important ones for human-capital formation. If conscious decisions are made at this point, they are made by parents, not children. Figure 7-3 is therefore a better picture of adult decision-making in human-capital investment than of the total process of human-capital formation.[5] With this proviso, "equal opportunity" would mean that everyone faced the *same* supply schedule for funds for investment in human capital — "levelling up" would imply that everyone has the advantages of S_3.

7.2.6 Inequality of Ability

Inequality of ability can also be represented in Figure 7-3, by curves A_1, A_2 and A_3. A person of high ability (A_1) might be hypothesized to benefit more (i.e., have a higher marginal rate of return) from each additional year of training. A person of lower ability (A_3) might get a lower marginal rate of return.[6] If we had instituted effective equal opportunity (i.e., everyone faces S_3), but people were of unequal abilities, then society would become an educational meritocracy, where high ability people had Y_4 years of training, average people had Y_3 and low ability people had Y_5.

In fact, we have both unequal opportunities and unequal abilities in the

---

[4]With the possible exception of economics!

[5]Alternatively Figure 7-3 could model the decision-making of parents if one assumed that all parents had the same degree of altruism — i.e., if true costs of investment were always inflated by the same fraction to yield "perceived" cost.

[6]It is not as obvious as it may seem that high ability people benefit more from training. Bowles and Gintis (1976: 107) cite some evidence that people of different abilities benefit about equally from more education — presumably high ability people learn more in school but need school less in order to learn.

real world. Figure 7-3 therefore illustrates nine possible combinations of ability and background, and the intersection points of A_1, A_2, A_3 and S_1, S_2, S_3 represent nine among the many possible combinations of rates of return and years of training, any of which might be selected by rational individuals, depending on their particular circumstances. Mincer (1974: 27) in fact argues that empirically "there is little if any correlation between rates of return and quantity invested," since both inequality of opportunity and of ability are important.[7]

7.2.7 Summary

The "human capital" approach to earnings inequality argues that higher earnings are the result of past investments and that people choose which human-capital investments to make in themselves on the basis of their own individual preferences. Human-capital authors tend, as Mincer put it, to define economics as "the analysis of constrained choices" (1976: 137), and see labour economics as the analysis of constrained choice with respect to human resources — with the emphasis firmly on the choices rather than the constraints.

Predictions on the result of these choices are, however, greatly complicated by the existence of "psychic income," the empirical ambiguity of compensating differentials, and the simultaneous presence of inequality of opportunity and of ability. In addition, as Blinder (1974) pointed out, if one assumes people like leisure as well as income, then their choices will not be based solely on maximizing earnings. Nevertheless, one important prediction is fairly clear: even if labour markets possessed no institutional imperfections and if all individuals had equal opportunity to finance their training, still some inequalities in the net present value of lifetime monetary earnings would persist in a market system. This remaining "inequality of result" would, in the human-capital view, be attributable either to differences in rewards arising from unequal ability (about which, they argue, one cannot do very much, without deserting the market mechanism) or to differences in individual tastes (about which, in the libertarian viewpoint, one *ought not* to do very much).[8]

---

[7]The discussion here refers to marginal returns to training which will only equal average returns to training if either the supply or demand schedules are perfectly elastic (e.g., S_3 or A_3 are horizontal). Equation F7:2 below and almost all empirical work in fact refer to an individual's average rate of return.

[8]Simulation studies such as Blinder's (1974) have concluded that an appreciable portion of U.S. lifetime inequality is due to differences in taste, but that "disparities in wages dominate all other causes of inequality" (p. 125).

7.3 The Distribution of Earnings

7.3.1 A Simple Model

If one ignores the complications of psychic income, risk, tastes, etc., the human-capital school predicts that individual earning capacity will be determined by the equation

F7:2 $$E^*_j = E_0 + r_j\, HK_j$$

where E^*_j is the earnings capacity of the jth individual.

In other words, earnings capacity (E^*) is the sum of the earnings capacity of unskilled labour (E_0), plus the rate of return (r_j) times the stock of human capital an individual possesses (HK_j). If we assume. (a) that actual earnings are equal to earning capacity and (b) that years of schooling represent the stock of human capital, this formula can be manipulated into the form (where S_j represents an individual's years of schooling):

F7:3 $$\ln E_j = \ln E_0 + r_j s_j$$

This is a special, very simple specification. Chiswick (1968) and Mincer (1970) have argued that it can become a model of income distribution if one takes the variance of both sides of the equation and calculates formula F7:4

$$\sigma^2\,(\ln E_j) = \bar{r}^2\sigma^2(s) + \bar{s}^2\sigma^2(r) + \sigma^2(s)\sigma^2(r)$$

where $\bar{r}, \bar{s}$ are the average rates of return and years of schooling and $\sigma^2(r)$, $\sigma^2(s)$, $\sigma^2(\ln E_j)$ are the inequality in (i.e., the variances of) the rates of return, years of schooling and natural log of earnings.

Although this is the simplest formulation of the human-capital approach to income distribution, it still has a number of clear and important predictions. If the distribution of schooling is symmetric, the distribution of earnings will be skewed — i.e., it will have a long "tail" to the right as in Figure 2-2. Holding all other variables constant, formula F7:4 also predicts that as the inequality of schooling decreases inequality in earnings will also decrease; that as the inequality in rates of return to schooling decrease inequality in earnings will also decrease; that as the average level of schooling increases the degree of earnings inequality will tend to increase. The first two relationships may seem obvious, but the third may not. Inequality increases as the average level of schooling increases, *ceteris paribus,* since an increase in the average level of schooling magnifies the impact of any inequality which exists in the rate of return to schooling among individuals. Hence, if we observe that the inequality of schooling has decreased at the same time as its average level has increased, (as has happened since World War II in North America), this model predicts that these two factors would have offsetting impacts on the distribution of income — the former tends to decrease earnings inequality, while the latter tends to increase it.

Chiswick (1974) reports the results of tests of this model against U.S., Dutch and Canadian income distribution data. Mincer comments, however, "The heroic statistical specification of the schooling model yields very low explanatory power and biased estimates of rates of return" (1970: 16).

7.3.2 A More Complex Model

The simple schooling model of equation F7:3 restricts the production of human capital to years of formal education, but learning does not only occur in school. In practice, on-the-job training is often more important. Human-capital theorists see a similar sort of investment process underway in the production of on-the-job training which explains, in their view, the increase in earnings with age which is observed in most occupations.

On-the-job training can produce skills which are *specific* to the firm where an individual is employed or *general* enough that they are of potential value to other employers. An example of firm-specific skill might be the knowledge of a particular firm's accounting system, while experience as a machinist will usually develop skills valuable to several potential employers. The human-capital school sees training as costly and argues that the cost of specific training will be borne by the firm. However, the firm will not be willing to bear the cost of general training since, once trained, workers could threaten to leave and demand a wage equal to their marginal product. The firm would get no return on its investment in general training.

Individuals are then seen as paying for "general" on-the-job training by deciding what fraction (k_j) of their time they wish to devote to the production of human capital and what fraction $(l-k_j)$ they wish to devote to the production of current income. Earnings capacity (E^*) must therefore be distinguished from actual earnings (E).

F7:5
$$E_j = (l-k_j)E_j^*$$

It is argued that k_j tends to decrease with age, since further investment in on-the-job training becomes less worth while the closer one is to retirement. The speed at which k_j decreases cannot, however, be unambiguously predicted from theory, and analysis can easily become quite complex. Mincer (1974: 86), for example, presents four possible specifications of earnings functions, which correspond to different specifications of the human-capital investment profile. The preferred specification is F7:6 which embodies the assumption that the fraction of time put to human-capital investment (k_{it}) declines with experience (t) at an exponential rate β. Neglecting the subscript for the jth individual for simplicity, it is:

F7:6 $\ln E_t = \ln E_o + rs + \dfrac{rk_o}{\beta} + \dfrac{rk_o}{\beta} e^{-Bt} + \ln(1 - k_o e^{-Bt})$

assuming $k_t = k_o e^{-Bt}$

If one introduces the idea that a person's human-capital stock "depreciates" with time at a constant rate d, perhaps due to physical aging and infirmity, or to the lapse of memory with time, or to the progress of current technology, this becomes:

F7:7 $\ln E_t = \ln E_o + (r-d)s - dt + \dfrac{rk_o^*}{\beta} (1 - e^{-Bt}) + \ln(1 - k_t^*)$

There is, of course, no theoretical reason why human capital might not depreciate exponentially and/or investment ratios might not fall linearly (or otherwise).[9] In practice, the choice between these (and other) assumptions is made on the basis of which one gives the better fit to the data at hand — an approach defended by Blinder (1976).

Using a human-capital framework, Mincer (1974) succeeded in explaining some 55 per cent of the variance of log earnings of non-farm white males in the U.S., with a regression which used as variables only years of education, age, and weeks worked. This remarkably good result is often cited as conclusive evidence for a human-capital approach.[10] ("Rates of depreciation" and investment ratios are logically quite important to human-capital *theory*, but do not enter the regressions, since unlike current monetary earnings, experience, or education they cannot be observed directly.)

7.3.3 Criticisms

Formulae such as equations F7:6 and F7:7 predict individual earnings, and obviously become even more intricate when the variance of both sides is taken in order to predict the distribution of earnings (e.g., see Chiswick and Mincer, 1972).[11] At this point, some (e.g., Blaug, 1976) pause to ask whether the theory is still "scientific" in the sense that it is potentially refutable. They wonder whether it has become so cluttered with ad hoc imputations

---

[9]Chiswick and Mincer (1972) in fact, assume K_i decreases linearly with time.

[10]Wolff (1976), on the other hand, found that for operatives, clerical workers and other occupations making up about one-half the U.S. labour force there is little payoff to experience or education.

[11]To make things tractable, Chiswick and Mincer (1972) must, for example, make the unappetizing assumption that an individual's rate of return to school and post-school investments is uncorrelated. Schultz (1971: 27) has argued that much of the empirical success of these models of income distribution is in fact due to a "weeks worked" variable which he argues cannot be properly considered part of the human-capital framework.

that any "bad" empirical results can be handled by a new "technical" assumption.[12] More fundamentally, the institutionalists (Chapter 8) question the whole notion of individual decision making in on-the-job training and the reason why earnings typically increase with age — i.e., they explain Mincer's (1974) results in terms of credentials and seniority.

A final source of criticism is the viewpoint that whatever the merits of the human-capital theory of individual earnings, it cannot be a complete theory of the *distribution* of earnings. A theory of distribution must predict not only that there will be rich and poor, but how many rich and poor there will be. Under simplifying assumptions, the human-capital theory can predict relative wage rates, but nothing in it can predict *how many* people will work at those wage rates. Demand for training depends on wage ratios *and* tastes, demand for trained people depends on wage ratios *and* technology — neither tastes nor technology are discussed within the model.

For example, given the cost of university education and the cost of capital, a human-capital theorist might predict that, in equilibrium, the wages of university graduates and high school graduates would be in a certain ratio, but the theory cannot predict how many people will find it worth while, at that wage ratio, to go to college or how many college graduates industry will want to employ. When Chiswick and Mincer argue, for example, that "if everyone were a college graduate . . . inequality would increase by 0,1074 points" (1972, s45), they are assuming that the wages of BA graduates would remain the same even if everyone had a BA — in effect, an infinitely elastic demand for that type of labour must exist. This does not seem reasonable. Using current data one might be able to predict an *individual's* increase in earnings due to college graduation on the assumption that he or she is a small part of the total labour market and other people's behaviour remains unchanged, but can one predict the result of changes in the aggregate using these marginal relationships?[13]

If we wish only to consider very marginal changes in labour supply there is probably not much error introduced if we simply assume that the return to education remains unaltered. If we wish to consider non-marginal changes in the supply of characteristics, it makes a great difference what we assume about labour demand.

---

[12]Mincer, for example, comments, "A low correlation between investment in human capital and earnings would not constitute a rejection of the human capital hypothesis" (1974: 138), since this might be "due" to unequal opportunity. Similarly the presence of "psychic returns" could "explain" almost anything — e.g., the earnings of academics, which have fallen continuously for a decade.

[13]A mathematical presentation of this argument can be found in Lucas (1977). At the theoretical level the human-capital response is to argue that the return to each unit of human capital is determined by aggregate supply and demand in the market for human capital, regardless of the holdings of particular individuals (Ben-Porath, 1967). That is, human capital differs in quantity but not in kind.

Figure 7-4   ALTERNATIVE DEMAND HYPOTHESES AND RELATIVE WAGES AND EMPLOYMENT OF UNIVERSITY EDUCATED LABOUR

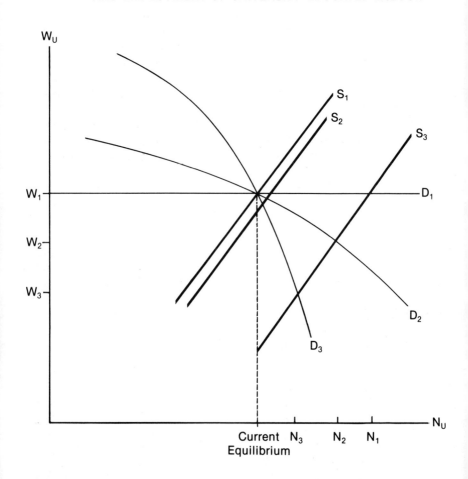

In Figure 7-4, for example, we plot on the vertical axis the relative wages of university graduates and on the horizontal axis the number of university graduates employed in the labour market. D_1 represents the hypothesis of a perfectly elastic demand for university graduates — i.e., an unchanged wage which can be estimated from current data on earnings. D_2 and D_3 represent alternative hypotheses of declining productivity of university-trained labour. If we consider an increase in supply from S_1 to S_2 there is not much difference between the wage ratios implied by D_1, D_2 or D_3. But if we are considering policies to deal with economic inequality (such as, for example, an equalization of opportunity throughout the educational system) we will often be considering shifts in labour supply such as that to S_3 — when it makes a great deal of difference which demand curve is appropriate (and when we will also get little assistance from econometric estimates made in the region of S_1).

The three alternative demand hypotheses imply not only different wage rates for university-trained labour (W_1, W_2 or W_3) but also that different numbers (N_1, N_2 or N_3) will be employed at these wage rates. Since the aggregate inequality of the earnings distribution depends not only on relative wages but also on the number at each wage, one cannot predict its degree of inequality until one has specified the shape of *both* the supply and demand schedules.

Debate on the importance of human capital is obviously highly contentious. Writers in the human-capital tradition tend to emphasize the "rigour" of its logical development and the variety of implications they can produce with relatively few (but crucial) assumptions. Their main conclusion is that if dollar-earnings paths cross (as in Figure 7-1), earnings inequality will decrease and then increase as a "cohort" of workers' age. Earnings inequality at the "overtaking point" will then reflect mostly differences in schooling, and on this basis, Mincer (1976: 151) argues that at least half of the total inequality in observed annual earnings in the U.S. can be attributed to differences in human capital — schooling accounting for approximately 20 per cent, and post-school "investments" for approximately 30 per cent.[14]

7.4 Of Families

7.4.1 The Family as a Productive Unit

The theory presented so far concerns *individual earnings,* but Chapter 2 referred to the distribution of *income* among *families.* This section therefore outlines a generalization of the human-capital approach as it is applied to family labour supply. Just as individuals maximize utility by deciding to work for others for money when money wages are attractive and to work for themselves when "home production" yields a higher return, so also do families make the same decision. Household tasks (e.g., painting the garage, minding the children) are productive — some people decide to do them themselves and some people decide to hire others, while earning the money to pay for these services by their own work in the labour market. Contemporary labour economics views this decision as an economic one, where individuals choose that use of their time which gives the greatest returns — either paid work in the labour market or unpaid work at home. (It is worth noting that unpaid labour at home can be a very large contributor to a family's real income — Gronau (1980) estimates that a housewife's work is worth an average 60% of family pre-tax income.) In a family, total income will be higher if the family members who can obtain higher money wages

---

[14]Elsewhere (1974: 134) he argues that the distribution of education and experience may account for two-thirds of the inequality of "normal" (longer-run) earnings.

for outside work specialize in paid employment while other family members specialize in production within the home. Whether from discrimination or due to lower stocks of human capital, women typically face lower wages than men (see Chapter 6.4). Some theorists (e.g., Gronau, 1977) often add the assumption that women are also more efficient in such home tasks as raising the children. Lower wages outside the home and higher productivity inside it are the neoclassical explanation of the household division of labour, in which men typically work outside the home and women tend to alternate paid work in the labour market and unpaid work in the home.

Over a family's lifetime, the relative returns to home and market work will change. The presence of young children, for example, creates additional demands on parents' time, and the "economic" model argues that it is primarily relative wage rates that cause women (rather than men) with young children to leave the paid labour force. As children grow older, they grow less demanding of time, and married women tend to re-enter the labour market (J. Smith, 1978).[15] Seen in dollar terms, family income obviously increases when women re-enter the paid labour force, but since the use of time in paid employment means the sacrifice of time for leisure or work around the home, the increase in family money income overstates the increase in family economic well-being. Conversely, inequality in family money income which is due to differences in the number of family earners will overstate inequality in family economic well-being.[16]

Recently, Garfinkel and Haveman (1977) have used the human-capital framework to try to estimate the importance of inequality in "earnings capacity" to the total inequality of money income. Arguing that an individual's potential wage can be predicted by their education, age, race, sex and location, they compute the earnings that a family would have if both husband and wife worked 2,000 hours per year. Adding this to the family's income from other sources, such as interest or dividends (but excluding government transfer payments), they compute the family's "earnings capacity" and compare the inequality of earnings capacity across U.S. family units to the inequality of money income across U.S. family units. Their finding is that "the distribution of earnings capacity is about four-fifths as unequal as the distribution of per transfer income" (1977: 3). The remaining 20 per cent of inequality (as measured by the Gini index) is due to differences in "capacity utilization" either because of child-care costs or differences in tastes (i.e., lack of work effort), and they argue that child-care costs are about two-thirds responsible.

---

[15]Women do not re-enter the labour market at the same wage as men of the same age, human capitalists argue, since their absence has cost them some years of on-the-job training. Indeed those women who anticipated, as children, these absences from the labour market would have had less incentive to invest initially in human capital of all sorts.

[16]In practice, increasing female labour force participation in Canada has tended to reduce the measured inequality of family money incomes, by increasing the share of low-income families in money income (see MacLeod, 1980).

7.4.2 The Next Generation

People often speak of being able to "afford" having children, and if one is willing to see a decision to have children as conceptually equivalent to a decision to purchase a car or other consumer durable (in the sense that both are seen as yielding a stream of utility in the future), the human-capital perspective can also be used to analyse family fertility. If children are a "normal" good, more will be desired at higher levels of income. The "price" of children is, however, expressed partly in terms of time (i.e., primarily their mother's time). This approach to fertility therefore argues that higher *family* incomes will mean that parents will have more children but than more highly educated women will have a higher "opportunity cost" of time and may tend to have fewer children.

Willis (1973), Becker and Tomes (1976) and others have also argued that in deciding the size of their families, parents face a trade-off between "child quality" and "child quantity." "Child quality" is produced, in their view, by parental purchase of such inputs as ballet lessons or private schooling or by the parents' own time. If parents have a taste for "child quality" they will, other things being equal, invest more in a fewer number of children. (Recall from Chapter 6 that many of these investments are made at a very early age, although the vague category of "investment" does not help us to distinguish between those deficiencies which can be remedied in later life and those which cannot.) Going a little further, Tomes (1980) has argued that parents who derive pleasure from their children's success (have altruistic tastes) will decide on the most effective means of passing on an inheritance — either by bequest of material wealth at their own death or by investing in their children's "quality" (human capital) over the childhood years. "Utility maximization" by parents is thus held to determine a simultaneous choice of family size, the human-capital formation of children, and material bequest.[17]

7.4.3 The Intergenerational Transmission of Economic Status

Many years ago, the English economist Alfred Marshall wrote:

> the investment of capital in the rearing and early training of the workers of England is limited by the resources of parents in the various grades of society, by their power of forecasting the future and by their willingness to sacrifice themselves for the sake of their children. (1913: 561)

---

[17]This approach can be seen as the development of a new language to describe old facts. "Tastes" can be so easily respecified, e.g., to incorporate social norms which emphasize the importance of male offspring, that virtually any real world fertility behaviour can find an explanation. The differences between childhood environments (see Chapter 6.3) have been reduced to a "tractable" two-dimensional quality/quantity choice, but some, e.g., Ryder (1973), wonder if this new language creates or obscures insight.

Marshall saw systematic biases in parental foresight, information, effort, access to capital (and contacts), and low rates of time discount of future earnings, which all favoured heavy investment by "the higher grades of society" in their children's training, and the opposite for "the lower ranks." As he put it:

> the professional classes especially, while generally eager to save some capital *for* their children are even more on the alert for opportunities of investing it *in* them (1913: 562)

while the children of the working classes "go to their graves with undeveloped abilities and faculties." Marshall emphasized, "the point on which we have specially to insist now is that this evil is cumulative" (ibid., p. 563), as poorly-trained, poorly-paid workers reproduce poorly-trained offspring in each generation, while those with better opportunities themselves tend also to invest more in their own children.

Recently, Becker and Tomes (1979) have formalized some of the same perceptions into an equilibrium model of the distribution of income across generations, within a market society with private ownership (i.e., a capitalist society). Where Marshall argued verbally, Becker and Tomes present their arguments mathematically, but with essentially the same conclusion, that families pass their status from generation to generation, largely by investing in their children.[18]

Specific predictions from the Becker and Tomes model depend on the empirical values of such parameters as a family's propensity to invest in children, the heritability of endowments of "social capital" such as business connections, etc., but its general perspective is clear. If one accepts Marshall's or Becker's and Tomes's analyses, they are arguing that unless government intervenes to invest in the human capital of children, a market economy with private ownership will be a dynastic society. The "life-chances" of an individual person will be in large measure determined by the dynasty or family line into which he or she is born, since dynasties differ in tastes for investment in children and in endowment of social capital. Becker and Tomes argue that skewness in the income distribution is due to higher-income families investing more in their children (and receiving more from their own parents) (1979: 1175). The fortunes of family lines are affected by transitory shocks such as "market luck" (i.e., variations in the returns their

---

[18]The major innovation in Becker and Tomes (1979) is the suggestion that the impact of progressive income taxes in one generation, has an impact on inequality in the succeeding generation, that is theoretically indeterminate (i.e., progressive taxation could increase inequality). Kanbur (1979: 791) derives a similarly ambiguous result within one generation, arguing that the impact of progressive taxation on inequality depends on society's degree of risk-aversion. The presentation of these counter-intuitive theoretical possibilities illustrates the importance of empirical evidence in economics.

assets bring in the market place) and "endowment luck" (such as random fluctuations in inherited ability), so some intergenerational mobility is possible (but temporary). In general, however, there is a substantial correlation between the incomes of grandparents, parents and children.

Of course, "equality of opportunity" in the labour market has usually been interpreted to mean that all persons, within a given generation, have an equal chance — in human-capital terms, an equal endowment of "social capital" and childhood human capital and equal costs of acquiring more human capital. Indeed, it is difficult to see what "equality of opportunity" could mean, if it does not mean equality of opportunity for individual persons. If the Becker/Tomes model is a good representation of a capitalist market economy it would indicate that "equality of opportunity" cannot be attained in such an economy, any more than "equality of result."[19]

7.5 Summary and Conclusion

Human-capital theory is one of the main components of "neoclassical" labour economics, which Cain (1976: 1216) defines as:

> the marginal productivity theory of demand — based on profit maximizing behaviour of employers — and a supply theory based on utility maximization of workers [which] . . . takes the form of (1) investment in human capital, which determines one's skill or occupation — the *kind* of work supplied and (2) labor/leisure choices, which determines the *amount* of one's labor supply.

The strengths of this approach lie in both the volume of theoretical and empirical work (literally hundreds of journal articles, books and monographs), and its extremely wide domain, which asserts insights into health economics, criminology, sociology, religious attendance and much else — as well as claiming to be an explanation both of individual earnings determination and the distribution of income.

The human-capital approach also provides an extremely close "fit" with other areas of neoclassical economic thought. The theory of optimal investment in human capital is almost identical, formally, with the theory of a firm's optimal investment in physical capital, hence techniques of optimization over time and under uncertainty which are used in other areas of economics can be readily transferred to this "special case." "Relative wages" in neoclassical labour models perform the same functions that relative prices do in models of the general economy as guides to optimization, embodying all the information necessary for firm and individual decision-

---

[19]Opinions on the desirability of "equal opportunity" may differ. Marshall, in his use of the word "evil" to describe this intergenerational transmission process, certainly left no doubt as to where he stood on the issue.

making and equilibrating supply and demand in the market place.[20] Most importantly, the focus of the human-capital approach is rational, individual choice. The determination of individual earnings and of the distribution of earnings are therefore seen as the result of rational individual choices — on skill-acquisition, on family labour force supply, and on "investment" in children.

Other interpretations, however, exist, two of which will be discussed in Chapter 8. A general criticism of the human-capital approach lies in the important logical role of such unobservable variables as "tastes" in the theory of family labour force supply or of "investment" in on-the-job training which make it difficult to construct definitive empirical tests of these approaches. Indeed, the very plasticity of the human-capital approach, its ability to generate new working hypotheses on unobservable variables to explain any and all new observations, opens it to the criticism that it has become more a working language of economists than a body of theory which can, ultimately, be refuted.

However, in Mincer's (1970:15) phrasing, one can make "important though not unconditional" statements about the perspective which a human-capital approach brings to the analysis of inequality:

(a) Individuals invest in their own future income, primarily by acquiring schooling and on-the-job training, although the amount they invest and the return they receive is dependent both on their abilities and on their opportunities.

(b) Greater schooling and on-the-job training increase worker productivity.

(c) Individual annual earnings can, to a considerable degree, be explained by experience, schooling and weeks worked.

(d) The increase in individual earnings with education and experience is due to greater productivity and is the pay-off for past individual investment decisions regarding academic and on-the-job training.

(e) Inequality in annual money incomes overstates "real" inequality. "Real" inequality is better measured by inequality in the present value of lifetime income.

(f) Inequality in money income (annual or lifetime) generally overstates inequality in utility, since low money earnings are typically compensated by high non-monetary returns (and vice versa).

(g) The aggregate degree of inequality in the earnings distribution can be seen as the summation of individual decisions on human-capital invest-

---

[20]The market for human capital, like the market for automobiles, does not really require that everyone be perfectly informed if it is to function effectively. If enough consumers at the margin respond to relative wages, relative occupational returns will tend to equalize. In addition, since discounting implies that returns which will be received in 30 or 40 years are heavily deflated in terms of present value, it is not really necessary for individuals to have firm forecasts of earnings in the far distant future.

ments and labour supply. Hence, a more equal distribution of education will tend to equalize the distribution of earnings.

(h) Family labour supply over the life-cycle, and male/female work roles within the family can be usefully analysed as utility-maximizing responses to labour market conditions (and especially to relative wage rates).

(i) Family income (as determined by family labour supply decisions and human-capital investments) and the opportunity cost of time are important determinants of fertility, and of the resources families invest in their children.

(j) Since individuals have differing tastes, opportunities and abilities they will make different investments in human capital. In the absence of government intervention *inequality of economic result is therefore inevitable in a capitalist market system.*

(k) Since families acquire different resources and make different decisions on investments in their children, in the absence of government intervention which equalizes investments in the human capital of children, *inequality of opportunity is inevitable in a capitalist market system.*

In a certain sense the last conclusion may appear surprising. The literature on human-capital investment in child quality has typically been approached from the viewpoint of parents, who make choices which affect their children's lives, rather than from the viewpoint of the children, whose choices are limited by the decisions of their parents. Nevertheless, the implication that inequality of opportunity is an inevitable part of unconstrained capitalism has often been stated over the years (e.g., Knight, 1923, 1951). It follows directly from the inequality of result in the labour market of one generation and the utility-maximizing choices of that generation. It follows also from a very different analysis of contemporary labour markets, to which we now turn.

Chapter 8

Institutional and Radical Perspectives

8.1 Introduction — An Analogy

Suppose that instead of being determined by complex market processes, individual earnings were determined by one's success at a simple task, such as hitting a baseball. In particular, suppose that at age 21 you faced a pitching machine which threw one thousand baseballs over the plate, and your earnings for the rest of your life were determined by the number of hits you obtained. Those who hit home runs every time become billionaires. Those who strike out become skid-row bums. The rest of us are somewhere in between.

Such a process might generate a distribution of earnings not unlike our own, and analysis of it could be approached from different sides. Those who emphasize ability (see Chapter 6) would argue that genetically-inherited ability is the primary reason for the inequality of batting averages and of income which one would observe. Tests of eye/hand co-ordination, reflexes and strength, and their similarity between parents and children might be used to test this theory. The policy implications would be ambiguous. Some might argue that one cannot do much to remedy inequalities in reflexes and co-ordination and therefore not much to equalize the distribution of income, but others would argue that one ought, for example, to provide eyeglasses to those with genetically weak eyesight.

By contrast, human-capital theorists (see Chapter 7) would examine the time that individuals had spend practising before the age of 21 and would argue that this investment of time would largely explain the differences one observed in batting averages. "Equal opportunity" would mean that every child is excused from household chores for an equal amount of batting practice time and all have equal access to expert coaching. But if people prefer not to practice, that of course is their business. A human-capital theorist would argue that even with equal opportunity, some inequalities of incomes would remain, as a result of differences in tastes and abilities which society should not seek to alter.

Most of the authors cited in this chapter would however, wonder whether the others have taken too much for granted. Does the machine pitch the ball at the same speed to everyone? Is the ball always the same size? Does everyone receive a bat of the same size to swing with? All these variables clearly affect the probability that any individual will be able to connect, regardless of their inherent ability or how hard they practice. In the extreme, those who are swinging with a broom stick handle at a marble which is travelling at bullet speed have the odds stacked against them! They will have to be of *exceptional* ability and perseverance if they are not to strike out.[1] For the vast majority the differences will be less large and in some cases quite subtle — for example, the difference between hitting a hard or a soft ball.

"Structural" approaches to the determination of income[2] emphasize the systematic differences in the probability of economic success which different individuals face. The authors cited in this chapter agree in emphasizing that these probabilities are in large measure beyond the control of individuals. They disagree in explaining why. Those who might be called the "neo-institutionalists" argue that is is primarily technological factors which determine the distribution of income and, secondarily, aspects of social class which determine where one places in that distribution. More radical interpretations emphasize the role of economic power in determining the technology of work and the division of labour.

8.2 Neo-Institutionalists

The institutional approach to labour economics has a long history, but in North America, its modern version stems from the work of Kerr (1950) and Reynolds (1951). They and other writers of the 1950s emphasized the "imperfections" of real-world labour markets and the importance of considering social factors and specific circumstances in the analysis of earnings determination. During the 1960s this school of thought was largely submerged by an onrushing tide of "human capital" literature whose stress lay, as we have seen, on the utility-maximizing decisions of individuals over time.[3] In 1971, however, Doeringer and Piore resurrected the notion

---

[1]Hank Aaron is reputed to have practised, as a boy, by hitting bottle caps over his house with a broomstick handle. Economic success is not impossible for the disadvantaged, just much more difficult and improbable.

[2]Note that a theory of income determination only has to predict the batting average of an individual, while a full theory of income distribution must predict as well the number of hitters at each batting average.

[3]The victory of the human-capital paradigm produced a dramatic change in the tools of labour economists. Where institutionalists tended to use a direct-survey methodology, to reason inductively from the evidence and to express their arguments verbally, their "human capital" successors have emphasized deductive, highly formalistic arguments and indirect inference from secondary data. Woodbury (1979) argues that this methodological difference remains the major gulf separating the two research traditions.

of an "internal labour market," which they defined as "an administrative unit within which the pricing and allocation of labour is governed by a set of administrative rules and procedures" (1971: 2). They estimated that over 80 per cent of U.S. workers were members of internal labour markets and argued that in emphasizing external labour markets contemporary labour economics was largely missing the boat on the real determinants of earnings.

8.2.1 The Internal Labour Market

In Figure 8-1 we present a schematic diagram of labour organization in a chemical plant. This plant is part of a larger organization and, as is normal, contains several operating sections. Within each section a number of "job ladders" exist, and we have presented two of the job ladders of the production department in some detail.[4] Typically, individuals are hired at a "port of entry" (usually at the bottom of a job ladder) and progress with experience, with increasing pay and responsibility at each stage. In blue-collar internal labour markets the primary criterion for promotion is seniority while managerial internal labour markets lay greater stress on ability (but balance that, usually, with an implicit guarantee of employment).[5]

Underlying the internal labour market is, in Doeringer and Piore's view, the technological fact of job specificity. They argue that the highly specialized nature of most modern production means that productivity improvements at the plant level usually come from a process of minor production modifications and adaptations to the idiosyncracies of local conditions. Knowledge of these locally-made improvements and an awareness of the different operating characteristics of particular pieces of equipment are not easily codified; in practice, nobody knows these details of work better than the workers themselves. Promotion up a job ladder means learning the skills of your new job and teaching your old skills to your replacement. In general it is not feasible for formal educational systems to perform this training function since the skills involved are so specialized. On the job, workers can learn by "osmosis," by filling in during vacations or illnesses and by informal demonstration (methods which can often be more effective than highly verbal classroom instruction).

But note that the "human capital" emphasis on individual decision-making regarding on-the-job training has vanished. On-the-job training is

---

[4]Figure 8-1 draws heavily on the work of Baron and Bielby (1980), who drew this particular case from a job analysis prepared by the U.S. Department of Labour in California in 1968.
[5]A third sort of internal labour market is operated through the "hiring halls" of craft unions — for example, in the construction trades. Elaborate rules decide which tradesmen will be allocated to which jobs, at what rate of pay, when tradesmen from outside the hiring halls' jurisdiction will be allowed to work on jobs in the area, etc.

PLANT'S INTERNAL LABOUR MARKET

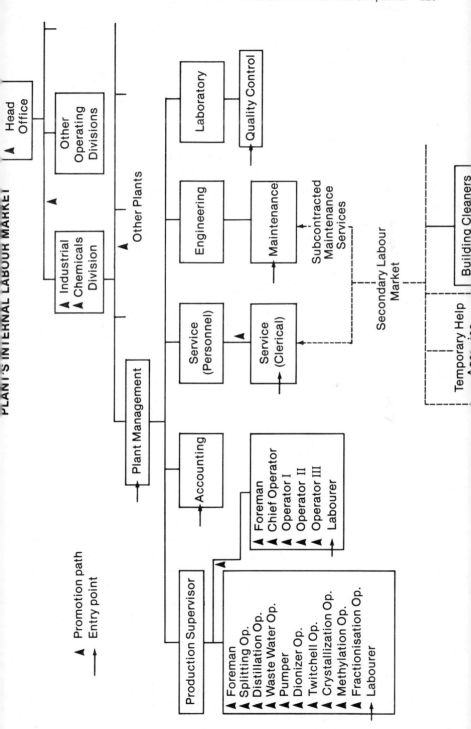

Promotion path
Entry point

Head Office

Other Operating Divisions

Industrial Chemicals Division

Other Plants

Plant Management

Laboratory

Quality Control

Engineering

Maintenance

Subcontracted Maintenance Services

Service (Personnel)

Service (Clerical)

Secondary Labour Market

Accounting

Building Cleaners

Temporary Help

Production Supervisor

Foreman
Chief Operator
Operator I
Operator II
Operator III
Labourer

Foreman
Splitting Op.
Distillation Op.
Waste Water Op.
Pumper
Dionizer Op.
Twitchell Op.
Crystallization Op.
Methylation Op.
Fractionisation Op.
Labourer

seen as a relatively costless by-product of employment, with management making such decisions as exist.[6] However, on-the-job training cannot exist without employment stability and it will not exist if the instructors (other workers) are reluctant to pass on their knowledge. As Williamson et al. (1975) have argued, the standard market solution cannot provide motivation for instruction since there are only a small number of participants involved in each training situation (due to specialization). Any attempt to create a price mechanism to reward workers for training their subordinates would soon degenerate into unproductive haggling over the "appropriate" price.[7] Any success in creating a competitive labour market within the firm would simply dry up the supply of training entirely. If worker A knows that passing on his knowledge of the job to worker B enables B to compete for A's job (e.g., by offering to do it at a slightly lower wage), then he is unlikely to help put himself out of a job by sharing knowledge. But increased productivity depends on effective transmission of these highly specialized skills. Technically sophisticated firms therefore have strong practical reasons for instituting seniority systems or employment guarantees which guarantee the individual worker that he can safely pass on his skills. In a seniority system, someone with lower or higher seniority is neither a threat nor threatened themselves by the competition of other workers, hence nothing is lost if one helps another to do his job — and no work group can function without some co-operation.

Stability of employment also means that people at a work site have an ongoing relationship with each other, i.e., they form a social group. As social animals, humans who interact with each other for any length of time tend to develop patterns of behaviour and to evolve group norms about the customary way of doing things. Patterns such as the normal length of a coffee break or the expected time to quit work are usually based mainly on the way things have been done in the past, but they can become very deeply ingrained — indeed, Doeringer and Piore refer to them as the "customary law" of a work place. Transgressing this customary law produces morale problems, which can have financial consequences. It is rarely sufficient for management to gain "perfunctory compliance" ("working to rule" almost invariably brings an organization to its knees), since beyond the most routine tasks it is usually impossible to formally describe all of a job's duties. Without some degree of internalization of the firm's goals, authority could

---

[6]The neoclassical reply is to argue that individuals choose firms which offer more or less on-the-job training, hence decide indirectly on investment in on-the-job training. Institutionalists tend to see this as highly unrealistic, arguing that the required information for such choices is usually not present, and jobs with training opportunities often pay more, not less, than jobs without them, and that high youth unemployment precludes such "choice for labour market entrants."

[7]Where large numbers of market participants exist, a competitive market generates a clear signal; where only a few are present, bargaining is inescapable.

not be delegated and unexpected developments could not be handled. Even firms without unions therefore tend to exhibit a tendency for "past practice" to continue, although a certain degree of codification of work rules is usually implied in a collective agreement.[8]

Pulling these ideas together, Thurow (1975:79) argues that 60 per cent of U.S. workers acquire *all* their job skills on the job and that "the labour market is not a market where fully developed skills bid for jobs. Rather it is primarily a market where supplies of trainable labour are matched with training opportunities that are in turn directly associated with the number of job openings that exist. Training opportunities only occur when there is a job opening that creates the demand for the skills in question." Turning the supply-side orientation of human-capital analysis neatly on its head, Thurow argues that typically a demand schedule exists for a job, but there is no independent supply schedule! In contrast to a neoclassical approach (which can be called a "worker sovereignty" model) he therefore sees the effective locus of decision-making on training (and relative wages) as being at the firm, rather than the individual, level.

If the dynamic efficiency gains (in long-run technological innovation and improved morale and labour productivity) of maintaining employment security in an internal labour market typically dominate short-run efficiency gains from hiring in an external labour market, people outside the internal labour market are simply shut out. Hence, for example, the existence of unemployed economists does not produce a bidding down of all economists' current wage rates and a new "marketing-clearing" equilibrium where business and government replace existing personnel from the pool of the unemployed. Instead, a variety of institutional mechanisms (tenure, Civil Service regulations, de facto employer policies — what Freedman (1976) calls labour market "shelters") protect those currently employed, and they in turn continue to use their very specialized areas of expertise for their employer's benefit.[9] Once inside the internal labour market (a faculty or government or business department), notions of parity with similarily qualified personnel (i.e., "wage contours") tend to dominate wage increases — for example, a university wage settlement which provides the same percentage increase for all departments, regardless of the current supply/demand situation of biologists vis-à-vis economists.

Many of the authors cited in Chapter 7 would, however, argue that

---

[8] As the almost universal existence of "past practice" clauses in collective agreements indicates, however, union agreements codify only part of the "customary law" of a workplace. By formalizing grievance procedures and by providing a mechanism for trading off benefits in one area for desired changes in work practices in other areas, unions may, in some instances, actually increase work flexibility (see Freeman, 1980).

[9] Competition certainly exists in the economist labour market, as in many others, at ports of entry, in the sense that real wages fluctuate but excess supply/demand may not be totally eliminated.

none of this is really new, it is rather simply *description* of the process of on-the-job training which they acknowledge to be important.[10] Nor do Doeringer and Piore deny totally the influence of market forces. The points at issue for earnings determination are really rather subtle: the speed with which wage rates adjust to excess supply (or demand) of particular types of labour, the importance people ascribe to relative wages compared to the absolute level of wages, and the degree of individual choice involved in the on-the-job training process. Neo-institutionalists argue that the internal wage structure of an establishment changes very slowly, that relative wages are extremely important and that there is in fact little individual choice involved in the on-the-job training process — while "neoclassical" writers, for the most part, take the opposite tack. In addition, institutionalist writers stress the importance of "past practice" for work organization and productivity. However, there is no clear criterion for determining when, for example, wages within a firm move "so slowly" in response to outside pressure to be "rigid" or "quickly enough" to be "responsive" to market forces. One's choice of perspective is, therefore, largely a matter of judgment at the present time.

8.2.2 The Role of Education

The institutionalist viewpoint argues that one's initial port of entry into the internal labour market is crucial to one's lifetime career. The main function of education is, in this view, that of screening workers for different possible levels of entry into the world of work. Even if almost all the skills people actually use in their jobs are learned on the job, still a *relatively* high level of education may indicate the *relative* ability of individuals, in particular their ability to absorb training. When technological progress is rapid and only dimly foreseeable beyond the short run, the ability to absorb new training or to adapt to new, as yet unknown, techniques becomes highly important. Access to management jobs, for example, will then tend to be restricted to those with a *relatively* high level of education. Hiring at this entry port will be determined, in large measure, by credentialism. The absolute level of education is not nearly so important as one's *relative* level of education. When only 5 per cent of the population had BAs they were the ones hired as trainee managers in business and government; when 20 per cent of the population has a BA it is the 5 per cent who have MBAs who are hired.

BA graduates are then pushed farther down in the educational queue, receiving the lower wages which accompany lower positions rather than a "general" rate of return on human capital. Inflation of educational qualifications then occurs throughout the job pyramid, from the increased

---

[10]For example, they argue that labour market "shelters" are due to firm-specific human capital, which an employer does not want to lose.

education required of potential policemen to the increased credentials required for elementary school teachers. In this competitive scramble, more education is a "defensive necessity" for each individual to secure a place in the job queue. Institutionalists argue, however, that the job hierarchy is not changed by all this jostling in the queue for desirable jobs — hence the considerable equalization of education since World War II has produced no corresponding change in the inequality of income distribution.

Formal models of labour markets where education is mainly a "signal" of potential ability have been developed by Arrow (1973), Spence (1974), Stiglitz (1975), and others.[11] A common conclusion of these models is that "economies with imperfect information differ in fundamental ways from economies with perfect information" (Stiglitz, 1975: 269). Several different equilibrium positions may exist in these models and in some equilibria everyone may be worse off as everyone "over-invests" in unproductive credentials. There is no guarantee that unaided market forces will push an economy to its optimum allocation of resources. These multiple equilibria differ in income inequality as well as in average income. What determines which equilibrium the model converges to? Past history (Spence) or particular parameter values (Arrow, Stiglitz), which may be determined institutionally, are crucial. These models, if taken seriously, then point to the role played by expectations formed on the basis of past behaviour and "arbitrary" social institutions in determining the degree of economic inequality.

In general, the "screening" perspective — that *relative* education indicates *relative* ability but does not change productivity — implies that equalization of opportunities for education will *not* equalize the distribution of earnings. It also implies that increases in the average level of education will not aid economic growth to any appreciable degree. "Investment in education" is therefore attacked on two fronts and it is argued (e.g., Taubman and Wales, 1973) that the "social" rate of return (in terms of increased output to society) to investment in education is less than the private return to the individuals involved. Part of the justification for the expansion of Canada's system of colleges and universities in the 1960s lay in the human-capital arguments that increased growth and equality would result; hence the screening/human-capital controversy is of considerable importance for policy.

Does education primarily create credentials or primarily impart skills? Obviously the issue is highly important. Wolff (1976) has demonstrated that only in a limited number of occupations does education affect earnings directly, as opposed to its general importance in limiting *entry* to an occupation. Riley (1979) comes to much the same conclusion but Layard and

---

[11] All of these authors would probably call themselves "neoclassical economists" if they had to pick a label.

Psarchopoulous (1974), among others, disagree. One can be certain the controversy will continue, but basically it is now a controversy over the *degree* to which education creates credentials vs. skills — few would contend that it does not do both.

8.2.3 Discrimination

Since the institutionalist view is that hiring decisions are largely based on estimated *potential* for future training rather than current skills, employers may well believe that "background characteristics" such as age, previous employment history, general personal demeanour, race, or sex are good predictors of future trainability. The standard neoclassical approach to such discrimination (see 6.4), is that if an employer is factually wrong in his belief he must pay for the privilege of discriminating, via higher wages unbalanced by higher productivity. The institutionalist perspective is that where there is in fact little difference in potential trainability and where wages are generally fairly rigidly set by the "wage contours" of the internal labour market, there is little cost to the employer in exercising a preference for a particular type of worker. Spence (1973) and Starrett (1976) have argued as well that an observed preference for whites over blacks, for example, in managerial positions will create informational feedbacks which decrease the perceived pay-off for blacks to invest in education, hence decrease their average level of education and reinforce the stereotype of uneducated blacks.[12]

In addition, personal contacts (what economists tend to call "informal information networks"; see Rees, (1966) or Granovetter (1974)) may well be the determining factor in which job a person entering the labour market actually gets. Accepting that initial job forecloses some options and opens up others. It is usually very difficult for an individual to evaluate fully the complex tree of decisions and future options involved, but those who have better contacts are clearly better off.

Hence the institutionalist model of individual income determination stresses education, seniority, background characteristics, personal contacts and an element of luck.[13] Their model of the income *distribution* stresses technology, and the sociology of wage determination. If we refer again to Figure 8-1, institutionalists tend to see the demand for these specific

---

[12]For a discussion of statistical discrimination see Aigner and Cain (1977).

[13]"Luck" might include, for example, the phase the business cycle is in when an individual enters the labour market. Institutionalists argue that employers react to booms and scarce supplies of labour by relaxing hiring qualifications, rather than by increasing entry level wages (raising wages would have a "ripple" effect on wages above the entry level). Members of minority groups or the poorly educated may be hired in such periods and, *if* they accumulate enough seniority, will escape lay-off in the recession. When labour is easily obtained, employers tend to demand higher qualifications, in many cases higher than some of their current workers could meet.

occupations and the job-ladder relationships between them as largely determined by technology. The state of technical and management knowledge at any point in time determines the number of possible choices of technology, plant layout, capital equipment, etc. open to a firm, but once made, that choice determines a matrix of labour inputs required.[14]

8.2.4 The Wage Structure

The technology of production may determine the number of people at each point in the job hierarchy, and "progression" up a job ladder may imply some increase in pay, but how much? It is the sociology of wage determination which, in the institutionalist view, determines relative wages within an internal labour market. They argue that relative wages depend heavily on notions of equity and "fair" treatment with respect to the custom of a workplace. Relative wages are thus heavily influenced by past history, hence the exact level of differentials is somewhat arbitrary, yet highly resistant to change once established. Past practice tends to define what is a "fair" remuneration for different shifts, for responsibility or for unpleasant working conditions, and job evaluation schemes both codify and lend an air of objectivity to those judgments. Institutionalists argue that employers are loath to risk the morale problems caused when an established wage structure is tampered with.

Lydall's (1959) model of the wage structure of a hierarchic organization argued that firms can be seen as composed of levels of supervisors, each of whose wages is proportionate (by a ratio p) to the total wages of the people under him. If the "span of control" of a supervisor (i.e., the number of people who report to the supervisor) is typically n and the wage of the ith level of supervisor is written as X_i, this amounts to saying:

F8:1
$$\frac{X_{i+1}}{nX_i} = p \qquad \text{hence} \qquad \frac{X_{i+1}}{X_i} = pn$$

The wage differential for responsibility is therefore dependent on n, which Lydall assumes is technically determined, and by p, which he argues is due to expectations — i.e., the sociology of the workplace.

---

[14]Baron and Bielby (1980) give examples where apparently similar California plants have different job structures. Phelps-Brown (1977: 34) notes that comparing similar French and German factories, the French use a higher ratio of non-manual to manual workers despite higher relative salaries of non-manual workers. Dore (1973) gives a fascinating account of the substantial differences in work organization between British and Japanese factories producing electrical generating equipment, which likewise escape simple explanation by relative wages or technological determinism. "Technology" therefore seems to impose fairly broad constraints, within which past practice, both national and company, plays a significant role.

Pareto's Law has long been known to be a reasonable approximation to the upper end of the distribution of wages and incomes.[15] Where y is the number of incomes exceeding any level of income x, and b and a are constants, it states (in its simplest form):

F8:2 $$Y = bx^{-a}$$

Lydall proves that $-a = \log(p)/\log(np)$ — i.e., that under the assumptions of his model the shape of the upper tail of the wage distribution is given by a combination of technology and the expectations of rewards for responsibility.[16]

There are fundamental differences between the way neoclassical and neo-institutional authors view the setting of wages. The neoclassical tradition argues that it is a reasonable approximation to say that supply and demand determine wages — labour demand is determined by marginal productivity[17], and labour supply by individuals maximizing their utility, subject to their own budget constraint, independent of the income of others. Thurow's verbal model (1975) and Stiglitz's (1975a) or Arrow's (1973) mathematical models argue that the marginal product of an individual is often very difficult (expensive) to calculate and may in fact be unknowable if the joint production of a group of workers is involved.

Thurow goes on to argue that even if constant returns to scale prevailed and marginal products were ascertainable, a profit-maximizing firm might not use them to construct a wage schedule, if such a schedule offended the norms of pay held by its labour force. (The cost of morale problems might mean the firm would be better off paying its traditional scale.) In contrast to a neoclassical approach, he feels that preferences are largely interdependent and that people care deeply about relative incomes,[18] hence institutional mechanisms are required for wage setting.

---

[15]Pareto (1896: 305) himself believed it to be applicable to the entire distribution of income, but was misled by his data (income tax returns), since income tax was then paid only by upper-income groups.

[16]The theory of optimal hierarchy and control structures for a profit-maximizing firm has been discussed by Stiglitz (1975b) and Calvo and Wellisz (1979).

[17]Strictly speaking, the marginal revenue product of labour equals the marginal cost of labour in profit-maximizing equilibrium, but the potential qualifications of imperfect product and/or labour markets are often ignored. As Oi (1962) noted when firm-specific human capital is involved the equation W=MP holds only in an expected value sense over the likely tenure of the job, not necessarily at any particular point in time.

[18]To take a particular example, independent preferences imply that doctors are indifferent as to how much plumbers make, while interdependent preferences imply that doctors get very upset if they think that plumbers make a higher hourly wage. One can test the realism of either assumption by querying any random sample of MDs.

8.2.5 The Secondary Labour Market

Up to this point, we have basically been discussing the "primary" labour market, where jobs are relatively well paid, with good fringe benefits, relatively pleasant working conditions, employment security and clearly defined grievance procedures and work discipline regulations. Institutionalists argue that this desirable package of employment rewards arises when the profit maximization of firms entails stable employment patterns and well defined internal labour markets, but a second major theme of early work is the presence of a "secondary labour market" whose jobs are much less desirable. Piore (1975: 141), for example, argues "Most industries appear to be operating as if they consistently faced a choice between two different techniques of production." One technique is capital and technology intensive, uses specific skills and highly differentiated work roles and is well adapted to long, stable production runs (hence generates stable employment and well-developed internal labour markets). The other option is less capital intensive, uses more general skills and more adaptable capital equipment and, being more flexible, can better cope with instabilities in market demand (hence generates unstable employment).

In the "secondary" or "dual" labour market, jobs are typically short term, unstable, with low pay, poor working conditions, arbitrary work discipline and few fringe benefits. Casual employment, sub-contractors of business services, marginal suppliers in unstable industries and some retail and service establishments are cited as examples.

In some respects, this analysis has a long history. John Stuart Mill emphasized the existence of "non-competing groups" and wrote "The really exhausting and the really repulsive labours, instead of being better paid than others, are almost invariably paid the worst of all, because performed by those who have no choice" (Mill, 1848: 372). Marshall referred to the occupational structure as a series of steps. He argued, "the dirtiness of some occupations is a cause of the lowness of wages in them" (1920: 558), since they would only be filled by unskilled workers with no other options and he saw "no more urgent social need" than the elimination of such jobs. The modern version of "dual labour market" analysis developed, however, in the late 1960s out of a perception of the employment problems of blacks in the urban ghettos of the United States. The quintessential secondary labour market employers, in this view, are the hiring halls for temporary labour which can often be found gathered around the edges of urban American ghettos. These hiring halls typically pay cash, by the day, for unskilled or at best semi-skilled labour on a first come, first served basis. No promise of work tomorrow is made by either party. More common (but less extreme) are the seasonal or short duration jobs, from fish-plant worker to security guard to gas station attendant, which offer little or no on-the-job training or prospects of advancement.

A major feature of this analysis is its emphasis on "feed-back" effects, from jobs to work attitudes and from past work history to future job options. Low pay and poor prospects for advancement mean that there is little pay-off to an individual in cultivating a good work record. As a result, habits of absenteeism and tardiness may become established, and voluntary job changes may restore some of the variety in work experience that the more fortunate members of the primary labour market achieve by progression up a job ladder. As the saying goes, a worker may then become "jack of all trades, master of none." Instability of employment can then create a vicious circle where there is little incentive for an employer to invest in on-the-job training and little incentive for a worker to stay, without prospects of future advancement. High turnover may also mean that work relationships appear arbitrary, since there is no chance for customs to become established among a stable social group. Bad morale and a general pattern of "negative exchange" or guerilla warfare between management and workers exacerbate the problem of low employee productivity.

Why would anyone stay in the secondary labour market, if they had a choice? For some, membership in the secondary segment of the labour market may be voluntary. Students (who are only in it for the summer), housewives (whose family roles may take priority) and temporary migrant workers may have no desire for employment stability or long term prospects of advancement. Others may not have a choice. Sexual or racial discrimination, the lack of educational credentials, unstable prior work history, a criminal record or an "irregular" immigration status[19] may well trap an individual in a succession of low wage, dead-end jobs interspersed with spells of unemployment. From the segmentation viewpoint, this is the basic problem of the working poor.

This "dualist" approach differs from the "human capital" analysis discussed in Chapter 7 on three important grounds:
(a) it argues that "bad" jobs are not paid more but rather are paid less than "good" jobs (hence inequality of utility is greater than inequality of money incomes would suggest);
(b) it feels that one's analysis should "make both technology and tastes integral parts of the economic process" (Piore 1974: 685);
(c) it postulates that one should see the labour market as composed of segments between which both outcomes and "rules of the game" differ.

8.2.6 Criticisms

It is, however, no easier for "dualists" than for "neoclassicals" to define unambiguously "good" and "bad" jobs (see 7.2.3). At the level of anecdote, both can offer examples of highly paid and poorly paid jobs which have poor

---

[19]Piore (1979) emphasized the plight of illegal aliens in the U.S.

working conditions, unstable employment and few fringe benefits. Since these characteristics do not always point to the same classification, the original description must be seen as an ideal type. As a result, in empirical work different writers in the dualist tradition emphasize different criteria. For example, Piore (1975) stresses employment instability, while Gordon (1980) focuses on control over own working time, and Edwards (1979) emphasizes job security. These different criteria blur the focus of a segmentation approach and expose it to the criticism that it lacks a unified theory.

The argument that technology necessarily splits possible production processes into two major options is probably as difficult for most people to swallow whole as a literal interpretation of the smooth "isoquant" of neoclassical micro-economic theory (which implies that an infinite range of production combinations exists). Interpreted as a metaphor, however, the segmentation approach is arguing that there are only a few processes which are viable options while the neoclassical approach feels there are quite a few. It is the identification of feedback effects from a firm's choice of technology which the critics of a dualist approach (Cain, 1976; Wachter, 1974) identify as one of its main theoretical contributions. A firm's choice of technology determines many aspects, such as stability, of the employment it offers, which affect the psychology and abilities of its employees (their "tastes" in the language of Chapter 7). These changes in employee attitudes and the work histories they acquire affect their future employment prospects (and Bowles and Gintis (1976) argue, the way they raise their children) in ways the employees could not be expected to foresee initially. In terms of one's judgment on economic inequalities, can they then be said to have chosen their eventual economic situation?

"Segments" are an idea which many economists find hard to accept. Many argue, with Marshall, that "nature does not make jumps" and feel that usually there are fine gradations between ideal types, and that one should more appropriately think of a continuum. They wonder also what defines the segments and what prevents people from moving between them.[20] One might agree that blacks and women receive different treatment in the labour market, but argue that the dividing lines there are at least fairly clear, and that such discrimination is a smaller topic than dualism claims to be.[21] It is also frustrating that there is no common view of the idea of "segments." American segmentation writers speak of segmentation of jobs (e.g., Edwards, 1979), segmentation of occupations (e.g., Piore, 1975), and segmentation of industries (e.g., Osterman, 1975), while the

---

[20]Mayhew/ Rosewell (1979) report finding substantial mobility.

[21]Leigh (1976, 1978) presents some of the few detailed empirical studies of dualism done by a non-convert. His largely negative conclusions are, however, based on the assumption that black workers are all "secondary" and whites are all "primary." Since virtually no dualists would agree with this specification, they tend to ignore his results.

principal Canadian research in this area focuses on segmentation of establishments (Clairmont and Wien, 1978). Hence many economists view segmentation as "a rich and provocative set of loosely connected empirical hypotheses" (Wachter, 1974: 680), which are not a threat to established theory (Cain, 1976).

In response, segmentation writers usually argue that theirs is an emergent literature and that it is too early to ask it to be as completely specified as its long-established alternative. Substantial revision has in fact already taken place. Piore (1975) and Edwards (1979) both now argue that one should think of three segments. In Edward's terms these are the secondary, subordinate primary and independent primary, each of roughly equal size. The secondary market is characterized by its low wage, casual, low-skilled nature (e.g., security guards, waitresses), the subordinate primary segment offers somewhat better paid, more secure jobs (e.g., auto workers), and the independent primary segment contains supervisors and professionals who have career prospects (1979: 162-183). Gordon (1980) argues from the radical perspective that the degree and type of labour market segmentation changes over time as economics develop and historical and political trends evolve. Other reformulations are sure to arise as the approach matures — but these reformulations expose the segmentation perspective to the same criticism we made of the neoclassical perspective, that is, it can be reformulated to cope with almost any empirical event and is more of a "working language" or "research tradition" than a strictly refutable theory.

8.2.7 Summary

The "neo-institutionalist" approach is composed of a number of strands of thought and a general perspective. It argues:
(a) that institutions (internal labour markets) generally allocate labour and set wages for most workers, without "much" pressure from market forces except at ports of entry;
(b) that education serves mainly as a credential to gain access to desirable jobs, hence equalizing access to education will have little effect on earnings inequality;
(c) that there is little tendency for market forces to eliminate discrimination;
(d) that wage inequality is heavily influenced by historically determined patterns and the sociology of the work place;
(e) that the labour market should be thought of as split into segments, within which outcomes differ greatly and between which little mobility is possible.
Rather than emphasizing the choices individuals make, its general perspective is to emphasize the constraints individuals face. Technology and social attitudes are therefore seen as the chief factors governing the degree

of earnings inequality we observe, and their explanation must be found in engineering and sociology. Institutionalists argue that the possibilities for reducing inequality are illustrated by the one major decline in economic inequality of recent times — i.e., that decline which occurred in the U.S. and Canada during the Second World War (Haley, 1968; Ostry 1979: 222) as a result, Thurow argues, of wartime wage controls reducing differentials but becoming, over time, accepted as "normal."

In method of analysis, conclusions and policy implications neo-institutionalism offers a different viewpoint to that of Chapter 7 but if taken separately its components can often be incorporated into neoclassical models. In its own way, it is "optimistic" on the subject of inequality. It sees equality of opportunity and greater equality of result as achievable, within present-day capitalist market systems, by a process of institutional reform (see 12.4.2).

8.3 A More Radical Interpretation

Edwards (1975) and Bowles and Gintis (1976) are representative of a group of radical writers who argue that it is not technology but the social relations implied by capitalism which create job ladders and segmented labour markets. These writers agree with the institutionalist description of primary and secondary labour markets and they agree that ascriptive characteristics such as race, sex or age, and credentials such as education, ration access to the job ladders of the primary market. Where they disagree with the institutionalists is in their conception of the role of technology. Institutionalists tend to see technology as an essentially neutral, exogenous element whose development depends largely on the inherent logic of scientific discovery. Radicals emphasize that the choice between existing techniques of production and between competing research and development projects for the development of new technology are both under the control of existing elites. They argue that the owners of industry have two main aims: to maximize profits and, more fundamentally, to maintain the control of the means of production which ensures they will continue to receive those profits.

Explaining the maintenance of social control is thus a key issue in the analysis of radical writers. As a result, their discussion is broadened to include issues of the distribution of political power, of the historical development of institutions and of the impact of work on individuals and their families, which are generally not touched on by other authors. Concentration of wealth and of control over industry (see Chapter 3.2) inevitably implies, in their view, a parallel concentration of effective political power. Formally, however, modern democracies have given most adults the right to vote. Centralized control and the growth of large corporations mean that economic organizations are authoritarian, that work is hierarchically organized and that any individual worker tends to lose touch with the final product. Normatively, however, the values of equality, of freedom and of finding a sense of satisfaction in one's work are deeply ingrained. How do capitalist societies deal with these contradictions?

Bowles and Gintis argue, "In capitalist society, to make the hierarchical division of labour appear just is no easy task; the autocratic organization of the enterprise clashes sharply with the ideals of equality, democracy and participation that pervade the political and legal spheres" (1976: 83). Yet the stability of any social system depends on its acceptance, i.e., the socialization of most individuals into values and perceptions which imply that the existing order of things either should not or cannot be changed. In capitalist societies, the school system plays a key role in educating children in what Bowles and Gintis call the "technocratic-meritocratic" perspective — i.e., the perception that the inequalities of economic life are technically necessary and that assignment to positions in the economic hierarchy is largely made on the basis of personal merit.

Radical writers tend to see few purely technological imperatives in the organization of work.[22] They admit that technology has developed so that most production processes are fragmented into many separate operations but they deny that technology had to develop in this way or that work relationships have to be organized in hierarchies of authority. They argue that experiments in work re-organization and in industrial democracy[23] indicate that productivity may well rise when workers share in decision-making and tasks are less finely divided. Following Marglin (1974), Bowles and Gintis argue that the primary purpose of the division of labour established during the Industrial Revolution was not to ensure efficiency but to guarantee that the capitalist controlled the whole production process and could collect his profit. Following Stone (1975), they argue that the internal labour market arose during the late nineteenth century as a mechanism to differentiate jobs that were essentially equal and thus fragment the working class into "dissimilar" segments.

The dividing line between "primary" and "secondary" employment is thus seen as a function more of class conflict than of technology. Union organization can change "secondary" jobs into "primary" jobs[24] and employers can shift jobs from primary labour markets to secondary, unless they are prevented.

When characteristics such as sex or race are, in practice, used to assign people to work roles and job ladders, and when status and pay are clearly differentiated within job ladders, the development of class con-

---

[22]Neoclassical writers share this scientific optimism but argue it is relative prices which determine choice of technique.

[23]For references, see Virmani (1979) or Newton/Leckie (1977).

[24]As when the United Farm Workers organized California farm workers, previously a "classic" competitive labour market, and won higher pay, a seniority system, improved working conditions, a hiring-hall system and grievance procedures.

sciousness is greatly impeded. These labour market mechanisms have, in the radical view, therefore played a key role in preventing the emergence of the revolutionary proletariat of which Marx wrote, but the stability of capitalism also requires that individuals are, on average, reconciled to their *personal* lot in life. Partly this reconciliation is accomplished by the different norms and aspirations acquired through one's family[25] but largely it is accomplished through the school system.

The school system is supposed to offer equality of opportunity to all, but in practice treats children of different backgrounds unequally (see Chapter 6). Unequal treatment by the school system helps to ensure intergenerational transmission of status, and the unconscious choices of parents on discipline strategy, lifestyle and values create distinct class and neighbourhood cultures which children acquire by "osmosis" and which guide them to particular occupational slots. Indeed, Bowles and Gintis argue that those people who move up the occupational ladder must adopt the mannerisms of their new socio-economic class (such as wearing a tie to work) if they are to "fit in," and that the real function of such mannerisms is to reinforce the authority relationships of a hierarchic society. They therefore argue that inequality of opportunity is inevitable in a capitalist society for people of different class backgrounds.

In addition, an important function of school is as a paradigm for later life — to convince the child that he or she is competing on an equal basis with peers, is assessed according to objective criteria and that those who are smarter and work harder are the ones who get the top marks (incomes). Failure is, therefore, important since it teaches students to lower their aspirations. Repeated failure can well convince students they are not cut out for the upper echelons — but remember that the institutionalists argue that the skills used there are very often learned on the job.

Bowles and Gintis argue that the most important lessons taught in school are the implicit ones. The importance of being on time and of obeying authority are emphasized in primary grades and in working-class high schools. Together with basic literacy and numeracy, they are the requirements of lower-level jobs in the economic hierarchy. Elite colleges and select private schools, on the other hand, emphasize self-direction and create a social milieu where students come to expect that they will achieve an elite position later in life. The educational system thus creates not only the credentials which allocate individuals to entry ports but also the habits and expectations which see this allocation as legitimate.

---

[25]Bowles and Gintis argue that the greater value placed on obedience, neatness, etc., and the conformity to external authority emphasized by working class parents merely represent the lessons they have themselves learned in their jobs, while the emphasis on responsibility, internal control, etc., of higher status parents reflects the attributes valued in their own occupational roles. Hence the transmission of different family values tends to ensure an inheritance of socio-economic status (1976: 146).

The radical analysis therefore addresses the issues of why the existing distribution of income is not equal, why this distribution is tolerated, why some individuals "get ahead" of others and why children tend to inherit their parents' socio-economic status. It does not address the issues of why the income distribution has a particular *degree* of inequality or why it is different in different countries other than to say that the degree of inequality in a capitalist society depends on its history and on the level of class consciousness and class struggle in that society.[26]

8.4 Discussion

Much of the radical analysis of modern labour markets is identical to that of neo-institutionalists (hence the same criticisms can be made), but their *perspective* is different. Where neo-institutionalists see technology as a relatively neutral but crucial force and are relatively optimistic that political actions could reduce inequality, radicals emphasize the distribution of economic power in modern societies (see Chapter 3:1) and argue that fundamental institutional change is required to produce appreciable decreases in inequality.

The radical and neoclassical approaches have both similarities and differences. Their methods of analysis could not be more different — the one verbal, inductive and sometimes dialectical, the other mathematical and deductive — but one will look in vain for an empirical test which could conclusively test (and possibly reject) either approach as a scheme of thought. "History" or "class-consciousness" in radical thought and "tastes" or "human capital" in neoclassical thought are sufficiently loosely specified concepts that either approach can elaborate explanations to almost any conceivable event. In some respects they can both best be seen as "working languages" or "frameworks" for discussion, and some things are easier to say in one language than in another.

Some things take on different names in the two languages, but remain the same empirical events. The advantaged "class background" referred to by Bowles and Gintis (1976) are the same advantages in parental attention, superior neighbourhood and schools and possible "connections" that Becker and Tomes (1979) refer to as a family's "endowment of social capital" and "investment" in their children. Empirically, radicals and neoclassicists disagree on whether to expect "breaks in the data" to exist which show clear differences between social classes, and how many borderline cases there are in a classification of class. They differ also in their emphasis on how many of the decisions which affect a child are under the conscious control of parents or under the control of others (such as school administrators) and

---

[26]The constancy of the U.S. income distribution is noted by Bowles and Gintis as an indicator of the failure of increased educational equality to promote meaningful social change, but they do not really explain it.

they differ on the degree to which people can be said to make conscious "decisions" on their children's or their own future. Nevertheless, from the point of view of the child, it does not make much difference if the choices are conscious or unconscious, and both agree that the family into which one is lucky (or unlucky) enough to be born exercises a major influence on eventual economic success.

What is perhaps most surprising, given the great differences in theoretical starting points and methods, are the common predictions — that a capitalist market system will produce neither equality of opportunity nor equality of result. Indeed both schools of thought now recognize that the distinction between "equality of opportunity" and "equality of result" can be maintained for only one generation in a capitalist market system. Since radical writers have generally attempted to integrate political and historical factors into their analysis, the "capitalist market system" as they see it *includes* the state and its operations. In their view the state is an indispensable part of modern economic life, training workers, providing "public goods" and most importantly, safeguarding property rights. They see political influence as being in large measure determined by economic power. Hence radicals argue that the contemporary operation of the state perpetuates inequality of opportunity and inequality of result, and that radical political change is necessary to change this bias.

Since neoclassical economists have generally left political analysis to the political scientists, their analysis is subtly different. They tend to define the "capitalist market system" as limited to the operation of markets, with private ownership of property. Such writers therefore tend not to discuss why the state intervenes in those markets. If parents (whose wealth is unequal) are the only ones to decide how much to "invest" in the early "human capital" of their offspring, then inequality of opportunity is inevitable in a "capitalist market system." If the state intervenes (e.g., by providing subsidized, enriched day-care for pre-school children or by subsidizing university education) this intervention may reduce, or may accentuate, inequality of opportunity (see Chapter 12.2). Which type of intervention to expect in a capitalist market system is an issue which neoclassical writers do not generally address.

Chapter 9

Earnings Determination — An Eclectic Summary

The problem of distribution is difficult; no solution of it, which is simple, can be true. Closer study has shown that what professed to be easy answers to it, were really partial answers to imaginary questions that might have arisen in other worlds than ours in which the conditions of life were very simple. But yet the work done in answering these questions was not wasted; for a very difficult problem can best be solved by being broken into pieces; and each of these simple questions contained a part of the great and difficult problem which we have to solve.

Alfred Marshall, Elements of the Economics of Industry.

9.1 Explanations: The Problem of Choice

9.1.1 Income Determination and Income Distribution

Chapters 2 to 4 discussed the extent of economic inequality and poverty in Canada; Chapters 5 to 8 presented some theories. There are two sets of questions to be asked. First, what factors produce the distribution of economic resources in Canada? In particular:
(a) Why do we have this degree of economic inequality in Canada?
(b) Why has income inequality been so constant over the period since the Second World War?
(c) Why do differences in inequality exist between countries and between regions of the same country?
   A second set of questions revolve around the factors which determine the economic resources of particular individuals and families. Specifically:
(a) Why do the children of poor parents have a greater chance of being poor themselves? How do the children of advantaged families inherit the status of their parents?
(b) Why do people with more education or more work experience tend to earn more than people with less education and less work experience?
(c) Why do women tend to earn less than men, blacks less than whites,

French-Canadians less than English-Canadians? Why do some people work all their lives for low wages?

Throughout the literature there is frequent confusion between theories which can answer either or both of these sets of questions — i.e., between theories which explain the determination of *individual* income and theories which explain the *distribution* of income. Not all theories can do both. If, for example, income were determined purely by a lottery, it would be a true theory to say that an individual's income was determined by whether or not he or she held a winning lottery ticket. A further theory, however, would be required in order to explain why there were a particular number of first, second, and third prizes and why they had those particular values — i.e., why a particular income *distribution* existed.

To cite a more realistic instance, one can consider the impact of unionization on individual earnings and on the distribution of income. A major aim of unions is to raise their members' wages, and several studies indicate that the average union/non-union wage differential is somewhere between 8 per cent and 15 per cent (Lewis, 1963:194; Rees, 1962:79; Starr, 1973, 1975).[1] One might then think that if a union were to organize a group of low-paid workers and to succeed in raising their wages relative to non-unionized workers, the distribution of income would become more equal, that is, low paid workers would now earn something closer to an average wage while wealthy capitalists would receive lower profits.

Within the neoclassical framework, however, Johnson and Mieszkowszki (1970), argue that it is not necessarily the case that a wage increase due to unionization increases the share of labour, and that union wage gains may be largely at the expense of non-union labour. In a general equilibrium framework, a wage increase in the union sector will cause prices to rise and demand to shift away from the goods the union sector produces. Only if the union sector is capital intensive will total returns to capital fall, since in this case unionization prompts a shift in demand toward relatively labour-intensive production (hence labour's share rises in aggregate and capital's share falls).

In this model the impact of a variable (unionization) in the individual earnings determination process may be quite different from its impact on the aggregate income distribution, once general equilibrium effects are

---

[1] There are of course, several estimates of average influences outside this range and much evidence that union impact differs widely between sectors. In addition, some argue that higher wages may help cause unionism, in the sense that highly paid, highly productive workers organize to protect their rights rather than simply going elsewhere (Freeman, 1980). Another argument is that higher union wages may mean higher qualifications demanded, hence on an "efficiency-units" basis, in the long run, unions do not raise wages. Obviously complex controversies continue — for useful summaries see Addison and Siebert (1979: 279-291) or Gundersen (1980: 307-324) — but for the present argument we need only assume that unions have some positive impact on their members' relative wages.

taken into account. Johnson and Mieszkowski (1970: 547) even suggest that partial unionization of the labour force may, under some assumptions, decrease absolutely the wages of *both* union and non-union labour, even though union members continue to earn more, *relative to*, non-union members.

As one can recall from Chapter 5, there is no consensus on the theory of the "functional" distribution of income, and the Johnson and Mieszkowski position is thus far from universally accepted. Certainly the post-Keynesian and Marxist perspectives would disagree, arguing that unionization more typically shifts factor shares in favour of labour. For the present discussion, however, the important point of this neoclassical argument is that the effect of a variable in determining relative individual earnings may not be generalizable to the distribution of income.

Similarly, men commonly earn more than women, but would equality between men and women in the labour market mean greater equality of earnings? Or would equality of opportunity simply mean that more men become low-paid secretaries and more women become high-paid executives? One must distinguish between theories which can explain the income distribution and theories which can explain individual income determination; only under such special assumptions as an infinitely elastic demand for all types of skills or human capital can the same theory suffice for both. A complete theory of income *distribution* must include a theory of individual income determination, hence both sorts of theories must be discussed. In practice, however, theories of individual income determination are much farther advanced than theories of the distribution of income and wealth.

9.1.2 Choosing One's Perspective

Our understanding of why individuals "get ahead" and why inequality exists is central to our understanding of the society around us, and it is a truism that there is no real agreement. Chapters 6, 7 and 8 presented some very different viewpoints on the determination of earnings, ones which will lead those who tend to value equality to very different conclusions about desirable social policy. Some of the chance or genetically-based theories outlined in Chapter 6 imply that not much can be done about earnings inequality, hence policies which attempt to alter distributive shares can do no good and may do much harm. The "human capital" viewpoint of Chapter 7 argues, however, that changes in the distribution of education and training can produce changes in the distribution of earnings, within our existing social and political structures. This "reformist" perspective is attacked by many of the writers cited in Chapter 8, who argue that earnings inequality is not inevitable, but that fundamental social and political changes are required in order to alter it.

How do we choose between these perspectives? In practice, many elements enter: the views of our family and the other social groups with whom we associate, our own social values on other issues, our degree of ignorance of the alternative theories which have been proposed and even such trivia as whether we like or dislike the individuals we meet who espouse a particular viewpoint. Ideally, however, we would choose rationally. Most economists would argue that the criteria we should apply in such a rational choice are: (a) that a theory be logically consistent, i.e., not be self-contradictory, (which implies that it be framed in specific enough language that one can tell); (b) that a theory produce predictions about the real world which are consistent with observed facts; (c) that a theory be at least potentially refutable.[2] Applying these criteria we may well find that none of the available theoretical alternatives is completely satisfactory — in particular, one can argue that such key concepts as "ability," "human capital" or "segments" can be defined in such a way as to enable theory to fit reality, whatever the reality.[3] Each of us must then make an individual judgment as to the least unsatisfactory approach or the "most promising" avenue for future research — one hopes it will be an informed judgment.

In Chapter 6, we examined the role of chance, ability, race and sex in earnings determination. Chapter 7 discussed the human-capital school whose focus is the supply of skills to the labour market while Chapter 8 presented a number of "structural" approaches which argue that the demand side of the economy (and especially the decisions on labour market policy made by firms) is the paramount factor determining income and wealth distribution. To some extent these theories simply emphasize different aspects of the earnings determination process, but they were posed separately, as alternative viewpoints, because they are often viewed as such by their exponents. Pragmatists may try to combine their insights, in the same way as one would make a stew of many ingredients, but one must do so with care. Those who have no dislike for the taste of illogic or inconsistency can combine these theories in virtually any fashion they desire, but others will notice the occasional incompatibility of assumptions between the different approaches. Tolerance or distaste for theoretical vagueness or the possibility of contradiction differs among economists, but in practice relatively few are total purists in their explanation of economic inequality. Even relative pragmatists, however, may disagree violently on what is the real "meat" of the inequality issue and what is the inessential flavouring which surrounds it.

---

[2]An example of a non-refutable, and hence, non-scientific theory is, "everything that happens is God's will." This theory explains everything but it predicts nothing. No skeptic can be convinced of the truth of this theory by an appeal to empirical evidence, since by construction of the theory, empirical evidence cannot refute the theory. Hence, belief or non-belief is a matter of faith.

[3]Hutchison (1960), Koopmans (1957), and Kuhn (1970) are all classic statements regarding the problems of evidence and inference in economics.

Figure 9–1 PATH DIAGRAM OF INFLUENCES ON INDIVIDUAL EARNINGS

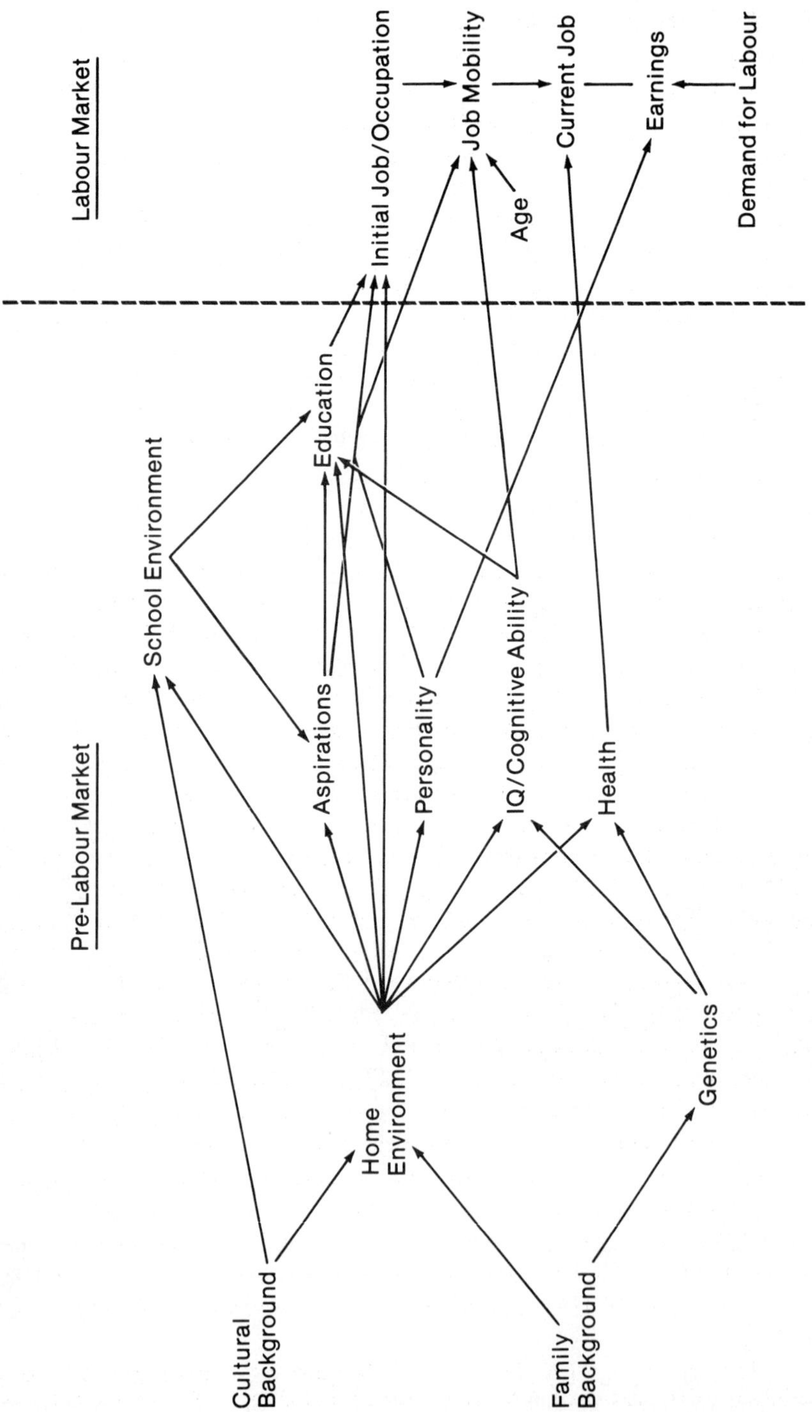

9.2 An Eclectic Approach

The discussion to this point can perhaps best be summarized in a diagram such as Figure 9-1. The determination of individual earnings is influenced by many factors, which imply both that individuals enter the labour market with very different characteristics, and have different experiences within it in terms of wage rates, unemployment and total earnings. Of course, the determination of family income depends also on inherited wealth, the returns to past savings and the earnings of all family members. Hence, this diagram, complex as it is, is not complex enough to explain the determination of family income. A fuller theory is also required to explain the *distribution* of family income, but drawing on the sources cited thus far, we can at least discuss the determination of individual earnings.

Under the heading of "cultural" influences, we can discuss the impact of an individual's background, outside of his or her immediate family, on eventual earnings. Numerous studies have observed differences between racial, religious and ethnic groups in average earnings. Francophone Canadians have lower earnings than anglophone Canadians, and Catholics tend to have lower earnings than Protestants (Kuch and Haessel, 1977). Individuals from rural backgrounds tend to earn less than individuals from urban backgrounds (Jencks, 1979), and individuals from the Atlantic provinces tend to earn less than individuals from central Canada (E.C.C., 1975). These differences mirror the differences in opportunity faced by people from different backgrounds; in general, the cultural environment of one's home is determined not simply by the idiosyncracies of one's parents, but also by the social community of which they are a part.

Among the measurable variables on family background, the most important seems to be the father's occupation. More generally, as Brittain (1977), Jencks (1979), and many others have noted, there is a strong tendency for children to inherit the economic status of their parents, as indicated by relative family income and parental education. This inheritance process is largely mediated through the school system (Husen, 1969), through a cumulative series of educational decisions which are strongly and consistently influenced by family factors (Parsons, 1975). Childhood environment is also influenced by the number of siblings present. Parents are responsible for an individual's genetic endowment, but this constitutes only part of "ability," and Jencks' evidence (1979: 121) indicates tests of cognitive ability have a relatively small *independent* effect on earnings.

"Home environment" is thus a complex entity with manifold impacts on future earnings. As Forcese (1975) noted, it interacts with school environment to shape an individual's aspirations, as well as having a primary role in forming personality and influencing health and cognitive ability.

The layman's term "personality" is typically disaggregated by economists into "tastes" and "abilities." One's taste for risk, one's tolerance (or desire) for change, and one's preference for the monetary versus the non-monetary aspects of jobs will affect career decisions at each fork in the road. All these tastes are systematically influenced by home environment. Bowles (1972), for example, conjectures that upper-class children are socialized to value more highly the non-monetary aspects of jobs.[4] Tastes for leisure versus monetary income also differ among individuals and influence both their choice of jobs and hours worked within those jobs. "Abilities", as in irritability, dependability, the ability to get along with others, the ability to delegate, the ability to organize and plan, are also often thought of as part of "personality" and largely formed within one's home environment.[5]

In some occupations, strength and dexterity are important for earnings, in others physical stamina may be important; clearly health is an important component of one's human capital. Despite the great importance of personal decisions (e.g., the self-inflicted wounds of smoking or alcohol abuse), a substantial fraction of one's health and physical constitution is shaped by one's genetics, early nutrition and the presence or lack of remedial medical attention in childhood.

The effect of home environment on cognitive ability and school achievement has been discussed in Chapter 6.3.4, but in addition, one's home environment may play an important role in initial job placement. The first job an individual obtains carries with it not only current wages but also a package of on-the-job training opportunities, promotion possibilities and an implied degree of job security. The formal qualifications required almost always include a minimum level of education and/or a field of special training, but since novice job seekers are often very poorly informed about alternatives, their access to information is also important. Rees (1966) and Granovetter (1974) have discussed the "informal" information networks of family, friends and neighbours and have emphasized that "contacts" are important in a majority of hiring decisions.

Once within the labour market, an individual's earnings are heavily affected by his or her degree of job mobility: geographic, occupational, industrial and hierarchic. Geographic mobility is very high in Canada, and Courchene (1974), and Grant and Vanderkamp (1976) have argued that much of it is a response to economic incentives. A person who is willing to move tends to receive higher earnings. Occupational mobility is also high in Canada, even among the highly trained. Ahamad et al. (1979) concluded on the basis of a 1973 survey of 96,000 degree-holders in Canada that "there is, in many cases, only a loose association between

---

[4]This implies that eventual money income underestimates the differences in options open to upper and lower class children.

[5]Lydall (1976: 29) emphasizes the "D factor" — drive, dynamism, determination, energy, industry, self-discipline — which is a combination both of personal abilities and aspirations. Jencks (1979, Ch. 5) discusses possible measures of "personality" and concludes that "leadership" as a student may be an important predictor of eventual adult earnings.

occupation and field of study" (1979:57).[6] Mobility between industries can also increase an individual's earnings, since some sectors (e.g., trade, services) have systematically lower wages than others (see Vanderkamp, 1977). Job mobility as a result of seniority is, however, the most important factor for the labour force as a whole, as individuals draw increased pay and benefits and move up a hierarchy of skill and responsibility with their individual employer. At the top of the earnings pyramid most earnings are almost totally defined by one's place in a hierarchic structure (as per Lydall, 1959).

Figure 9-1 is more complex than similar diagrams in Lydall (1976), Atkinson (1975) or Canterbury (1979), (although less complex than Meade, 1976: 147) but it is still highly reductive. Its essential point is that many influences operate on individual earnings, both before and within the labour market, and both directly and indirectly. Unravelling the relative importance of these influences is a highly complex task.[7] "Luck" enters at every turn — e.g., the good luck of being placed with an exceptional early teacher who may encourage a child to persevere in education or the bad luck of a disabling accident. (Of course, some schools have a higher proportion of good teachers and some jobs have a higher risk of disabling injuries.) At most one can hope to estimate the relative probabilities of different levels of earnings of a person with given characteristics. The most important characteristics determining individual earnings are socio-economic background and sex.

Figure 9-1 omits many of the complexities of the supply side of labour markets and omits also the complexities of the demand side.[8] It illustrates

---

[6]One might have expected that those with university degrees would be the most specialized, with the least likelihood of changing occupational fields, but some 32 per cent of those with university degrees had changed their broad occupational category between 1971 and 1973. Hierarchic mobility, i.e., movement into managerial roles, might account for some of this occupational change, but substantial movement was also noted out of managerial occupations.
[7]Economists tend to use multiple-regression analysis, at various stages of sophistication, while the preferred technique of sociologists is that of "path analysis," which imposes the restrictive assumption of linear relationships between all variables and an absence of interaction effects. In addition to the problem of appropriate specification of variables, functional forms and estimating technique (see Griliches, 1977), Chapters 10 and 11 of Jencks (1979) discuss the differences in parameter estimates, with *identically specified* regressions, which different surveys and research styles generate. Parameter estimates are thus a function not only of statistical technique but also of data collection and manipulation methods.
[8]For example, Taubman (1977: 438) mentions that nepotism may be important in determining earnings on the basis of the finding that one's father-in-law's education was a significant determinant of male earnings in the sample he studied. Any possible direct impact of family background on job mobility has been ignored in Figure 9-1 on the presumption that the most important effects of family background are felt before most individuals enter the labour market. Figure 9-1 also neglects, in an attempt to avoid excess complexity, most feedback effects. Physical health, for example, determines whether one can pass the medical examination that many employers impose before hiring, hence health affects earnings, but job-related injuries or diseases such as the coal miners' "Black Lung" imply that one's job may also affect one's health, and eventual earnings.

only influences on the characteristics individuals will bring with them to the labour market, but the price those characteristics will command depends also on the nature of labour demand. Labour demand is, in Marshall's phrase, the "other blade of the scissors." Higher wages in booming areas of the country lure labour from depressed areas, for example, but the size of the wage premium which exists will depend not only on the supply of mobile labour, but also on the demand functions of firms for workers. The degree of wage inequality is thus due to the interplay of supply *and* demand factors. Figure 9-1 cannot, therefore, be taken to imply that differences in earnings are solely due to differences in personal characteristics, as such differences can only be part of the answer

9.3 Summary

(a) Students of economic inequality usually wish to know not only why a society has a particular degree of aggregate inequality but also why specific sorts of individuals receive higher income or earnings than others. The former issue refers to the causes of the income *distribution*, the latter is that of the process of income (or earnings) *determination*. Only under restrictive assumptions can the theories which explain the latter be directly generalized to the former.

(b) Since a variety of explanations of the earnings determination process exist, choice of theory is inescapable. One can ask that such choice be based on reasonably full knowledge of the alternatives and that it be made in the light of specified and defensible criteria, but ultimately the choice is a personal one. As an empirical matter one can state with certainty that there are knowledgeable and intelligent people in all the intellectual camps discussed.

(c) As discussed in Chapter 8.4, different theoretical perspectives sometimes agree on a common prediction, probably because they must attempt to explain the same empirical regularities. Although different theories offer different interpretations they must all face the fact that socio-economic background and sex are systematically and strongly associated with differences in individual earnings.

Chapter 10

The Acquisition of Property

10.1 Introduction

Chapters 6 to 9 have discussed the determination and distribution of labour earnings but this is only part of income, and its inequality is only part of economic inequality. As Chapter 3 indicated, the inequality of wealth in Canada is considerably greater than the inequality of earnings. How do people acquire property? What factors govern the distribution of ownership of property? Section 10.2 discusses the "life-cycle" model of wealth accumulation which argues that most property is acquired by individual saving. Section 10.3 presents the theory of inheritance and Sections 10.4 and 10.5 discuss the evidence which exists on the presence of large inheritances and inheritance in general. The social institutions of property and inheritance have been among the most hotly debated of economic issues for generations, so in section 10.6 we discuss a few of the many ethical issues involved. Knowledge about the real world, theory about how it operates and values about how one wants it to operate are the ingredients of public policy. Section 10.7 presents some of the policy options which have been discussed regarding the institutions of property and inheritance.

10.2 The Life-Cycle Savings Model

In its simplest form, the "life-cycle savings model" argues that individuals will accumulate a stock of capital while working in order to finance their consumption while retired. Their wealth will therefore be at a maximum just before retirement and will decrease throughout their old age. Figure 10-1 graphs a typical individual's net worth according to this theory. Over the period OS the individual is going into debt in order to acquire human capital and to finance consumption during early periods of low earnings — hence his net worth is negative. At S, the individual begins to pay off these debts and by age M has succeeded. Over the period MR the individual saves for his retirement (at age R) and for the rest of his life lives on his savings.

Figure 10.1 presents a highly simplified version of the model since the exact pattern of wealth accumulation will depend on the rate of interest, on whether the individual wishes to maintain a constant, increasing or decreasing level of consumption over time, and on the number of family members to be supported (Irvine, 1978). The great function of capital

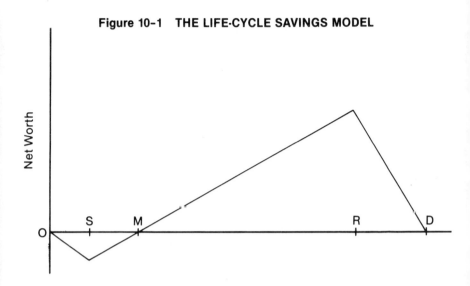

Figure 10-1   THE LIFE-CYCLE SAVINGS MODEL

markets is, in this view, to enable individuals to spread their consumption over their lifetime. Over the period MD, individuals are net lenders on capital markets, usually through intermediaries such as banks or pension funds, but ultimately to investers in human or physical capital. This model is then used as an explanation both of the aggregate level of wealth in a market society and of the distribution of wealth.

The specific predictions of the life-cycle model are that net worth will increase with age, and that the distribution of net worth will be more equal within age cohorts than within the general population. Although a small percentage of the population (the elderly) will own most of society's wealth, people of the same age will be at roughly the same point in the wealth accumulation process and will therefore have roughly equal net worth. One must say "roughly" since differences in ability will imply differences in lifetime earnings and differences in individual tastes will lead some people to consume more now and less in retirement (i.e., save less), while others accumulate more for their old age. The inequality of property ownership which we observe is therefore explained as due to a combination of individual tastes, lifetime earnings, and the natural cycle of life through which we all pass.

As tests of the theory, however, one must ask:
(a) can it explain the total volume of private savings which we observe?
(b) can it explain the inequality of wealth which we observe?

With respect to the aggregate level of private savings, White's recent (1978) simulation study indicates that the life-cycle model can only be part of the picture, explaining, at best, about 42 per cent of total private saving in the U.S. Concerning wealth distribution, Atkinson (1975: 141) comments, "concentration of wealth within age groups is not markedly less than in the population as a whole." Davies (1979: 241) notes, "only 5 per cent of the total (Canadian) wealth inequality on a per adult basis is due to differences between 10 year cohorts."[1]

It is true that average wealth increases as individuals age, but the life-cycle model cannot explain the large fraction of the population who have very low net worth at all ages.[2] Neither can the simple life-cycle savings model explain the existence of very large fortunes (see Chapter 3.2). (Indeed, Brittain (1978: 59-66) has noted that top wealth-holders in the U.S. continue to save well after retirement, contrary to a simple life-cycle model.) Since the life-cycle savings model fits neither the few who are rich nor the many who are poor, it is probably best to think of it as a model of middle-class behaviour. Overall, "neither the U.S. nor the British evidence proves a wealth-age relationship of the life-cycle type to be a major factor in generating inequality" (Brittain, 1978: 71) and one can say the same of Canada.

10.3 The Theory of the Inheritance of Property

Discussion of the inheritance of property is crucial to a study of economic inequality because property carries with it more than just income. Property gives security — to a far greater extent than human wealth. It gives flexibility and, if one has enough of it, it can give power. Wealth in the form of property is also qualitatively different from "human wealth."[3] The "human wealth" of an individual refers to the value of one's potential future earnings, and one must work in order to avail oneself of that potential. Saleable property, on the other hand, represents actual current command over resources. If one compares an individual with training which commands $10,000 per year in the labour market to a person whose property assets yield the same amount, it is clear that the option of leisure or a change of job or occupation is open to someone who owns property but not (i.e., not without sacrifice) to someone who has only their skills to rely on.

Income from property has therefore long had a different ethical status than income from labour earnings, especially if that property was inherited.

---

[1]Based on 1970 SCF data, using the coefficient of variation to measure inequality.

[2]Survey of Consumer Finance data indicates that in 1970, the percentage of Canadian families having net worth of $5,000 or less was 37.7 per cent among those families aged 35 to 44, 31.9 per cent among those 45 to 54, 30.8 per cent among those 55 to 64 and 32.4 per cent among those aged 65 and over (Statistics Canada, 13-547; p. 140).

[3]The term "wealth" is used in a variety of different senses in the literature. Sometimes it is used to mean only the ownership of property rights (such as those enumerated in 3.3) and sometimes it is used to mean the present value of all expectable future income streams. We have used the term "wealth" in the former sense, but to avoid any possibility of confusion we henceforth refer primarily to "property," alternating only to avoid tedium where the context should be clear.

As the old saw goes, "it is one thing for everyone to stand on their own two feet, and quite another for some to stand on their parent's shoulders."

Given the distribution of property ownership among one generation, however, what impact will inheritance produce on the wealth distribution of the next generation? As usual, the answer depends on a variety of factors.[4] In particular one must ask:

(a) How much wealth is passed from generation to generation?

(b) To whom are inheritances left?

(c) How are inheritances combined in current families?

(d) What is the rate of accumulation of inherited property?

Of course, one could also ask "Why do people leave inheritances at all? We all know that "you can't take it with you," so one might expect people who wanted to maximize their own utility to spend all their wealth in their own lifetime (or, at least, to die trying). However, although death is certain, its timing, of course, is not. Even those people who planned to spend it all before dying will include some who overestimate the years remaining to them and leave estates inadvertently (but only to the extent of their over-optimism — probably not very large estates on average).[5]

Most inheritances are, however, probably not the result of an accidental early meeting with the grim reaper. There appear to be a number of motivations. Firstly, there may be an unselfish, altruistic desire to increase the utility of someone else (usually one's children). In this case, one's bequest will tend to be greater the greater one's own human and property wealth is, the greater the degree of empathy one feels with one's heirs and the more they need an inheritance (i.e., the lower their income in the absence of an inheritance. See Shorrocks, 1979). A less admirable motivation, however, may be an aged individual's desire for power over potential heirs in his or her last years. Alternatively, an individual may have a "dynastic" sense of self and feel it important that both forebears and heirs occupy a certain social position. In this last case, individuals may have a "target" bequest which they wish to pass on, to "set their children up right," but for whatever motivation, it is the tastes of the elder generation which govern the inheritances of the younger.

Given a certain aggregate "taste" for bequests, Figure 10-2 illustrates the importance of alternative social patterns of inheritance, fertility, and marriage, for inter-generational stability of the wealth distribution. (It

---

[4]Wolfson (1977) examines these and other factors in a complex simulation model.

[5]In theory, individuals who are uncertain about their own life span could use their stock of wealth on retirement to purchase an annuity (i.e., a promise by a financial institution to pay a certain sum of money every year until their death). This demand for annuities should impel financial markets to supply a menu of annuities with different terms (perhaps including inflation indexing). In practice, financial markets do not offer a menu of inflation indexed annuities, perhaps because of "market failure" in the sense of Akerlof (1970) (see also Davies, 1981).

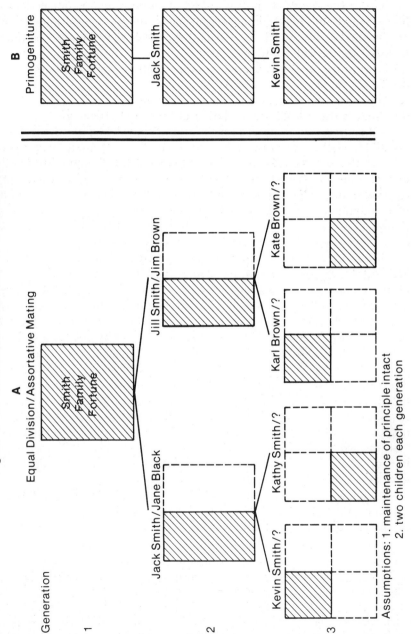

Figure 10-2 THREE GENERATIONS OF INHERITANCE

A Equal Division/Assortative Mating

B Primogeniture

Generation

Assumptions: 1. maintenance of principle intact
2. two children each generation

assumes that consumption equals only the interest on inherited property, so the principal neither grows nor diminishes.) In some societies, primogeniture has been the rule — i.e., the eldest son inherits all the family's property and other children receive either nothing or only minimal shares. This is the surest way to perpetuate the existence of large fortunes, as each generation's eldest son simply passes his inheritance, intact, to his own eldest son. Although prevalent among the nobility until recent times, there is little evidence that such an inheritance pattern is typical today, at least in developed countries.

If all children share their parents' estates, one must examine the size of each share, and how many children there are to divide the inheritance among. Menchik (1980) argues that the norm, in the United States at least, is equal sharing. Panel A of Figure 10-2 embodies as well the assumption that each generation has two children, one male and one female. If equal sharing is the rule, the shaded boxes illustrate the spreading of the original Smith family fortune among children and grandchildren which occurs with the passage of generations. Obviously, the greater the average size of family, the smaller the average share of each succeeding generation.

If a society's norm is equal sharing, however, families will inherit on both sides. "Assortative mating" refers to the tendency for individuals to marry people from similar social backgrounds. Perfect assortative mating implies that individuals always marry people with the same amount of family wealth, hence husbands and wives both have inheritances of equal size from their own parents. The shaded areas of Figure 10-2 represent inheritances received by the spouses of Smith offspring. As the size of the total boxes indicates, the combination of perfect assortative mating and equal sharing among children implies inherited fortunes will not diminish, i.e., the same tendency for the perpetuation of wealth inequality will exist as under primogeniture. Under primogeniture, the Smiths, the Browns, the Blocks and other families not pictured in Figure 10-2 would pass their fortune intact to their eldest sons. Under equal sharing with assortative mating, sons have to share their parents' estates with their sisters, but they marry their "socio-economic sisters" who bring a similar amount of property with them into the marriage.

However, if (to use a Victorian term) the children of well-off families "marry beneath themselves," family fortunes are fragmented over generations and wealth will tend to be spread more equally over the population. The more random (in the socio-economic sense) marriages are, the greater is the tendency for the distribution of inherited property to be equalized over generations.[6]

---

[6]If marriages are in fact negatively assortative — i.e., rich men systematically marry poor women and poor men systematically marry rich women — then the distribution of inherited wealth will equalize very rapidly. Blinder (1973) argues that the degree of assortative mating or social stratification in marriage is in practice a more important determinant of wealth equalization than societal inheritance patterns.

And, although it is more romantic to think of peasants marrying princesses and millionaires marrying their maids, it is much more normal for people to marry someone with broadly similar attitudes, habits and assumptions about day-to-day style of life. Residence in the same neighbourhood, attendance at the same schools and universities, and membership in the same social network of clubs, fraternities, and sororities all help to ensure that people are exposed during their susceptible years to compatible prospective mates. Some indication of this is given by the correlation of socio-economic status scores, which among the fathers of U.S. couples is between 0.39 and 0.70 (Blinder, 1973: 625), and the correlation of spouses' educations, which in Britain is about 0.56 (Layard and Zabalza, 1979).

Finally, one must examine the rate of accumulation (or dispersal) of inherited wealth. Figure 10-2 embodies the restrictive assumption that each generation consumes only the interest on their inheritance and maintains the capital intact for future generations. If an heir's rate of consumption is particularly high, even the largest of fortunes can be squandered in a remarkably short period. (Tebbell (1962) cites the dissipation of the Dodge fortune, as well as some other highly entertaining examples). On the other hand, large fortunes generate large incomes (which are particularly large if the rate of return received by large investors is greater than that received by small savers).[7] The total stock of inherited fortunes will increase over time only if, on average, heirs realize a rate of return greater than their taxes and their consumption from inherited wealth.[8]

If, however, one is interested in assessing the fraction of wealth that has been inherited and the fraction which is "self-made," it is difficult to classify those fortunes that are currently large but which accumulated rapidly from relatively small inheritances. In Canada, Paul Desmarais (see Chapter 3.2) is an example. Inheriting a small, struggling bus company from his grandfather when he was in his early twenties, he turned it into a profitable operation, merged it with a larger one, then merged it with a still larger one (Booth, 1980). In one sense, he realized a very high rate of return on his capital, which was originally inherited. Others in similar situations have, of course, failed. Like a high stakes poker game, success in finance depends on both ability and on luck, and "you can't win if you can't bet."

---

[7] As one of the Bronfmans put it, "To turn one dollar into a dollar ten, that's work; to turn $100,000,000 into $110,000,000, it's inevitable" Newman (1978). Lower transactions costs for financial investments, better access to information, preferred treatment by government authorities or the presence of monopoly profits, (Comanor, 1975) may all contribute to higher rates of return for large investers.

[8] In Canada inheritance taxes have been abolished (except for the province of Quebec). Capital gains tax is payable on assets which pass on death, but if the asset in question is a bond or preferred share with fixed money value, there is usually no capital gains and hence no tax. With foresight, even the future capital gains on such assets as business equity can be transferred tax-free to one's heirs (see Cooper 1979: 13-19).

Thurow (1975) explains the making of very large fortunes as the result of a "random walk" where luck dictates that some able, hard-working, individuals are in the right place at the right time and realize very high rates of return on their assets. He argues that many people have ability and work hard, but when we examine large fortunes we do not observe the efforts or skills of the unlucky, only the lucky. In his view, large fortunes arise when markets capitalize the high rates of return lucky enterprises generate. (In the next generation these become stable, inherited fortunes).[9]

Many businessmen argue that acquiring one's initial stake is the hardest stage, since without inheritance of some sort one must do it by patient saving from labour earnings. This takes time, and a person who has to save for some years to start a business obviously has that many fewer years to make the business grow. The "initial conditions" of Thurow's random walk may be the inheritance of an estate which is much smaller than the fortune to which it grows. Families in the top 5 per cent or 10 per cent of the wealth distribution may move up much more easily if inheritance gives one generation the start it needs in business. Alternatively, if family contacts enable a business to start or to grow, inheritance may take the form of access to capital rather than capital itself.[10] Inheritance may therefore play a very complex role in wealth distribution, but even the simpler case of direct property transfers on death is difficult enough to estimate empirically.

10.4 The Inheritance of Large Fortunes

In the great majority of cases, the large fortunes of one generation belong to the children of those who possess the large fortunes of the preceding generation. Josiah C. Wedgwood, The Economics of Inheritance, 1929.

As is clear from Wedgwood's emphasis on "large fortunes," there has always been great interest in the inheritances of the very rich. The possession of vast amounts of property carries with it "riches," in the sense of large amounts of discretionary purchasing power, (which excites the envy of the less fortunate), and "power," in the sense of the ability to wield economic influence, (which can arouse anxiety among the less favoured). There are therefore really two issues in the study of inheritance; first, what fraction of "large fortunes" are inherited, and second, the impact of inheritance on the distribution of income and wealth in general. One

---

[9]Footnote 4 of Chapter 6 outlines the mathematics of the impact of a chance process on the inequality of income, or of wealth.

[10]Conrad Black, of Argus Corp. for instance, while still a graduate student, was able to borrow on his own recognizance to buy a number of small town Quebec newspapers, on which he made a good deal of money, but his father's wealth as a director of Argus was well known (Ross, 1979).

problem with studies of inheritance is that some techniques are better suited to address the first and some better suited to address the second.[11] (In practice, the available Canadian literature emphasizes the impact of inheritance on the distribution of income and wealth in general.)

Of course, Canada's very largest fortunes are few enough in number (see Table 3-5) that one is tempted simply to enquire how each of them was accumulated. Newman (1975: 269-295) provides brief biographies of each of Canada's centi-millionaires which indicate that only one (Roman) of the 19 fortunes which he lists was acquired by its present holders without the assistance of a substantial inheritance. In *at least* a dozen instances, the inheritances of the current generation were of roughly the same order of magnitude as their present holdings, i.e., one can say they inherited practically all their property.[12] In many instances, however, these fortunes are not particularly old ones, having their origins with the previous generation (e.g., Bronfman, Thomson, Irving). One perspective on the Canadian super-rich therefore argues that the acquisition of very large fortunes was a feature of the more unrestricted capitalism of the early part of this century. If so, increased barriers to business entry and the resistance of a now entrenched elite may be closing the doors to this exclusive club (Clement, 1975). On the other hand, "new money" may simply not be as well-known. The immense profit opportunities presented to the oil and natural gas industry by the increase in energy prices since 1973 would, for example, only recently have been capitalized into large personal fortunes.

"Self-made" fortunes can arise in a number of ways. Atkinson (1975) has argued that first among these is the development of a new process (e.g., microelectronics, Xerox machines) which is immensely profitable.[13] In the United States the owners of such new processes have often become extremely wealthy, but we do not observe the same pattern in Canada. A majority of Canada's manufacturing industry is owned abroad, and its technology has, up to now, largely been imported. Great Canadian fortunes have therefore more typically been made in the exploitation of raw materials (e.g., uranium, oil), in distribution and merchandising (e.g., Eatons, Weston, Wolfe) and especially in finance (e.g., the Argus empire, Desmarais, the Richardsons).

If a large fortune is to be accumulated from small beginnings, a very high rate of return is required on investment. In some industries, the

---

[11]Survey evidence, as in Brittain (1977), for example, may be quite a reliable indicator for those who have inherited very little, but the natural human desire to emphasize one's own achievements probably produces an understatement of inheritance among the more favoured.

[12]Bronfman, Weston, Thomson, Eaton, Irving, Webster, Rathgeb, Molson, Richardson, Meighen, McConnel, Harvie.

[13]The technical and material progress which this opportunity for profit is said to encourage has long been one of the main justifications of a capitalist system (see Schumpeter, 1942).

high rate which we observe to have been made on existing fortunes is more like the winning ticket of a lottery than the average return for the industry in question. Quite a few prospectors, for example, die poor for every one who strikes it rich. The average rate of return for an industry is the average of both those who make very little and those who make a great deal.[14] Some industries may, however, have an above normal rate of return as the result of technical innovation or a secular shift in demand patterns. Railways in the nineteenth century, the auto industry in the early twentieth century and urban construction in postwar Canada are all examples of industries which grew rapidly in a relatively short period, where individual entrepreneurs had an especially good chance to accumulate large stocks of capital. If the economy is a competitive one, these opportunities for extraordinary profit are essentially transitory, but if barriers to entry prevent outside competitors from joining the industry and thereby diluting the bonanza, much larger fortunes may be acquired.

Historically, many of the polemics directed against capitalism have been attacks on monopoly profits and the concentrations of wealth they create. Recently, Comanor and Smiley (1975) have attempted to estimate the impact of monopoly profits on the distribution of ownership of property in the United States, arguing that the future monopoly profits of corporations are capitalized into the prices of the shares of those corporations and thereby influence the distribution of wealth in the economy as a whole. Under alternative assumptions concerning the degree of monopoly in the United States, they argue that the presence of monopoly elements in American industry has a substantial impact on the distribution of wealth. Their estimate is that between two-fifths and two-thirds of the wealth of the top 0.27 per cent of households is capitalized monopoly profits, and between 20 per cent and 50 per cent of the wealth share of the top 2.4 per cent is similarly due to the presence of monopoly.[15] It is precisely these top wealth holders for whom inheritance is most important. Osman (1977: 49) for example, argues "intergenerational wealth transfers are not an important asset source for 97.5 per cent of the population; however, for the top 2.5 per cent of U.S. consumer units, who own 43 per cent of the nation's wealth, they appear to be an important asset source, and an important possible reason for the persistent inequality in the distribution of wealth observed from generation to generation."

In Britain, Wedgwood (1929) and Harbury (1962, 1973, 1976) have traced the antecedents of large fortunes using estate data. Harbury's tech-

---

[14]Of the $100 million plus fortunes on Newman's list, two originated in mineral discoveries — Roman (uranium) and Harvie (oil) — neither actually discovered the property involved (Newman 1975: 270, 280).

[15]These estimates have been questioned by Thomas (1980). Recall from Chapter 4 that concentration levels in Canadian industry are typically higher than in the U.S.

nique was to draw a sample of the names of deceased males who left net worth of one hundred thousand pounds or more from the registry of wills probated in 1956, 1957, 1965 and 1973 (this is approximately the top 0.1 per cent of estates). Harbury then identified the fathers of these men and searched estate records, until he located details of the estates left by them. By comparison of the estate of the father with that of the son, he sought to examine the importance of initial inheritance to wealth accumulation. He concluded that no very appreciable change had occurred in the relative fraction of self-made fortunes between Wedgwood's similar studies of the 1920s and the mid-1950s or the mid-1960s. Over all, some 67 per cent of sons leaving an estate greater than a hundred thousand pounds had fathers whose estates were at least twenty-five thousand pounds (in constant prices), although less than one per cent of the population at large had fathers with that much wealth. By 1973, some decrease in the percentage of wealthy sons who had wealthy fathers had occurred (to 58%), but Harbury is unsure whether that reflects a real decrease in intergenerational wealth transmission or simply a growth of gifts, trusts, and other methods of estate tax avoidance (Harbury, 1976: 326). Harbury was also able to establish that about one in eight of top wealth leavers may have had poor fathers, but were able to marry into money. Harbury qualifies his conclusion by noting that he has not been able to consider gifts between living persons, trusts or "social inheritance," but his primary conclusion is that inherited property remains the most significant determinant of large fortunes.

In the U.S., Menchick (1979) has somewhat reversed Harbury's prodecure by starting from a sample of the large estates which were left in the 1930s and 1940s and examining the probate records of the estates left by their children. He finds that wealthy children tend to have wealthy parents, although there is a tendency (which depends partially on how many children there are in a family to share the inheritance) for children not to have quite as much wealth as their parents.[16] There appears to be some "regression to the mean"; if your parents left an estate 100 per cent larger than my parents did, on average you will leave an estate some 75 per cent larger than mine.[17] Menchick speculates, however, that the inheritance of earnings capacity and of property are correlated and can reinforce one another to produce more similarity between parent and child wealth than either would produce alone. But examination of the impact of inheritance

---

[16]The raw correlation between parent and child wealth is about 0.5, but if account is taken of the biases introduced when a truncated sample is drawn, Menchik argues the true correlation is more likely about 0.8 — i.e., very high.

[17]Recall from Chapter 4 that Cooper (1979) has called the U.S. estate tax a "voluntary" tax and that inheritance tax rates have increased. Increased sophistication in tax-free intergenerational wealth transfers could produce an apparent, but illusory, regression to the mean in estates.

in general demands that we examine more than just the estates of the wealthy.

10.5 Inheritance and the Distribution of Lifetime Resources

Concentrating attention on "large fortunes" emphasizes only part of the total picture of income and wealth distribution. The majority of people die leaving either no estate or an estate made up largely of such assets as a house, a car, home furnishings and, perhaps, a small amount of cash. Indeed, in many ways, it is more accurate to think of many individuals as leaving "negative bequests," since those people who require financial assistance in their old age are receiving wealth transfers *from* their children rather than bequeathing property to them.[18] Taking the population as a whole, what impact does inheritance have on the entire distribution of wealth and lifetime income?

Since to acquire property one must either inherit it or save it from one's own current income, Oulton (1976) followed Atkinson (1971) and argued by elimination that inheritance must be a major source of inequality in the distribution of wealth. Oulton argued that if we take the simple life-cycle model of section 10.2 seriously, inequality in wealth holdings is created by inequalities in earnings, the rate of return on savings from those earnings, and one's position in the lifetime saving/dissaving process. He calculated the distribution of wealth which the life-cycle model would imply under alternative assumptions on these variables and observed that inequality in the resulting estimated distribution of wealth (measured by the coefficient of variation) was, if interest rates were equal, less than 20 per cent of the inequality one observed in reality. The residual he ascribed to the inheritance of property.

Davies and Shorrocks (1978) agreed with Oulton that the life-cycle model does not adequately explain the distribution of wealth but argued that his methodology ascribed all remaining, unmeasured influences to inheritance, ignored possible interaction effects between the inheritance of earnings and of property and was potentially sensitive to the measure of inequality adopted. Indeed, any simple model of only two or three variables which "explains" the distribution of wealth is always open to the criticism that it has omitted the "most important" factor. Davies (1980) therefore set out to model explicitly the process of the acquisition of property and to

---

[18]Clearly there are limits on the extent to which one can rely on one's children's charity, hence models of intergenerational wealth transfers, such as Shorrocks' (1979), constrain the possibility of leaving negative bequests. A "choice" model of this situation may, however, be misleading, since although most people probably have a very strong desire "not to be a burden on their children," some may have no other option in their old age.

assess rigorously the contribution of inheritance to overall inequality in Canada.[19]

Davies' simulation study takes a great many variables into explicit account within a basically neoclassical "life-cycle" methodology. Economic growth and tax rates, different rates of return on human capital and the correlations between inherited property and human wealth, between the inheritances of spouses, and between tastes for bequest and lifetime income are all taken from actual data or available estimates. Tastes, either for income now versus income later or for one's own consumption versus consumption of one's children, are allowed to vary between individuals and their importance estimated. The range of experiments of alternative assumptions is vast (which is one of the problems involved in communicating the results of simulation studies) but Davies' particular interest is in the impact of inheritance on the Canadian distribution of wealth and income.

Davies performed the conceptual experiment of asking what the Canadian distribution of wealth would look like: (1) if inheritance of property were equalized; (2) if the institution of unequal inheritances were abolished; and (3) if unequal opportunity were eliminated. Unequal inheritance, by itself, appears to have an impact on the distribution of wealth of the same order of magnitude as differences in tastes, rate of return on assets, earnings and age. Davies argues that all of these factors have distinct impacts on the distribution of wealth and it is difficult to rank their importance if one controls for each separately. Eliminating the *institution* of unequal inheritance has a much greater impact, however, since it implies that not only do people receive the same amount from their parents but they also bequeath the same amount to their own children (hence higher income families accumulate less wealth themselves). Davies concludes, "equalizing inheritances for *both* parents and children has such a large impact that one would be justified in attributing to the *institution* of unequal

---

[19]Simulation models involve the creation of an artificial panel of households, whose different statistical characteristics resemble the differences in the population at large, as well as the "calibration" of assumed decision rules (such as for savings as a percentage of income) which govern their future behaviour. In such a computer simulation, each member of a panel is "aged" one year at a time and their new characteristics noted (for example, after one year's savings a household's stock of wealth has increased). The total simulated behaviour of the sample is then checked against real data (e.g., the total simulated savings of all households in the artificial sample is compared to actual total savings) and if there is a discrepancy the assumed decision rules (for example the savings rate,) are changed. The final result of a successful simulation, after a large number of calibrating runs, is a computer model whose aggregate characteristics mirror those of the actual economy fairly closely. Hence one can evaluate the impact of a variable (such as inheritance) by making new and artificial assumptions regarding it and comparing the new behaviour of the panel of households with their behaviour under "normal" conditions.

inheritance a dominant effect on the distribution of wealth" (1980: 24).[20] Eliminating unequal opportunity, i.e., eliminating unequal inheritance from one's parents and inequality in the rate of return on assets, has an impact on the distribution of wealth "almost as large" as eliminating the institution of inheritance.

Since income from property is only part of total income, it is more meaningful to examine the impact of the inheritance of property on the present value of lifetime resources (i.e., total lifetime earnings discounted to the age of 20 plus the discounted value of inherited property). Wages and salaries form, in aggregate, approximately 77 per cent of the money income of Canadian family units (see 5.2) and are the largest part of lifetime resources. Discounting, moreover, implies that inherited property received late in one's own life has a much lower present value at age 20 than its current dollar value when it is received. If one's parents die at 70, for example, one can usually expect to be at least 40 before receiving inherited property. Discounting the value of this inheritance to age 20 will usually produce a fairly low present value. For the bulk of the population, therefore, inherited wealth has a fairly small impact on the present value of total lifetime resources, evaluated at age 20. It has a somewhat larger impact on the extremes of the distribution.

In Davies' simulation, the equalization of inheritances from one's parents would produce a decrease in the share of the top quintile in total lifetime resources from 40.4 per cent to 38.1 per cent and an increase in the share of the bottom 20 per cent of the population from 5.3 per cent to 6.5 per cent. Inequality as measured by the coefficient of variation or the Gini ratio would decline by approximately 10 per cent. This small impact of inheritance must, however, be interpreted with some caution since one suspects it is partially a function of the point in time at which comparisons are made. Discounting at 3.6 per cent per year (as in Davies) implies that a dollar received at age 45 has a present value at age 20 of roughly 41 cents. Any inequality in inheritances received at 45 is thus "scaled down" in comparison to inequality in current earnings, if lifetime resources are calculated as at age 20. If one calculated the impact of inheritances on the inequality of resources, for the rest of their lives, of people aged 45, it would be larger than the impact on lifetime resources, discounted to age 20.

Should one evaluate the impact of inheritance as of the point most individuals become "adults" or as of the point they receive their inheritances (if any)? Does the knowledge that an inheritance is coming, or that family financial resources are available in an emergency, offer a security to those

---

[20]If the institution of unequal inheritance were abolished Davies' simulation indicates that the share of the top one per cent in the wealth distribution would be 6.3 per cent (compared to the actual 19.6 per cent), the share of the top 10 per cent would be 33.6 per cent (actual 58 per cent) and the share of the top 20 per cent would be 52.3 per cent (actual 74 per cent).

from wealthy families that others do not have? Lifetime income, discounted to age 20, will not guide us on these issues but one can point out a conundrum if it is used as a criterion — if all inheritances were received at age 20, Wolfson (1978) shows that the aggregate inequality of the wealth distribution would decrease, (since 20-year-olds have, on average, less wealth than older groups). However, the impact of inheritance on the distribution of lifetime resources (as measured by Davies) would increase since inheritances would no longer be "scaled down," and inequality of lifetime resources would, therefore, increase! By contrast, equalizing earnings would decrease the share of the top 20 per cent of families to 23.3 per cent of lifetime resources (discounted to age 20) and increase the share of the bottom 20 per cent to 18.8 per cent — fairly close to absolute equality. For the bulk of the population (although *not* for the inheritors of large fortunes) inherited property is a significant cause of economic inequality, but one which is much smaller in importance than the inequality of earnings in the labour market.

10.6 On Property

The discussion up to this point has concluded that the inheritance of property is chiefly important for the top 2.5 per cent or so, the "upper tail" of the distributions of income and wealth. For the vast majority, hence for the distribution as a whole, the inheritance of earning power is far more important than the inheritance of property. But the astute reader may perhaps have asked "what is property?"

Property is clearly not things[21] themselves (since they exist regardless of whether anyone owns them) nor is it the possession of things (since one can use what is not one's property). Rather, as MacPherson puts it, "What distinguishes property from mere momentary possession is that property is a claim that will be enforced by society or the state, by custom or convention or law" (1978: 3). Private property is then a person's socially enforceable claim to use, or to exclude others from the use of, or to receive the benefits of, certain rights. Or as Tawney put it,

> Property is the most ambiguous of categories. It covers a multitude of rights which have nothing in common except that they are exercised by persons and enforced by the State. Apart from these formal characteristics, they vary indefinitely in economic character, in social effect, and in moral justification. They may be conditional like the grant of patent rights, or absolute like the ownership of ground rents, terminable like copyright, or permanent like a freehold, as comprehensive as sovereignty or as restricted as an easement, as intimate and

---

[21]In some cases knowledge (e.g., knowledge of a company's processes) can be "property"; property is not restricted to material objects.

personal as the ownership of clothes and books, or as remote and intangible as shares in a goldmine or rubber plantation. It is idle, therefore, to present a case for or against private property without specifying the particular forms of property to which reference is made. (1920: 136)

Property as an enforceable claim implies that there must be someone to enforce it, which in modern times means the state. It is therefore both a political and a social phenomenon and its definition varies across societies and, over time, within the same society. Many African tribal societies, for example, recognize private property rights in land, but only so long as the land is being productively used and not sold outside the community (Elias, 1962). English and Scottish landlords used to possess, along with their land, the right to nominate the priest for the parish which it comprised (Cohen, 1927). The modern institution of property is shorn of these appendages. Modern property rights are not conditional on any social function, nor do they exclude the right to dispose of, as well as to use.[22]

Any social institution, such as property or the inheritance of it, requires some ethical justification. Tawney argues that the primary justification of property is a functional one; it contributes to human happiness by guaranteeing the security of man's labour, by ensuring that individuals can prosper from their own exertions. He traces the history of its justification in the defence of the right of English farmers and working men to receive the product of their labours. Land or tools which were used by the owner for the purposes of production were plainly indispensable to the primary social purposes of providing food and clothing. The security which came with an assurance, via the institution of property, that improvements to them would yield benefits to their owners in future years was both a benefit to most individuals (at a time when ownership was widely dispersed) and a condition of the increasing prosperity of the nation.

To the extent that they have any property, it is this sort of "active" property that the vast majority of Canadians are familiar with. Indeed, if the life-cycle savings model were an accurate picture of the wealth generation process in total, all wealth would be the product of individuals' saving from the earnings of their own exertions and this historic justification of property would be applicable to the present day. But the life-cycle savings model can only explain a small part of the aggregate distribution of property. And the "functional" justification of property is a two-edged sword, since it does *not* justify "passive" property, or property as pure ownership unlinked to the performance of any social function. As John Stuart Mill argued:

---

[22]See Macpherson (1978:10). Any social institution changes over time and property rights are no exception; witness anti-pollution laws which increasingly restrict individuals' rights to physically dispose of their assets.

Private property, in every defence made of it, is supposed to mean, the guarantee to individuals, of the fruits of their own labour and abstinence. The guarantee to them of the fruits of the labour and abstinence of others, transmitted to them without any merit or exertion of their own, is not of the essence of the institution, but a mere incidental consequence, which when it reaches a certain height, does not promote, but conflicts with the ends which render private property legitimate. (1841: 359)

In the incomes of the very wealthy, some income arises from their labour and some income arises merely from their possession of wealth. In Canadian society, the makers of high-level business decisions are often very well rewarded.[23] But the excess of income over and above the salary of a paid manager with equal responsibility is, in Tawney's terms, a return to "passive" property. Accumulation from that excess is merely an increase in the stock of functionless ownership.

The inheritance of such property can therefore be judged somewhat differently from the inheritances with which the vast majority of Canadians are familiar (i.e., nil or, for the more fortunate, the family home or farm, the home furnishings passed down through generations or, perhaps, the small family business). In part, the law recognizes such a distinction. Such property as the family farm or family home receives special consideration in Canada. Other countries exempt entirely estates under a certain amount from taxation.[24] Many societies therefore draw ethical and legal distinctions between types of inherited property which, although somewhat vague, do roughly correspond to our empirical distinction between the inheritance of "large fortunes" and inheritance in general.

---

[23]In 1979, R. H. Lawrence of Westcoast Petroleum received $665,000, R. M. McManis of Husky Oil got $648,229 and J. A. Armstrong of Imperial Oil was paid $615,530. The 49 Canadian companies who have to report to the U.S. Securities and Exchange Commission employed at least 133 executives earning over $100,000. Privately-held companies and those listed on only Canadian stock exchanges do not have to report executive salaries (Robinson, 1980). Whether these salaries and bonuses are "too high" for the social function performed, whether the positions were unfairly obtained, (Edgar Bronfman paid himself $788,979 as C.E.O. of Seagrams) and whether society is best served by "top-down" business decision-making are serious questions but in the text we address only the issue of economic returns to pure ownership.

[24]In Canada, the federal government has vacated the field of succession duties and most provinces have ceased to levy them. Capital gains tax is deemed payable on death (and hence is often confused with a succession duty) but it is not really a succession duty, merely a tax on the increased value of assets that could have been collected earlier but is deferred when assets are not sold in the market. Nevertheless, this class of exemptions is made. Other countries routinely exempt from succession duties properties of various types, and less than certain account — e.g., in 1977 estates under $120,000 in the U.S. were not taxed (Harrison, 1979).

10.7 Public Policies

If competitive capitalism can be described as a race, then "equal opportunity" would imply that we all should start from about the same place. Chapter 6 discussed the head-start that a good family background can give a child even before he or she enters the labour market, but these advantages are often subtle and not easily quantified. By contrast, the inheritance of large fortunes gives some individuals a very clear and obvious lead in the economic race (see Table 3-3). Public policy has occasionally tried to intervene to even these odds — not so much because of the quantitative importance of large fortunes to the distribution of economic welfare (see 10.5), but more because of their symbolic importance for the myth of equal opportunity, and because of a continued anxiety about the impact of a hereditary class of privilege on democratic institutions.[25]

Most often, estates have been taxed by the state. In the U.S., nominal rates of taxation go as high as 77 per cent on estates over $10 million (Cooper, 1979:1). These high rates might be thought enough to ensure that large fortunes are broken up over time but Cooper (1979) has argued that loopholes in the law are sufficiently numerous to ensure that these rates are largely cosmetic. The du Pont fortune, for example, which dates from the founding of the family firm in 1802, is still approximately $500,000,000 and has paid an effective estate tax, over the two last generations, of only about 5 per cent (Cooper, 1979: 1). Despite very high rates of estate taxation in Britain in recent years the Grosvenor family still own the 12,500 acres of Cheshire which they acquired in 1068 and 300 of the 500 acres of downtown London which they obtained in 1677. The family fortune is estimated at between £200 million and £500 million in total but is largely in the hands of 11 trusts, (of which family members are the beneficiaries). As a result, Gerald Grosvenor (Sixth Duke of Westminster) has received an estate on which no estate duty was paid through the deaths of the Third, Fourth and Fifth Dukes (Cunningham, 1979). Of course, except for Quebec, Canada has deserted the field of estate taxation entirely and collects only capital gains tax (really a deferred tax) at half the rate of ordinary income tax. "Tightening up" (in Britain or the U.S.) or imposing (in Canada) an estate tax is therefore one possible policy to break up large fortunes.

Alternatively, one might encourage wealthy individuals to divide their estates into more separate pieces. Mill (1848: 378) argued society should set a ceiling on the maximum bequest a person could make to any of his or her heirs, implying that no individual could inherit excessive wealth and large fortunes would be divided among many heirs. Alternatively, if inheritances were taxed as income in the hands of individuals, rather than estates being

---

[25]The small financial yield of estate duties is thus largely irrelevant to whether they should be imposed, just as a small number of heroin dealers convicted is a poor argument for heroin legalization.

taxed before division among individuals, there might be some incentive for donors to split their estates among more people, thereby hastening the process of the fragmentation of large fortunes over generations.

In essence, the higher the tax rate on inheritances the higher is the "price" to put $1 in the hands of one's heirs. If the size of the estate as a whole is taxed, then heirs are paid from what remains after tax is paid and the "price" of a $1 bequest is the same no matter who it goes to. If the inheritances of individuals are taxed and if that tax depends on the individual's income, then a higher-income individual will pay a higher inheritance tax, i.e., the "price" of bequeathing $1 to that person will be higher than the "price" of leaving $1 to someone else with lower income. The difference in "price" will be approximately the difference in their marginal tax rates. Hence the impact on inheritance patterns of an inheritance tax system versus a succession duty system depends on the "price-elasticity" of bequests and the difference in "prices" among one's potential heirs, as well as on the utility which one derives from the future utility of one's heirs. There is apparently a tendency already for parents to favour slightly in their wills those of their children who have lower expected earnings (Tomes, 1980), and taxing inheritances as income might encourage this tendency.[26]

If excessive concentration of wealth is to be diminished, a tax on wealth can be imposed, much as we already impose municipal taxes on the value of one's home, and some jurisdictions in the U.S. tax the value of one's car. These taxes fall on the assets in which the poorest 80 per cent of families hold most of their wealth, but Norway, Denmark and Sweden all impose a comprehensive wealth tax (but exempt wealth under a certain level). Potentially, this is a powerful tool for the equalization of the wealth distribution[27] since, like the income tax, it can have exemptions large enough to leave most life-cycle savings untouched or rates progressive enough to bear most heavily on the largest fortunes (e.g., a tax of 0 per cent on net worth under $150,000, 0.5 per cent on net worth between $150,000 and $1,000,000, 0.75 per cent on wealth over $1,000,000, etc.).

The nationalization of large enterprises, i.e., the (forced) purchase of the shares of all large companies has also often been proposed as a remedy for inequality. As a remedy for inequalities of wealth, however, such a measure would only be effective if compensation payments were substantially below the market value of the shares purchased. If government bonds were, for example, issued to pay for the shares purchased, nationalization with full compensation would simply change the financial portfolios of the previous owners, replacing shares with bonds. As a remedy for inequalities of income, nationalization would only have an effect if the rate

---

[26]However, this result was based on a very small U.S. sample.
[27]Although in some countries under-reporting of wealth appears significant (Harrison, 1979:1).

of return on bonds issued as compensation payments was substantially below the rate of return previously obtained on shares. Some differential in rate of return would be "fair," since the new assets (bonds) are risk-free while the old assets (shares) were exposed to the risk that companies would go bankrupt, but full compensation would imply that the differential in rates reflects only the change in risks associated with the two types of assets.

Okun (1975: 53) estimates that nationalization (with compensation) of all U.S. corporate assets would imply a net transfer of income away from former property-owners of roughly 1 per cent of GNP. If added entirely to the incomes of the poorest 20 per cent, this is not insignificant. It is, however, less than normal year-to-year change in the economy's growth rate.[28]

The real issue in nationalization is, however, not inequality of income or wealth but inequality of power. Socialists argue that great inequalities of economic power (see 3.2) necessarily produce inequalities in effective political influence.[29] By now, there has been sufficient international experience with nationalization that socialists rarely see nationalization as a panacea. Rather, most socialists see nationalization as enabling, but not guaranteeing, (i.e., a necessary, but not sufficient, condition for) a more democratic organization of work, and an emphasis on values such as workplace safety or a clean environment which are not adequately reflected in the monetary profit and loss calculations of capitalism. Some socialists (e.g., Bowles and Gintis, 1975) also argue that only if the public owns and controls productive enterprises can one make a reasonable start on reducing inequalities, both of "result" in the workplace and of opportunity outside it.

Nationalization without compensation, i.e., confiscation, is a more radical brand of socialism, but it is hard to envisage in a non-revolutionary situation. A revolutionary situation, however, would require a drastic change in economic and social conditions (e.g., a depression which reduced the income share of the majority to 20 per cent or so). One cannot reasonably estimate the impact of confiscation on our *current* distribution of income or wealth therefore, since the impact of confiscation would be relative to those distributional shares which would produce it as a response.

If one examines the impact of confiscation on the *current* distribution of property one sees a very clear reason why it has not occurred. Suppose that *all* the property of the top 5 per cent Canadian adults had been simply confiscated in 1980. This would not affect directly the poorest 95 per cent,

---

[28]If government bonds received as compensation can be left as inheritances, the problem of inherited wealth is not solved by nationalization, although it would probably become easier to collect estate taxes.

[29]Those who believe that markets are highly competitive and provide severe constraints on economic power and that economic power cannot be translated into political power obviously find such arguments unconvincing.

and Davies' (1979) estimates, updated for growth (see Table 3-3) indicate it would produce roughly $333.9 billion for redistribution. As a lump sum this is a huge amount, but if it were divided among the poorest 80 per cent of Canadian adults (some 13,224,000 people) it would be sufficient to bring their average wealth up to $40,910. This would be a large gain for the poorest 40 per cent, whose estimated net worth in 1980 averaged $1,002, but a much smaller gain for the next 40 percent, whose estimated net worth was an average $30,377. It is extremely unlikely that this middle class would support such a confiscation when the current gains to them are so small.[30] Even though their wealth is likely to be almost entirely equity in a house, or a car, and they feel themselves to be just "getting by," their potential monetary gain from such a revolutionary confiscation is a good deal less than from a continuation of capitalist growth, if it occurs. In fact, if this middle 40 per cent in 1980 were the same people as the middle 40 per cent in 1970 (an extreme assumption which would ignore any possible life-cycle savings) one can calculate that over the 1970s they increased their property by an average $12,614 in 1980 dollars. Relative to potential losses in their employment income (from dislocation of economic activity), or to the prospects of continued growth, confiscation is not likely to be appealing to the middle classes. If, however, growth becomes less likely and unemployment becomes more probable, confiscation would appear a better bargain.

10.8 Summary

(a) The life-cycle savings model argues that individual savings for the retirement years account for the bulk of private wealth and that inequality of property ownership is largely due to age and individual tastes.

(b) The life-cycle savings model can explain only a small fraction of private savings and only a small portion of the inequality of property ownership.

(c) The tendency for inherited property to become concentrated or to be fragmented over generations depends on average family size, social patterns of inheritance, the degree of assortative mating and the rate of return (minus consumption) on inherited wealth.

(d) Inherited property is an important part of the assets of the top 2.5 per cent to top 5 per cent of the wealth distribution but for the vast majority of the population the inheritance of property is a fairly small part of lifetime economic resources.

---

[30]Since there is a substantial range of property even within these intervals it is somewhat misleading to simply subtract averages. Some would gain by far more than the average difference and some by much less.

(e) A substantial portion (SCF estimates would indicate 30 to 35 per cent) of the population own very little personal property at any age. A small fraction (2.5 per cent to 5 per cent) inherit most of their property, and are joined at the top of the wealth pyramid by a few "self-made" fortunes. The acquisition of personal property (houses, automobiles, consumer durables, bank balances) over the life-cycle and the building up of pension rights provide the main sources of property for a broad "middle class," for whom the "social inheritance" of earning power is far more important.

(f) Since the inheritance of property is highly important for a small wealthy minority and fairly unimportant for the large majority, it is less important than inequalities in earnings for many measures of *aggregate* inequality.

(g) Property is a social institution whose definition changes over time. There is a long history of ethical distinctions being drawn between different types of property, in particular between property acquired by savings from labour earnings and property acquired by inheritance.

(h) Estate duties, inheritance taxes, wealth taxes, nationalization and confiscation are some of the measures that have been proposed to prevent a concentration of inherited property.

Chapter 11

Underdevelopment, Growth, and Inequality

I went to Senhor Manuel, carrying some cans to sell. Everything that I find in the garbage I sell. He gave me 13 cruzeiros. I kept thinking that I had to buy bread, soap, and milk for Vera Eunice. The 13 cruzeiros wouldn't make it. I returned home, or rather to my shack, nervous and exhausted. I thought of the worrisome life that I led. Carrying paper, washing clothes for the children, staying in the street all day long. Yet I'm always lacking things, Vera doesn't have shoes and she doesn't like to go barefoot. For at least two years I've wanted to buy a meat grinder. And a sewing machine.

I was feeling ill and wished I could lie down. But the poor don't rest nor are they permitted the pleasure of relaxation.

Maria Carolina de Jesus, Child of the Dark, 1962.

11.1 Global Economic Inequality

Maria Carolina de Jesus made her living, as thousands do, collecting scrap paper in the streets of Sao Paulo. In 1958 her diary was discovered and published by a Brazilian reporter. She became famous and moved away from the *favela* into a brick house. But millions remain behind, anonymous.

No book on inequality can be complete without a discussion of the greatest inequality, that between rich and poor nations in the world today. If we look beyond Canada's borders we see a world where hundreds of millions of people struggle to remain at the very margin of subsistence. Table 11-1 presents the average national income per capita of 72 countries in 1975. Since inequality within these countries is often very substantial, even relatively prosperous nations, such as Brazil, contain large numbers of people whose standard of living is as low as the average in such nations as Bangladesh or Chad.

Ahluwalia (1976b:12) used income distribution statistics on 44 countries in Asia, Africa and Latin America and calculated that in 1969 there were some 371.4 million people in those countries (30.5 per cent of the total population) who had annual incomes less than $50 (U.S.) per year. Almost half (47.9 per cent) — that is, 583.2 million people — had an annual income

Table 11-1

ESTIMATED PER CAPITA NATIONAL INCOME — SELECTED COUNTRIES
(U. S. DOLLARS — 1975)

Middle East South Asia		Africa		Europe		America		Oceania and East Asia	
India	136	Algeria*	803	Austria*	5,576	Canada*	7,485	Australia*	6,582
Pakistan	181	Angola	404	Belgium*	7,449	U.S.A.*	7,686	New Zealand	4,092
Bangladesh	108	Burundi	88	Denmark*	8,199	Mexico*	1,010		
		Chad	165	Finland*	5,660			Burma	91
Iran	1,600	Egypt	308	France*	6,380	Bolivia	415	Hong Kong	1,599
Iraq	1,159	Ethiopia	91	Germany*	7,465	Brazil	1,095	Indonesia	200
Jordan	457	Ghana	464	Greece*	2,701	Chile	421	Kampuchea	140
Kuwait	11,431	Kenya	213	Ireland*	2,711	Columbia	499	S. Korea	519
Saudi Arabia	4,371	Mozambique	275	Italy*	3,076	Ecuador	566	Laos	86
Turkey	873	Nigeria	373	Netherlands*	6,989	Guatemala	522	Phillipines	333
Afghanistan	160	Somalia	151	Norway*	7,253	Haiti	174	Singapore	2,279
Israel	3,232	Sudan	304	Spain*	2,896	Nicaragua	678	Sri Lanka	238
Syria	702	Tanzania	159	Sweden*	8,369	Paraguay	536	Thailand	323
Yemen	168	Zaire	127	Switzerland*	8,918	Peru	507		
Nepal	115	Zimbabwe	474	United Kingdom*	3,898	Venezuela	2,128		
Japan*	4,293								

*-1977 data
Source (U.N. 1978: 14-17)

of $75 or less. Since these 44 countries make up only about 60 per cent of the population of the developing countries, excluding China, and since population growth between 1970 and 1977 has added some 450 million to the total population of developing nations, (U.N.:, 1979:8) the number of people in absolute poverty in the Third World is certainly far greater today.

In human terms, an income this low usually means a life that revolves around heavy agricultural labour. If the rains are timely, if no pests affect the crop and if illness does not strike, with hard work (and if they own their own land) the fortunate can aspire to purchase a transistor radio, a bicycle or a tin roof for their house. But if the crop fails, disaster may loom. Once appeals to relatives or neighbours are exhausted, they will be driven to the money lender or to join the fruitless migration to the cities, there to swell the total of the occasionally employed. And if illness should strike, based on life-long malnutrition, unsafe drinking water, endemic diseases such as malaria or bilharzia, or something as commonplace as an infected tooth, the vast majority of rural people will find no convenient hospitals or doctors to care for them. If they are lucky, they recover, if not, even the most ordinary of accidents can produce infections and complications which make the difference between being able to work hard enough to acquire a few small possessions, and life at the extreme margin. Daily life, for the poor of the Third World, is therefore not only devoid of the material comforts we take for granted, it is also *precarious* to a degree which Canadians, insulated by wealth and the welfare state, can hardly imagine.

In aggregate statistical terms Whalley (1979: 273) has calculated that the top 10 per cent of the world's population receive roughly 60 per cent of the world's income while the bottom 20 per cent receive about 0.9 per cent, if one converts currencies at official exchange rates. However, the prices of some goods may be lower in less developed countries, so these estimates must be corrected for "purchasing power parity." Since some goods, such as the services of servants, cannot be traded on world markets, their prices in poor countries may be very low. Hence even people with a low dollar income can afford to buy them. Correcting for the increase in consumption enabled by such lower prices produces an "amended" estimate — 50 per cent of the world's income is consumed by the top 10 per cent and roughly 1.8 per cent by the poorest 20 per cent. The distribution of world income is still far more unequal than the distribution of income within Canada.

11.2 Inequality and Economic Development

Inequality in Canada, substantial as it is, is much less glaringly obvious than inequality within the less developed countries. Canada has no counterpart to the homeless beggars of Calcutta, who sleep on the streets only yards from the walled gardens of the wealthy, or to the shanty towns of Rio de Janeiro, within shouting distance of luxury apartments and villas.

One of the most shocking aspects, to many Canadians, of travel in the Third World is the contrast between the lifestyles of the elite, who may live on a scale unknown in servantless North America, and the masses, whose poverty is hard to describe.

In the very poorest countries, however, the elite is only a tiny fraction of the population and if the great majority of the population are more or less at a subsistence level of living, *their* incomes will be roughly equal. Hence statistical measures of inequality, such as the Gini index, will show a relatively low level of inequality. This is "equal hardship" for most, but statistically, the smaller the elite is, the smaller is its weight in the index of aggregate inequality. As growth occurs, however, some of the population climb above bare subsistence, while some remain behind. The *share* of the poorest in total income then tends to fall, even if their absolute income may not (see Ahluwalia 1976a). As development proceeds, a larger and larger fraction of the population becomes educated and urbanized, employed in the modern cash economy rather than working in peasant agriculture. If the economy can make the transition to developed status, the number of prosperous peasants and skilled urban workers may grow to the point where the income share of the poor starts to rise and inequality begins to fall.

Kuznets (1955) therefore hypothesized that the structural changes associated with development (chiefly industrialization, increased education and urbanization) would produce first an increase, then a decrease in inequality as average incomes rose (i.e., a graph of inequality against average income would resemble an upside-down U). By this argument, Marx's prediction of the "immiserization of the proletariat" and an increase in inequality refers only to the initial stages of capitalist development; eventually we will have more equality *and* more growth.

Figure 11-1 is taken from Ahluwalia (1976b) who examined the relationship between average income and income shares for a sample of 66 countries. Ahluwalia examined as well the impact of an economy's structure on inequality. Socialist countries have considerably less inequality at all income levels, and higher education levels also produce a decrease in inequality — but heavier dependence on agriculture is associated with more inequality. There is some mild support for the Kuznets' hypothesis in Figure 11-1, but the share of the top 20 per cent falls quite gently as incomes rise above $400 per capita and the share of the bottom 40 per cent rises with equal slowness.

Although theoretical arguments can be mustered in support of the Kuznets' hypothesis (see Robinson, 1976), Kuznets himself only proposed it as a historical generalization. As Fei, Ranis and Kuo (1978) point out, income is the sum of returns to different factors, hence income inequality is a weighted sum of inequality in factor returns. The impact of development on inequality depends on how the inequalities in the ownership of land,

Figure 11-1 VARIATIONS IN INCOME SHARES

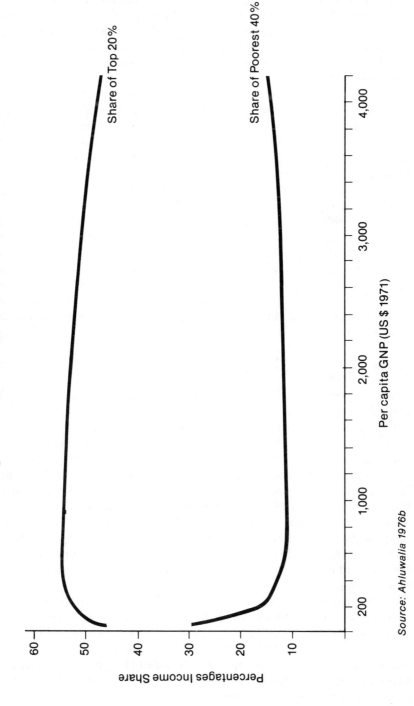

Share of Top 20%

Share of Poorest 40%

Per capita GNP (US $ 1971)

Percentages Income Share

Source: Ahluwalia 1976b

labour and capital change relative to one another as well as on the changes in relative returns to each. The aggregate impact of development on income inequality is thus necessarily complex and depends on the specific trends in factor returns in each country. In the case of Taiwan, increasing income equality has accompanied growth throughout its transition from a peasant agriculture, surplus labour economy to an industrializing one.

There is therefore nothing inevitable about inequality "having to get worse before it gets better." In a primarily agricultural economy (as most less developed countries are), land ownership is the key to inequality in rural areas, where most of the population lives. Landless farm labourers and tenant farmers are the poorest of the poor while, especially in Latin America, great landowners may live in almost feudal splendour. Land reform and an emphasis on rural development can be key factors enabling growth with equality; as Johnston and Kilby put it "There is now a general consensus that almost never does land reform decrease production, occasionally it has a neutral affect, most often it has a positive impact" (1975: 162). Many government spending programs (such as in medical care) provide considerably greater total benefits if more equally spread among the population than if concentrated in a few high cost locations. Hence, many (e.g., Chenery, 1976) argue that land reform, an emphasis on agricultural production and egalitarian social policies are the most rapid path to, economic development.

11.3 Equality and/or Growth?

In Canada, however, people argue as to whether we can afford to aid the poor of the less developed countries or even the poor of our own. Gillespie (1976) has observed that a myth has become entrenched in the Canadian body politic, namely, that Canadian governments have increasingly redistributed income towards the poor (see Chapter 12 for a discussion of the evidence). In the popular press this myth has often formed the basis for an "analysis" — that redistribution has gone "too far" and is the cause of Canada's current low growth rates. Since, as we saw in Chapter 10, the monetary gains from growth in the 1970s have exceeded the potential financial gains from radical redistribution for a large middle-class segment of the population, this is a crucial issue. Up to now, improvements in the standard of living of "middle Canada" have come with a constant share of a growing pie.

If the pie ceases to grow, however, pressure for distributional change may mount. As Cornwall (1977) has argued, until the 1970s economic growth meant that an expansion of public services (such as health care and old age pensions) could be achieved at the same time as increases in individual incomes. Growth therefore enabled the preservation of social harmony, despite a commercialization of society which has undermined traditional social ties. As Cornwall puts it:

with a rapidly expanding output to be divided up, the traditional arguments for a redistribution of output of those with an anti-capitalist bent were blunted. The result was an implicit, if somewhat shaky, alliance not only between labour and management but also between various labour groups and different sectors of the economy . . . . However, a lack of economic growth introduces a zero sum game . . . given a declining sense of national solidarity or "common shared experience"; increasing class, group, occupational and sectoral antagonisms can only be expected . . . (with) a higher risk of political instability. (1977: 210)

Is there a trade-off between equality and growth?[1] Ahluwalia concludes his cross-sectional study of 66 countries by saying, "The cross-section evidence does not support the view that a high rate of economic growth has an adverse affect upon relative equality. Quite the contrary, the rate of growth of GDP in our sample was positively related to the share of the lowest 40 per cent, suggesting that the objectives of growth and equity may not be in conflict" (1976b: 17). Of course, it might be objected that this study includes so many less developed countries that the regression results are dominated by them, hence one ought not to generalize this conclusion to developed nations. Figure 11-2 therefore presents a plot of the inequality (as measured by the Gini index) within OECD nations (see Table 2-3) compared to their per-capita growth rate. If there is a relationship, it is not nearly as obvious as the myths would have it. The country with fastest growth (Japan) has roughly average inequality, as does the country with slowest growth (the U.K.) — the country with greatest equality (Holland) has the third highest growth rate, but not that much higher than the most unequal nation (France). In short, no obvious pattern exists.[2]

But, of course, one can turn the issue around and ask, why would we expect more unequal societies to grow faster? The one-word answer is usually "incentives" — incentives to save and invest more, to work longer and to be more entrepreneurial. Let us examine each in turn.

11.3.1 Incentives to Capital

Ensuring an adequate supply of capital, it has been argued, is one reason

---

[1]As Okun says "Trade-offs are the central study of the economist." (1975:1), perhaps so central that economists may see trade-offs even where none exist.

[2]From Chapter 2 one will recall that several aggregative measures of inequality exist, which may rank inequality differently. Indeed, Roberti (1974) has examined the details of movements in income shares in OECD nations and cautioned against the use of any single summary statistic. Growth in GDP per capita is also less than satisfactory since it may reflect such good fortune as favourable movements in international terms of trade or the finding of North Sea oil. The rate of growth in labour productivity is what one would really like to relate to inequality, but its measurement is at least as controversial as that of inequality. Figure 11-2 is meant merely to indicate the lack of a simple partial relation between growth and inequality.

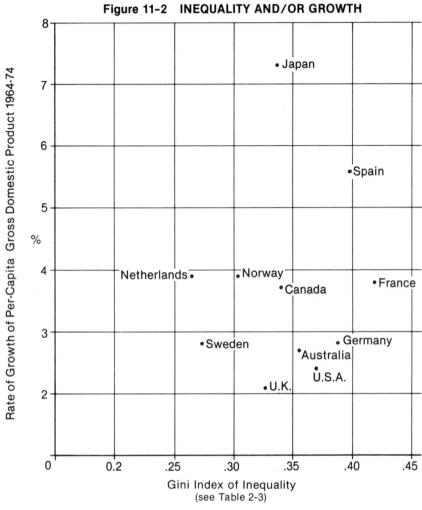

Figure 11-2 INEQUALITY AND/OR GROWTH

Sources: Sawyer (1975)
OECD National Accounts — 1975

for decreasing the tax burden on upper income groups. Low income groups must consume almost all their income, hence the greater part of private savings comes from the top end of the income distribution. A larger share of income for them, it is argued, would increase savings, increase the incentive to invest and thereby increase growth. Okun, for one, categorically rejects this argument as a fake: "the nation can have the level of saving and investment it wants with more or less redistribution, so long as it is willing to twist some other dials" (1975: 99).

Government budget surpluses and corporate retained earnings, as well as private savings, are the sources of domestic savings in the economy as a whole. *If* particular redistributive measures decrease total private saving, adjustments in other tax or spending measures may become necessary, but there need be no effect on long-term capital formation.

11.3.2 Incentives for Effort

Increased incentives for "effort" are also often advanced as a justification for decreased emphasis on equality. If income tax rates are high, is this not a disincentive to work more hours, hence a disincentive to expanded output? Shouldn't a decrease in income tax rates, especially for upper income groups, increase their supply of labour (and hence their output)? But might not things work the other way? Might not a cut in income taxes mean that one can finance the same style of life with fewer hours of work and have more hours of leisure to enjoy? The effect of a change in income tax rates on labour supply is theoretically quite indeterminate, depending entirely on an individual's tastes.[3]

Figure 11-3 illustrates the simplified case of a "flat-rate" income tax (a constant percentage of income) and compares two persons' consumption of "leisure" before and after a cut in income tax rates, on the assumption that they can freely vary their hours of work. Indifference curves, their personal trade-offs between income and leisure are graphed as U_1 and U_2. Person A reacts to the cut in income tax rates by increasing his demand for leisure from L_1 hours to L_2 hours (i.e., decreasing work effort). Even though the higher after-tax wage rate means it is more lucrative to substitute leisure for work at the margin, still this person's tastes are such that he prefers to take some of his potential higher income in the form of increased leisure. (i.e., the income effect outweighs the substitution effect). Person B reacts differently and decreases her demand for leisure from L_1 to L_2, i.e., increases her work effort (the substitution effect dominates).

The crucial issue, of course, is which of these theoretical possibilities is more common in reality. Studies of highly-paid professionals (who can vary their hours of work), and of samples of the population at large do not produce any clear evidence of substantial "disincentive" effects of high income tax rates on working hours (Break, 1974). Thurow puts the point unequivocally, "high (income) taxes either do not affect work effort or might even increase work effort among executives and professionals. People work as hard or harder (after a tax increase) to restore their previous incomes or to obtain their income goals" (1975: 49).

---

[3]More complex models (e.g. Kanbur, 1979; Becker/Tomes; 1979) may present the possibility that increased income taxes may not reduce inequality, but these remain theoretical conjectures.

Figure 11-3   INDIVIDUAL RESPONSES TO AN INCOME TAX CUT

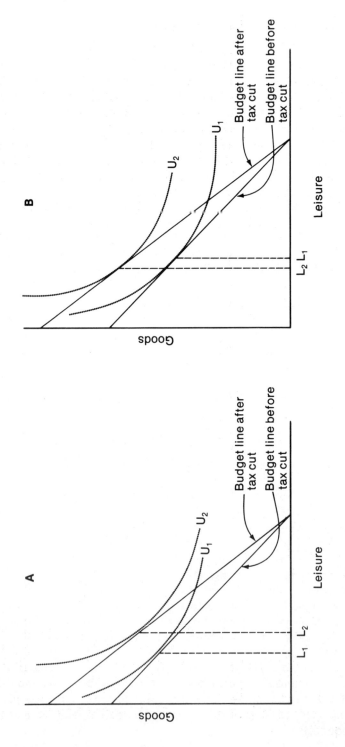

11.3.3 Incentives for Entrepreneurs

The supply of entrepreneurial ability is an especially important aspect of the supply of labour, but one that is not as well understood by economists as it should be, perhaps because in a perfectly informed, perfectly competitive market there is really no room for entrepreneurship. Leff (1979) notes that the issue has "virtually disappeared from the literature" in recent years, although it had been prominent in the discussion of development economics. Current wisdom appears to be that the supply of entrepreneurship in developing economies is not a serious constraint, although entrepreneurial activity has taken a wide variety of institutional forms, in both public and private ownership of industry.

Schumpeter, however, (1934: 74-94) placed the entrepreneur, the person who puts together *new* productive combinations, at the centre of his theory of economic development, but he argued that the entrepreneur's motives could not be analysed in terms of careful marginal calculations of benefit and cost. Rather, Schumpeter saw the entrepreneur's function as that of economic leadership, and his motivation as the desire to found a private (economic) kingdom of power and independence, a will to conquer and the joy of creating and getting things done. These are complex motivations, only tenuously linked to the careful labour/leisure choices pictured in Figure 11-3. Break (1974: 90), among others, has argued that it is the details of tax legislation, such as its treatment of capital gains in new small businesses *relative to* the tax rate on wages and salaries, which may affect the supply of entrepreneurship, rather than the aggregate degree of progressivity in the tax schedule or the overall degree of post-tax income equality.

In summary, the verdict on the theory that economic growth is negatively related to economic inequality must be the Scottish one of "not proven." And, of course, the alternative viewpoint (also "not proven") argues that some policies which increase equality will also encourage growth. Institutionalists, for example, contend that the view that existing incomes reflect the rational decisions of well-informed individuals operating in perfectly competitive markets with equal opportunity is merely a professor's myth. Rather, they see a world of unequal opportunity and highly imperfect markets, hence a world where there is nothing "optimal" about the existing income distribution, either in equity or efficiency terms. If many people now work in jobs that use only a fraction of their abilities, improved access to training and education will aid both growth and equality. If a substantial "under-class" is trapped in the secondary labour market, accelerated growth is necessary to draw them into primary labour market jobs and start them in the process of on-the-job training which produces future productivity growth — and greater income equality. In this view, economic inequality represents, at least partially, wasted economic potential. Increases in the "earnings capacity" of low income people, and the "good jobs" capacity of the economy can give us both more growth and more equality.

11.4 Summary

(a) The distribution of income among the population of the world is far more unequal than the distribution of income within Canada. The low average income of many nations, and the inequality of income within those nations, mean that hundreds of millions of people must subsist on annual incomes in the range of $50 to $75 per capita.

(b) As a historical generalization, one can say that economic inequality has usually first increased, then decreased during the process of development. However there is nothing inevitable about this pattern and many authors argue that redistributive measures such as land reform may accelerate growth.

(c) Above per capita GNP levels of approximately $400 per year, a rise in annual per capita income is statistically associated with a decline in inequality. Among the most highly developed nations it is hard to detect any simple empirical relationship between average incomes, or growth of incomes, and inequality.

(d) Economic theory, either neoclassical or neo-institutional, offers no unambiguous prediction as to whether inequality and growth will be postively or negatively correlated.

(e) Economic growth may therefore be necessary if the current degree of economic inequality in Canada is to be tolerated, but there is little evidence that such a degree of economic inequality is necessary for economic growth.

Chapter 12

Government and and Inequality

12.1 Government and Inequality

Some of the roles played by the state in influencing economic inequality have already been alluded to. The state in Canada largely finances the education whose attainment is a major element of earnings determination (see Chapters 6 to 9); it safeguards the property rights which distribute income from property (Chapter 5 and 10), and its redistributive policies have been blamed for slow growth (Chapter 11), to name only a few of its impacts on economic inequality. In Chapter 8 we also noted that opinions may differ as to what kind of action to expect from government in a country like Canada, but it is clear that if economic inequality is to be altered from the path it would otherwise take some form of state action will be required.

In this chapter we do not attempt to outline political theory of what actions Canadian governments will take on the issue of economic inequality. Rather, we consider only the impacts of the actions they have taken (12.2 and 12.3) and a few of the actions they could take (12.4). Of the wide range of possible government policies, we consider only three: the contingent tuition repayment plan, an incomes policy, and a negative income tax. Even these three, however, are controversial enough.

12.2 The Current Impact of Government

In Chapter 2, Table 2.3 compared the distribution of income of different nations after accounting for the impact of direct taxes, but this is only part of the picture. Income taxes are highly visible, but other taxes also affect the distribution of income. For example, sales taxes constitute a larger fraction of the income of the poor than of the rich. As well, governments provide services to individuals which are not captured in statistics on the distribution of money income. Comparing Canada and the U.S., for example, Table 2.3 would not reveal that in Canada medicare pays most medical bills, while in the U.S. they must be largely financed from personal income.

If "income" were comprehensively defined, as "command over resources" it would include the value of the medical care one is eligible to receive. How would a comprehensive definition of income affect the degree of measured inequality in Canada? How has government intervention affected the distribution of income over time?

Medicare, for example, was generally expected to benefit primarily the poor, since we all need some medical care and a system of private payment restricts the access to medical care of those who have lower incomes. Manga (1978: 34), however, found in a 1974-75 study of public medicare in Ontario that upper-income families received more medical care than low-income families. Upper-income families also make greater use of specialists than lower-income families. These differences in utilization may be explained by a greater awareness of medical dangers among the more educated and a greater insistence on access to care among the middle classes. Such differences in utilization, even when the service has the same money cost to both rich and poor, may mean that medicare is less redistributive in practice than was hoped at its inception.

Boulet and Henderson (1979), however, note that family size is larger for higher-income families and that the poor have a greater need for health services. Their conclusion is that when one looks at *individuals* the medicare scheme redistributes income towards the poor. Of course, the redistributive impact of medicare depends partly on how it is financed. To the extent that provincial funding comes from premiums (as in Ontario, Quebec, Alberta and B.C.) the share of cost borne by the poor is increased. In addition, since these studies were completed, doctors in several provinces have been allowed to "overbill," which implies that the poor now pay more, partly in money and partly in the medical services they are forced to forego (see Barer et al., 1979:49).

Governments also finance education and thereby provide benefits to the children of different income groups. Primary and secondary public schools are wholly government financed in Canada, but post-secondary institutions are also heavily subsidized. Tuition payments are usually not more than 15 per cent of operating expenses. During the 1960s expanded access to higher education was seen as a major way of reducing economic inequality. Nominally, student aid plans enable the benefits of university education to be received by students from all income groups. In practice, however, there is a heavy bias to the relatively well-off in attendance at universities (see Chapter 6). In 1974, for example, 55 per cent of children from well-off families (annual income over $25,000) attended post-secondary institutions while only 11.6 per cent of children over 18 from poor families (i.e., income under $5,000) did so. Among students attending post-secondary training, those from well-off backgrounds were much more likely to attend university than other training institutions (Statistics Canada, 13-561:45). The probability of attending university is therefore much higher for the children of upper-income families, a bias which is partly due to the joint influence of schools and parents on the aspirations of children (see Forcese, 1975: 57-82) and partly due to the cost of financing

Table 12-1

TAXES PAID AS A PERCENTAGE OF FAMILY INCOME, 1969

Tax Source	Under $2,000	$2,000 2,999	$3,000 3,999	$4,000 4,999	$5,000 5,999	$6,000 6,999	$7,000 7,999	$8,000 8,999	$9,000 9,999	$10,000 10,999	$11,000 11,999	$12,000 14,999	$15,000 & over	All Classes
								%						
Corporate profits tax														
— federal	3.9	2.6	3.0	2.9	1.8	2.8	2.0	1.9	2.0	2.3	2.3	2.0	5.8	3.2
— provincial	1.2	0.9	1.0	0.9	0.6	0.9	0.6	0.6	0.7	0.8	0.8	0.7	1.9	1.1
Personal income tax														
— federal	0.9	1.9	3.1	4.4	6.0	6.5	7.6	8.3	8.9	9.3	9.4	10.5	10.8	8.5
— provincial	0.3	0.8	1.2	1.7	2.3	2.5	3.0	3.2	3.5	3.6	3.6	4.1	4.2	3.3
General sales tax														
— federal	7.2	4.5	4.4	4.3	4.2	4.0	4.1	4.1	3.8	3.8	3.8	3.5	2.5	3.6
— provincial	5.4	3.4	3.3	3.2	3.1	3.0	3.0	3.0	2.8	2.8	2.8	2.6	1.9	2.7
Selective excise taxes	6.1	4.4	4.9	5.1	6.1	5.2	4.9	4.9	4.7	4.4	4.4	4.0	2.7	4.2
Import duties	2.9	1.9	1.7	1.6	1.6	1.4	1.5	1.5	1.4	1.3	1.3	1.2	0.8	1.3
Health insurance premiums	2.8	1.8	1.5	1.3	1.3	1.2	1.0	1.0	1.0	0.9	0.8	0.8	0.6	0.9
Property taxes	11.6	7.6	6.3	5.6	5.0	4.5	4.5	4.6	4.4	4.2	4.0	3.8	3.5	4.5
Motor vehicle taxes	0.9	0.8	0.7	0.8	0.8	0.8	0.7	0.7	0.6	0.6	0.6	0.5	0.3	0.6
Natural resource taxes	1.5	1.0	1.0	0.9	0.8	0.8	0.8	0.7	0.7	0.7	0.7	0.7	1.0	0.8
Municipal business taxes	0.9	0.6	0.5	0.5	0.5	0.5	0.5	0.5	0.4	0.4	0.4	0.4	0.3	0.4
Social security taxes														
— federal	0.8	0.7	0.9	1.1	1.3	1.2	1.4	1.4	1.3	1.3	1.4	1.3	0.9	1.2
— provincial	0.6	0.4	0.5	0.5	0.5	0.5	0.6	0.6	0.5	0.5	0.5	0.5	0.4	0.5
— CPP/QPP	1.3	1.1	1.3	1.5	1.8	1.7	1.9	1.9	1.8	1.8	1.9	1.8	1.3	1.6
Other	0.3	0.3	0.3	0.2	0.2	0.2	0.2	0.2	0.2	0.2	0.2	0.2	0.1	0.2
TOTAL	48.7	34.6	35.3	36.6	37.8	37.8	38.1	39.0	38.7	39.0	38.9	38.9	40.3	38.9

Source: Adapted from Allan Maslove. *The Pattern of Taxation in Canada,* Economic Council of Canada, 1972.

Table 12-2

DISTRIBUTION OF TOTAL BEFORE-TAX BENEFITS OF
THE TOTAL SOCIAL SECURITY SYSTEM ACROSS
ALL ECONOMIC FAMILIES ORDERED BY TOTAL INCOME
AFTER TAX, BY QUINTILE, 1971-75

Quintile	**Before Tax Benefits** %			
	1971	1973	1974	1975
Bottom	25.1	24.4	24.0	23.4
Second	28.9	26.4	25.1	25.2
Middle	17.5	17.4	17.1	18.2
Fourth	14.2	15.8	17.1	16.2
Top	14.3	16.0	16.7	17.0
Total	100.0	100.0	100.0	100.0

Source: Ross, 1980.

higher education. Mehmet (1978: 16) also points out that not only are children from upper-income backgrounds more likely to attend university, they also tend to specialize in those areas within university which have the highest expected incomes after graduation (e.g., medicine and law). The monetary benefits of university education therefore accrue disproportionately to upper-income families, although the costs of financing the university system are borne by the taxes paid by all segments of society (see Table 12-1).

Mehmet concludes, therefore, "the principal net gainers from the university system are the middle and upper income groups at the expense of the lower income groups. In this sense the university system is a large public expenditure programme in which the relatively poor groups tend to subsidize the relatively rich" (1978: 45).

Medicare may redistribute income towards the poor, while subsidies to university education may redistribute income towards the rich, but these are just two of the many impacts of governments on Canadian society — who gains the most on balance? Gillespie (1966, 1976, 1978, 1980), Maslove (1972), Dodge (1975), and others have tried to estimate the net fiscal incidence of government on the income distribution of Canada. Their basic methodology is to calculate (i) the amount of government services, plus (ii) transfer payments, minus (iii) taxes paid by each income group, and express total incidence (i + ii - iii) as a proportion of income from other sources. Net fiscal incidence is then:

F12:1
$$NFI_i = \frac{(B_i + R_i - T_i)}{Y_i}$$

NFI_i net fiscal incidence on income group i
B_i government services received by income group i
R_i government transfers received by i
T_i taxes paid to all levels of government by i
Y_i income of group i (excluding transfer payments)

Naturally, these calculations involve a whole host of detailed assumptions. Transfers (R) are relatively easy to calculate, but on the tax side (T) one can argue about who *really* pays the corporate income tax, shareholders (via decreased dividends) or consumers (via increased prices)? On the benefits side (B) one can query whether it is automobile owners or the consumers of products transported by trucks who benefit from government expenditure on roads. Each assumption implies a somewhat different fiscal incidence since shareholders are much better off, and automobile owners are somewhat better off, than consumers in general. (However, Gillespie (1980: 39) argues that the overall conclusions of his work are unchanged, even under alternative sets of assumptions.)

Figure 12-1 is drawn from Gillespie (1976) and illustrates his result that the total impact of government taxes, transfers and expenditures is redistributive, the lowest-income classes getting net benefits and the highest bearing net costs. The different levels of government vary in their expenditure patterns and tax sources, hence they vary also in their fiscal incidence. If the municipal property tax is seen as a tax on shelter it will bear most heavily on low-income groups, while income taxes paid to federal and provincial governments are a higher fraction of high incomes. Since personal income tax is perhaps the most visible of tax levies, the impression exists that Canada's tax system is quite progressive (i.e., takes an increasing share of higher incomes). Table 12-1 is reproduced from Ross (1980) and indicates that the progressivity of the total tax system is, in fact, rather slight.

The redistributive impact of government's activities arises primarily on the spending side, through the social security system. Table 12-2 is also taken from Ross (1980) and indicates that although more of the social security system payments do tend to go to lower-income groups, this redistributive impact lessened during the early 1970s primarily because of the increasing importance of programs whose benefits are not linked to family income.

Indeed, by 1977/78, when an interprovincial task force compiled an inventory of the 50 Canadian social security programs of different levels of government which made $16.7 billion in payments to Canadians,[1] only 21.5 per cent of those payments were made under programs where benefits

---

[1] In addition, at least 30 programs provide benefits in kind.

Figure 12–1   FISCAL INCIDENCE

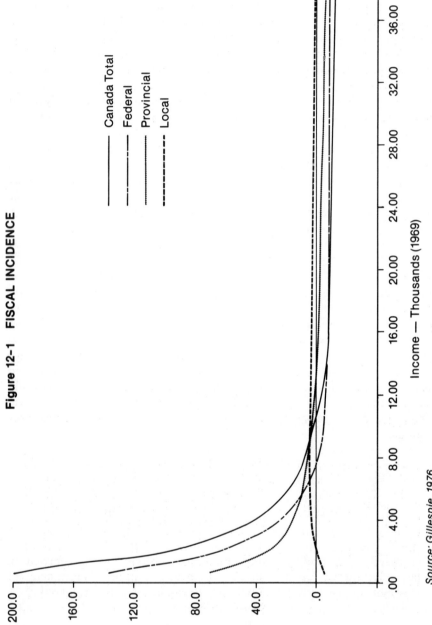

Legend:
Canada Total
Federal
Provincial
Local

Effective Incidence — PC

Income — Thousands (1969)

Source: Gillespie, 1976

were directly tied to family income CICS, 1980: 36). Provincial and municipal social assistance ("welfare") was only 12 per cent of total social security spending, the vast majority of which went to "demogrant" programs (like family allowance or old age pension) which are available to everyone or "social insurance" programs (such as unemployment insurance, Canada Pension or workman's compensation) where benefits are based on previous earnings. Hence, although it was estimated that some 30 per cent of Canada's population received some form of social security benefits other than family allowance at one time or another during 1977/78, only about half of these people found "transfer payments a vital source of income" (CICS, 1980: 3).

The *total* net fiscal incidence of the government (i.e., B + R - T/Y) on different sections of the income distribution is given by Table 12-3 (from Gillespie, 1980) which examines the total impact of government on various sections of the Lorenz curve of the income distribution. Group I comprises the poorest 21.7 per cent of families while Group 5 is the richest 5 per cent. Panel A illustrates the share of total income redistributed from (-) or to (+) a segment of family units, while Panel B illustrates the share, per 1 per cent of families, in that group, which was redistributed.

A critical assumption underlying fiscal incidence studies, however, is that both earnings and returns to capital (i.e., total income — Y) would remain unchanged even if all levels of government in Canada were to disappear. One can imagine Canadian society without a medicare system or without subsidies to university education, but can one imagine a modern society without government of any kind? In addition, government may not be simply a neutral observer of the distribution of national income between labour and capital. Marxists, for example, argue that it is systematically biased towards capital (see Chapter 8). Government programs may also affect the level and distribution of earnings. Kuznets has argued, for example:

> once a progressive income tax has been in effect for some time and is accepted as a form of redistribution, the range of employee compensation flowing directly from the productive process is likely to be at least partly adjusted to it — similarly after the establishment of free benefits, such as state paid medical and educational services, there may be more ready acceptance of low rates of compensation flowing out of the production process. Thus inequality in the distribution of employee compensation as it originates in the production process may be wider merely because of the extension of progressive income taxation at one end and the provision of free benefits at the other, i.e., because of the expected "redistribution." (1966: 197)

At least in the medium term, therefore, *changes* in government programs which produce *changes* in fiscal incidence over a period of time are the most interesting statistics, (i.e., columns (5) and (6) of Table 12-3)

Table 12:3

FISCAL INCIDENCE IN CANADA, TOTAL GOVERNMENT SECTOR, 1951-69, USING THE LORENZ CURVE METHODOLOGY

Line	Lorenz Grouping (Income Class)	Family Units in Lorenz Group (1)	Fiscal Incidence 1951 (2)	Fiscal Incidence 1961 (3)	Fiscal Incidence 1969 (4)	Change in Fiscal Incidence 1951-61 (5)	Change in Fiscal Incidence 1961-69 (6)
				(Percentages)			
Panel A — Share of Total Income Redistributed within Each Lorenz Grouping							
1	Group One (Lowest)	21.7	1.6	2.6	3.6	+1.0	+1.0
2	Group Two (Lower-Middle)	25.5	0.8	2.6	2.9	+1.8	+0.3
3	Group Three (Middle)	25.5	0.6	0.1	-0.2	-0.5	-0.3
4	Group Four (Upper-Middle)	22.2	-1.4	-2.1	-4.0	-0.7	-1.9
5	Group Five (Highest)	5.0	-1.7	-3.2	-2.2	-1.5	+1.0
6	Total	100.0	0.0	0.0	0.0	0.0	0.0
Panel B — Share of Total Income Redistributed for a Percentile of Family Units within each Lorenz Grouping							
7	Group One (Lowest)	1.0	.074	.120	.166	+.046	+.046
8	Group Two (Lower-Middle)	1.0	.031	.102	.114	+.071	+.012
9	Group Three (Middle)	1.0	.024	.004	-.008	-.020	-.012
10	Group Four (Upper-Middle)	1.0	-.063	-.095	-.180	-.032	-.086
11	Group Five (Highest)	1.0	-.340	-.640	-.440	-.300	+.200
12	Total	1.0	0.0	0.0	0.0	0.0	0.0

Source: Gillespie (1980)

rather than an (unrealistic) estimate of incidence at a point in time. In this regard, Gillespie argues that it is a myth that Canadian governments have become more redistributive in recent years. He calculates that "the redistributive mechanism of the public sector during the 1960s generated major gains to rich Canadians: each rich Canadian family gained three times more than each poor Canadian family and six times more than each Canadian in the lower middle income class" (1976:433). During the 1950s, on the other hand, changes in fiscal incidence generally benefited low income groups. In short, "those families who gained substantially relative to others during the 1950s experienced a reversal of fortune during the 1960s. During the 1970s it is quite likely that the command over resources of the lowest income families deteriorated relative to other families" (Gillespie, 1980:41). As Reuber (1978) has also concluded, without a serious political intent to decrease income inequality the activities of Canadian governments have, on balance, had little impact on a remarkably stable income distribution.

12.3 Distributional Implications of Regulation

In addition to its taxation, transfer and expenditure policies, government also regulates the economy. Regulation may affect the rate of return to specific factors, their probability of unemployment and the prices of goods (which are consumed in different proportions by different groups in the population). All these can affect the distribution of economic welfare, although the estimation of the size of such effects can be quite complex.

As one of many potential examples, consider the case of quotas on the import of low-priced clothing from abroad. By limiting import competition, such quotas preserve the value of equity capital tied up in the Canadian clothing industry, thereby benefiting the owners of the companies involved. Restricting foreign competition also preserves some current jobs. The benefit of job maintenance to the people involved is, for the period they could expect to be unemployed, the difference between their wage while working and their income as unemployed.[2]

On the other hand, the increase in clothing prices caused by quotas increases the cost of living of consumers in general, and especially that of large, low-income households. The distributional impact of such a policy then depends on the size of gains to owners (and where in the wealth distribution they stand), the size of gains to workers (and whether they belong, on balance, to high or low income households) and the size of losses to consumers (and how these are distributed).

Assessing the balance of these impacts is obviously not an easy task. It requires fairly sophisticated analysis, and demands substantial amounts

---

[2]From their private point of view their income while unemployed would equal unemployment insurance plus the value of their time in "home production" minus depreciation of human capital minus the psychic costs of unemployment.

of statistical information, both of which are scarce, and especially scarce relative to the range of policies which need analysis. Furthermore, many have argued that it is the dynamic effects of trade restrictions which are most important, both in restricting the growth of national income and in shielding domestic producers from the pressures of international competition. Trade restrictions may influence the long-run level of inequality in the wealth distribution, as well as lessen the constraints which market forces place on the exercise of economic power.

The distributional implications of such policies as air pollution regulations (Gianessi, Peskin and Wolff, 1977), have also been assessed by researchers, but the *total* distributional impact of government regulation is hard to ascertain. The total impact is composed of the effects of many regulatory policies and it is quite unclear what the economy would look like, or indeed if it could function, if all regulation, from meat plant inspection to airline fare regulation, were abolished. It is clear, however, that income distribution is a distinctly subsidiary issue in the framing of many regulations. In section 12.4, however, we consider the potential impacts of policies aimed explicitly at inequality.

12.4 What Could Government Do?

Corresponding to the many actual policies which influence economic inequality is a multitude of possible policies to alter it. Since Chapter 10.6 has already discussed some of the ways the inequality of wealth might be altered, we will consider here only policies affecting the distribution of earnings. Naturally, one's view of which of the theories outlined in Chapters 6 to 8 best analyses the earnings determination process will crucially affect the policies one recommends. Section 12.4.1 therefore outlines one policy which might be recommended by a neoclassical approach (the contingent tuition repayment plan), while section 12.4.2 discusses an approach which might be favoured by institutionalists (an incomes policy). On these particular policies the sides are clearly drawn and each would consider the other's proposal to be at best useless and possibly a recipe for economic disaster. On some policies, however, there is widespread support from both camps. Section 12.4.3 discusses briefly the theory and evidence of a Negative Income Tax.

12.4.1 The Contingent Tuition Repayment Plan

Okun (1975) is one of the many who have argued that the ends of both equity and efficiency are served by moving closer to the ideal of "equal opportunity" in access to higher education. In his view, inability to finance higher education means able people from poor backgrounds are less productive workers than if they could attend university.

One possible remedy is to enable students to finance their university years (tuition and expenses) by agreeing to pay a small increase in their income tax rate in later life. Those who do financially less well after university are therefore not burdened with a load of debt, while the increase in taxes is calculated so that taking the ne'er-do-wells and the affluent among the graduates together, on average, each year's university class will pay for its own education expenses.

This plan therefore enables students from poor backgrounds to finance their education and removes much of the financial risk of going to college — both of which are likely to be important for a student from a poor background. If tuition fees were increased to cover the whole of university expenditures, it would also mean that the recipients of the financial benefits of university paid, as a group, for those benefits, rather than taxpayers at large, thus tending to equalize the lifetime income distribution (see 12.2 above). As well as equalizing "result" by equalizing earnings and by reducing tax inequalities, such a program is intended to equalize the opportunity of people from different socio-economic backgrounds to enter upper-level administrative and professional positions.

Forcese (1975:73), and other sociologists argue, however, that streaming in primary and high school has largely foreclosed the option of university for many working-class children well before they could benefit from such a plan. Even were this not the case, if education is largely a credential, one can expect little impact on inequality of result if its supply increases (see 8.2.2). Thus institutionalists doubt whether such a program would materially affect either inequality of opportunity or inequality of result.

12.4.2 An Egalitarian Incomes Policy

For institutionalists, the lesson to be learned from the decline in earnings inequality during the wage control period of World War II is:

> If the public does in fact want a more equal distribution of earnings, the public can quickly have it at very low cost. Wages can be equalized without massive long-run investments in education and manpower programs. The wage structure can be quickly altered the way it was during World War II to reflect a new pattern of interdependent preferences. To some extent the wage policies of World War II were a deliberate — and successful — attempt to change the sociology of what constitutes "fair" wage differentials. (Thurow, 1975: 192)

The key is "whether the public wants it." Under wartime conditions a consensus for equal sharing of a national effort may enable substantial changes in relative wages, and the new wage structure will "stick" when it has persisted for a few years. Under peacetime conditions a "solidaristic" wage policy (as in Sweden or Holland — see Ulman and Flanagan, 1975) may set national pay scales, with somewhat larger percentage increases for the lower paid. Over time this will compress wage differentials and lessen earnings inequality. Over time, public attitudes on "appropriate" pay differentials will also change as the new pay structure is accepted as "normal." In time, a more equal earnings distribution will become entrenched. If, however, the speed of compression of wage differentials outpaces the rate of change in wage norms, discontent may emerge. One may then have, as in Sweden, strikes of the university educated which aim to maintain or increase their earnings differential over lower-paid workers.

An egalitarian incomes policy is thus a gradualistic method for decreasing earnings differentials. To the extent that "wages drift," (local pay settlements above the national scale), favours the highly paid, its impact on the earnings distribution will be blunted.[3] Incomes policies have, however, been widely adopted, and their rationalization has often been that of equity — i.e., in attempting to limit inflation and to control more strictly the earnings of upper-income groups, it is argued that incomes policies decrease the inequality of the distribution of real income (see Chapter 3.4.3).

To this argument, and especially to controls on wages and prices, many economists have a vehement reaction. Lipsey's (1977) discussion of the wage and profit margin controls in force in Canada from 1975 to 1978 is a case in point. He argues strongly that controls are at best temporarily effective in delaying inflation (i.e., a temporary reduction of at most, 1 per cent to 2 per cent in the inflation rate) and that in general, prices are much more difficult than wages to control.[4] As a result of wages being held down while prices continue to rise, controls tend to mean a shift in the distribution of national income from labour to capital. For this reason, controls in capitalist societies are often opposed by trade-union groups.[5] In the longer run, Lipsey argues, controls introduce distortions into the economy which decrease allocative efficiency and, therefore, growth. He argues they produce a more politicized income distribution process in which "he who makes a big noise gets" (Lipsey, 1977:11). The politically inarticulate and the unorganized therefore get, he feels, a smaller share of a smaller pie (and one can recall from Chapter 4 that low income groups tend to be less politically active). From his perspective, egalitarian attempts to control incomes have very high costs and very uncertain benefits. Even those who have less faith than Lipsey in the "free market" will agree that fair controls require an effective political mechanism to ensure that they benefit low income groups in fact as well as in rhetoric.

---

[3]"Wages drift" can amount to between 25 per cent and 50 per cent of settlements agreed by centralized bargaining (Malles, 1973: 101).

[4]In Canada the Anti-Inflation Board during 1975 to 1978 placed no direct control on prices. Profit margins were subject to ceilings but the option of bases on which they might be calculated meant very few firms had to roll back prices. Wage increases were however held down by between 3.2 per cent and 4.5 per cent (Reid, 1979; Auld et al., 1979).

[5]If, however, the capital stock is publicly owned, an increase in enterprise profits passes through to government revenue, enabling either a general decrease in taxes or an increase in public expenditure.

The institutionalist reply is, of course, that market forces presently play a fairly weak role in the determination of most people's relative wages, hence there is little loss in allocative efficiency when institutional mechanisms are, in effect, co-ordinated at a national level. However, national co-ordination will produce a more equitable income distribution only if this is the demand of the political process to which it is responsive. Incomes policies are therefore not a panacea, since to be effectively redistributive they require a prior set of political changes.

12.4.3 Negative Income Tax Proposals

On tuition payment plans or income policies there is little agreement, but many economists of varying views have supported some version of a Negative Income Tax. Partly this is due to widespread dissatisfaction with current methods of income support. Panel A of Table 12-4 and Figure 12-2 are based on Reuber (1976: Table 11) who examined the income support programs for which a single parent of two would be potentially eligible in Ontario in 1975. Since there are a variety of programs, each with its own regulations, many people may not actually be claiming all the benefits they might be entitled to. In general, however, benefits under these programs are reduced substantially as an individual's income rises, and there is little incentive to engage in paid work in the labour market.

Indeed, if earnings should rise above a relatively low ceiling, ($3,600), a single parent would lose benefit entitlement altogether and her income[6] would fall. She would be working more, but getting less. Suppose, for example, her wage was $4 per hour. Working 18 hours per week for 50 weeks, the total value of her income (subsidies included) would be $10,414; but if she decided to work another two hours per week, she would be cut off family benefits and her income would fall to just over $9,135. She would not regain her previous level of benefits until she increased her work effort to 46.8 hours per week i.e., a full six-day-work week. In addition, if there is any uncertainty involved in her job and she might possibly be laid off in the future, she must compare the certainty of family benefits with the uncertainty and delay of finding another job or re-establishing benefit entitlement.

Obviously there are severe disincentives to work built into such benefits. Part-time or limited temporary low-wage work is the only thing that pays at all, but such work generally does not generate the experience or on-the-job training required for the stable, high-paying jobs which would

---

[6]One must say "her income" since only a minute number of men could in 1975 receive family benefits, and that by special Ministerial direction. "Income" from other sources is negligible for this population, hence "income" and "earnings" can be used interchangeably.

Table 12-4

WELFARE/SUBSIDY SYSTEM VS. NEGATIVE INCOME TAX

	WELFARE/SUBSIDY SYSTEM[1] (A)					NEGATIVE INCOME TAX SYSTEM[2] (B)			
Earned Income 1	Family Benefits 2	Subsidies* 3	Family Allow. & Tax Credit 4	Income Tax 5	Total Income (1+2+3+4+5)	Tax Credit 6	Tax (@60%) 7	Net Payment 8	Total Income (1+8)
$ 0	3,936	1,884	794	0	6,614	5,616	0	5,616	5,616
1,440	3,756	2,684**	794	0	8,674	5,616	864	4,752	6,192
2,880	2,676	3,484	794	0	9,834	5,616	1,728	3,888	6,768
3,600	2,136	3,884	794	0	10,414	5,616	2,160	3,456	7,416
3,960	0	4,381	794	0	9,135	5,616	2,376	3,240	7,200
4,320	0	4,189	794	- 252	9,051	5,616	2,592	3,024	7,344
5,040	0	3,910	794	- 425	9,319	5,616	3,024	2,592	7,632
6,480	0	3,120	794	- 738	9,650	5,616	3,888	1,728	8,208
7,920	0	2,337	794	-1,023	10,038	5,616	4,752	864	8,784
9,360	0	1,582	794	-1,318	10,418	5,616	5,616	0	9,360
10,800	0	844	794	-1,637	10,801	5,616	6,480	-864	9,936

* Subsidies = Day care + housing + OHIP premium subsidies.
** Subsidies increase due to increased use of day care — assumes person receives all subsidies for which eligible.
[1]Based on Mother, two children — one 0 to 9 years and one 10 to 15 years, Ontario, 1975.
[2]Based on $468 per month tax credit, 60 per cent tax rate on earnings.
Source: Reuber, 1976.

Figure 12-2 ALTERNATIVE INCOME SUPPORT SYSTEMS

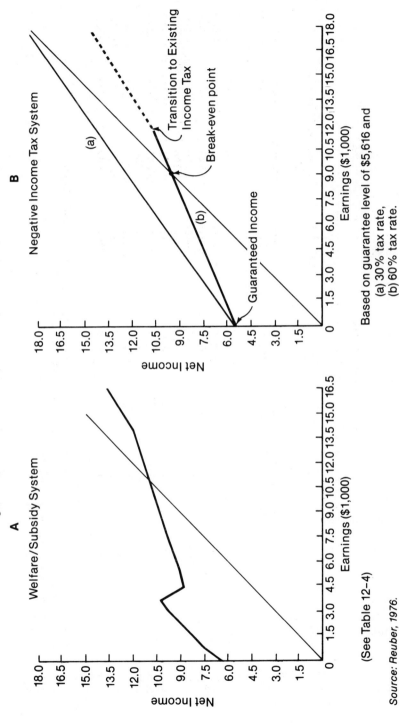

A

Welfare/Subsidy System

Net Income

18.0
16.5
15.0
13.5
12.0
10.5
9.0
7.5
6.0
4.5
3.0
1.5
0

1.5 3.0 4.5 6.0 7.5 9.0 10.5 12.0 13.5 15.0 16.5
Earnings ($1,000)

(See Table 12-4)

Source: Reuber, 1976.

B

Negative Income Tax System

Net Income

18.0
16.5
15.0
13.5
12.0
10.5
9.0
7.5
6.0
4.5
3.0
1.5

(a)

(b)

Transition to Existing Income Tax

Break-even point

Guaranteed Income

0 1.5 3.0 4.5 6.0 7.5 9.0 10.5 12.0 13.5 15.0 16.5 18.0
Earnings ($1,000)

Based on guarantee level of $5,616 and
(a) 30% tax rate,
(b) 60% tax rate.

enable one to escape welfare altogether. Although many researchers (e.g., Steinberg, 1974) have found that only a small minority of the welfare population could enter the paid-labour force in any event, surely these disincentives to work are a perverse feature of any society which claims a "work ethic."

As a reform, "guaranteed annual income" or "negative income tax" schemes have often been proposed. Many variants exist, but they have in common the feature that government would guarantee a minimum level of income to all and make payments of that full amount to those with no earnings. For those with earnings, government payments would be reduced by a "tax rate" on money earnings. Such a scheme is often called a Negative Income Tax scheme since above a certain break-even level of income an individual makes positive tax payments to government, while below it an individual receives transfers ("negative" tax payments).

If, for example, such a scheme had been in place in Ontario in 1975 with a tax credit or "guarantee level" of $468 per month (just above the stingiest of Canada's four poverty lines),[7] and a "tax rate" on earnings of 60 per cent, total income would be represented by line (b) in panel B of Figure 12-2 and the figures of Table 12-4 (panel B). A family with no earnings would receive the full "guarantee level" of $5,616 while a family with earned income of $9,360 would be at the "break even" point and would neither receive payments nor pay taxes. Higher income families would pay tax. If the scheme was administered through the income tax system all three families would fill out the same forms. Some would get cheques in the mail, some would send them in, but there would be no stigma to receiving a tax credit and no nosey welfare officers to supervise the lives of the poor. No one would have to declare themselves an "economic failure" to gain benefits. In an "automatic" program the arbitrary criteria which exclude many "working poor" from benefits would disappear, which would have the incidental benefit of ending the resentment of "welfare" felt by many of today's working poor.

Gains in self-respect are impossible to quantify but money income would be given by the formula:

F12:2   Net Income = [Guarantee level - (tax rate x earnings)] + earnings

The combination of tax rate and guarantee level which are chosen are the crucial economic parameters of a Negative Income Tax (NIT) system. Together they determine the break-even point, hence the fraction of the population which receives payments under the scheme. In Figure 12-2 panel

---

[7]For a family of three in 1975 the Statistics Canada updated poverty line (i.e., the 70 per cent spent on necessities criterion) was $5,577, the Statistics Canada revised poverty line was $6,311, the C.C.S.D. line was $7,119, and the Senate Committee poverty line was $7,973.

B, for example, lines (a) and (b) represent an NIT with the same guarantee level ($5,616), but (a) involves a tax rate of 30 per cent, hence a break-even point of $18,720 while line (b) represents a tax rate of 60 per cent and a break-even point of $9,360. In 1975, (b) would have implied that roughly 23 per cent of Canadian three-person families received payments, while (a) implies about 55 per cent received payments.

Clearly the budgetary cost of an NIT program will be crucially affected by how many receive benefits, hence there are strong pressures on governments to keep the break-even point low. But if a poverty-line income (however meagre) is to be guaranteed to those unable to earn, this implies a high tax rate is required, which reduces the "work incentives" the plan was supposed to provide. In addition, although panel B of Table 12-4 illustrates the desirable fact that incomes under an NIT always increase as earnings increase, a comparison with panel A indicates that even though *cash* payments are greater under an NIT than those under family benefits, if an NIT such as (b) were to replace *all* existing welfare/subsidy programs some of the poor might be worse off than under the actual 1975 welfare/subsidy system.[8] As a method of reducing inequality, therefore, the parameters of a Negative Income Tax (i.e., its tax credit guarantee and its implicit tax rate), and which existing programs are replaced by it, are vitally important.

Indeed it is unlikely that an NIT could ever replace all current social welfare programs, since the needs of some (e.g., the physically handicapped) both cost more and are so specific that they require special attention. In addition, the details of payment mechanisms and payment periods (monthly, quarterly, yearly?) are crucial to many households. If the guarantee level is to vary with household size one must also define "household" — is it to be legally married couples only (as in the current Income Tax Act) or does it include common-law spouses or all people living together? Finally, an NIT, if it is to be administered via the income tax mechanism, must be "harmonized" with tax law and the current tax scheme adjusted, if people are not to be both receiving negative tax supplements while paying ordinary income tax.

A variety of NIT schemes have been introduced in planned experiments (see Hum (1980) for a brief description), and such "housekeeping" details have been shown to be quite important to the plans' impacts. Economists, however, have tended to emphasize the issue of whether an NIT would substantially reduce labour supply, since if it did the economic consequences (in reduced output) and the political fall-out (in resentment of "welfare bums") would be serious.

Clearly the size of the impact of an NIT on labour supply depends on the particular program parameters adopted. The level of tax credit guarantee

---

[8]One must say "might" since only a fraction of those eligible for subsidized housing or day care actually receive those benefits.

set implies an "income" effect, (i.e., people who are now better off may consume more leisure) while the tax rate chosen implies a "substitution" effect, (i.e., an hour of labour, at the margin, may yield a lower return). The number of experiments conducted and the variety of results obtained have by now created an entire specialist literature on this topic alone. The interested student can start with Hum (1980), who provides a concise recent synopsis, or Masters and Garfinkel (1977), who offer a book-length treatment. Our even briefer summary notes that the labour supply effects of an NIT differ significantly by demographic group. Older male workers work very nearly the same hours in an NIT experimental scheme or under "control" programs. Women, especially married women with children, and younger men may reduce their paid work hours more substantially, but since they tend to work less to begin with, their reduced labour supply is a smaller fraction of the total. In aggregate, Masters and Garfinkel estimate an NIT with a poverty line base and a 50 per cent tax rate would reduce paid work hours in the U.S. by 2.5 per cent to 4.3 per cent (1977: 239), an effect they argue is small, relative to the general reductions in work hours achieved during the past few decades due to a shorter work week.

In terms of lost output to the economy, a labour supply decrease of 2.5 per cent could be achieved by a 1/40 decrease in everyone's work hours or achieved by 2.5 per cent of the labour force ceasing work entirely. In political terms, however, these would excite quite different reactions from the public. In political terms, society also distinguishes between the "leisure" of different ages and sexes, and between the absence from paid employment of those with and without children. There is little resentment, for example, at a 70-year-old who lives on government old age pension or a single parent who receives family benefits, but considerable animosity exists to ablebodied males of working age who do not seriously try to find a job. These differences in social expectations may explain why the Guaranteed Income Supplement, which is basically a Negative Income Tax scheme for the old, can be introduced with little fuss, while proposals for a comprehensive Negative Income Tax remain stalled.

Indeed, the Child Tax Credit introduced in 1979 also has some features of an NIT — i.e., a general tax credit, and a "tax rate" based on family income. Its deficiencies are its very small size ($200 per child) and its payment on a once-a-year basis. However, the Family Allowance program (which is by now a Canadian institution) is basically a "demo-grant," paid conveniently to all families on a regular monthly basis. If it were increased drastically in size it could form the guaranteed minimum base of an NIT scheme for families with children. If it were taxed on a family income basis, the tax rate could be adjusted (as with the Child Tax Credit) so as to provide net benefits only to relatively low-income households. Since families with children are a socially acceptable target group for income transfers, and since the mechanism is long established and well accepted, a relatively minor piecemeal reform could effectively institute a Negative Income Tax for a substantial fraction of the Canadian population. Such a reform might be easier to achieve than a comprehensive Negative Income Tax which would also provide benefits to younger single people and childless couples.

Akerlof (1978) has argued that a scheme which "tags" certain target groups can provide greater benefits to that group and can be more socially efficient, than a program which is required to be universalistic. Income support programs for younger adults without dependants may well require (politically) a different structure (e.g., a work test or training component) than a program for families with children.[9]

12.5 Summary

(a) Governments provide services to individuals, transfer income to individuals, and tax the income of individuals — all these activities affect the distribution of economic well-being. Some activities (such as the subsidization of colleges and universities) appear on balance to transfer real resources to higher-income families while others (such as medicare) transfer resources to poor families. If one assumes that labour earnings and capital income would be unchanged even in the absence of government, the "net incidence" of government activities is to redistribute income from rich to poor, although the amount of such redistribution has declined in recent years. Part of the explanation for this decline lies in the increasing importance of social security transfer programs whose benefits are not tied to family income, coupled with a tax system which in aggregate takes a roughly constant proportion of family income at all income levels.

(b) In addition to their tax, transfer and expenditure activities, governments also regulate economic activity. The distributional impact of such regulation is hard to assess, but is unlikely to be negligible.

(c) Those who argue from a "human capital" perspective tend to feel that government policies to equalize incomes should emphasize the equalization of opportunities and the removal of market imperfections. They contend that a "contingent tuition repayment plan" or other policies which equalized the cost to individuals of higher education would increase both the efficiency and the equity of the labour market, enabling growth and equality. Since an "institutionalist" or a "radical" analysis argues that university education very often serves mainly as a credential, it implies that such policies would be costly but ineffective.

---

[9]To the extent that an NIT scheme for families with children provided greater benefits than a companion scheme for childless adults there would be an incentive to transfer — i.e., have children. Whether this is desirable depends partially on social attitudes to population growth and the estimated elasticity of birth rates with respect to income.

(d) One "institutional" approach to equalizing wages is to institute an "incomes policy" which, over time, would allow greater increases to the low-paid. Neoclassical economists, however, feel controls are ineffective, impede the efficiency of market forces and further politicize the income distribution process.

(e) Many economists of all persuasions support some form of "negative income tax." A basic guarantee available to all, decreased by a "tax" on earned income, would increase work incentives and eliminate much of the stigma of current social security programs. A high "guarantee level" (to prevent poverty) and a low tax rate (to preserve incentives) tend, however, to imply a program which is very costly — unless its operation is restricted to a socially acceptable target group such as only those families who have children.

Chapter 13

A Personal Conclusion

There are many books and articles which focus on particular aspects of the theory of economic inequality, and relatively few on the facts of economic inequality as they exist in Canada. This book has attempted, therefore, to present a broad overview of the theory of economic inequality and a relatively narrow focus on the Canadian facts. In Chapters 2 and 3, it was noted that there are many dimensions to "economic inequality" — hence the choice of the "facts" which require explanation is neither easy nor obvious. Indeed, since some alternative definitions of the "facts" of inequality will tend to alter our perception of its extent and since some "facts" only make sense within a particular theoretical framework, both one's perception of the extent of inequality and one's perspective on its causes are tied up with the definitions by which one attempts to measure it.

By the criterion of annual income, as distributed among Canadian family units, economic inequality has remained roughly constant since the Second World War. Measures of economic inequality in wealth, in riches or in power are much less easy to obtain. Where available, however, they show a higher degree of inequality than inequality in annual incomes, while inequality in lifetime income or annual income after government taxes, transfers and expenditures is somewhat lower. Despite the many changes in the Canadian economy which have occurred over the 1945-80 period, there is little evidence that economic inequality in Canada, by any of the above measures, has decreased appreciably.

One implication of this is that if one sees "poverty" as being economic deprivation relative to the prevailing living standards of the community, these 35 years of economic growth have not eliminated it. As discussed in Chapter 4, poverty, like inequality, can be defined in a number of ways. A "relativistic" conception of poverty implies that poverty is not a diminishing problem in Canada, and that the extent of poverty depends directly on the degree of inequality in the distribution of economic resources.

Who the poor are, i.e., who it is that occupies the bottom place in our unchanged aggregate distribution, depends largely on the workings of the labour market. Although a majority of those currently poor are outside the current labour force, nevertheless for single parents, and the aged poor, as well as the "working poor," the labour market's past operations are a key ingredient in their current poverty status. An effective analysis of the incidence of poverty must therefore start, in a market economy, with the earnings determination process — i.e., the determination of returns in the only market in which most people have anything to sell (i.e., their labour).

Empirically, Chapter 5 demonstrated that the vast majority (77 per cent) of the personal income of Canadians comes from labour earnings. Chapters 6 to 9 therefore focus on earnings, and especially the determination of earnings as seen by the neoclassical, institutional and radical research traditions. In some respects, these different approaches can be seen as alternative languages with which to analyse earnings inequality. Just as a language will evolve new vocabulary, new syntax and new grammar for a previously unknown event, for which no term is available, so also can each of the major research traditions generate new maintained hypotheses and new theoretical models to cope with the strain of "anomalous" research results (see Kuhn, 1970). What Blaug (1976) calls the "hard core" of a theoretical approach (to distinguish if from the "protective belt" of subsidiary assumptions or working models which can easily be jettisoned) is in each case somewhat amorphous.[1] New evidence can therefore be assimilated within each major research tradition, and just as one can trace the evolution of languages back over the generations so also can one trace the development of the major research traditions.

Over time, a "borrowing" of vocabulary enriches languages, and over time concepts such as "internal labour markets," have been borrowed from one school of thought by another.[2] Choosing a theoretical framework or research tradition with which to analyse earnings inequality is, at one level, therefore much like choosing which language to learn. (Most learn the language they are taught in school and few take the trouble to become bilingual.) Partly one's choice will be based on what one wants to talk about, since some things are much harder to say in one language than in another (e.g., wage rigidity and unemployment is much more difficult to explain in a neoclassical than in an institutional framework — see Solow (1980)). Partly one's choice will also depend on whom one wants to talk to. Since the neoclassical approach dominates North American universities' economics departments, arguments framed in its terms find a readier acceptance in academia, while the institutional approach has more currency in business and government. A final factor may be one's aesthetic sense of which language offers greater clarity and ease of expression, which "tells us the most in the fewest words" and which produces the most useful conjectures to test against the data.

---

[1]Compare, for example, the concepts "human capital" and "segments." Both are capable of a great many theoretical, and even more empirical, specifications.
[2]Just as, however, the use of French words in English is often accompanied by a subtle shift in their meaning, so also do concepts originating in one theoretical context change subtly when used in another. Purists, moreover, often dislike intensely the patois which can result.

At another level, however, one must be aware that one's choice of research tradition may create or accentuate bias. Within the neoclassical tradition, for example, the fact that it is difficult to define or to speak of "exploitation" or "power" may mean initially that it is easier to study other issues. Since it appears to be human nature to emphasize the importance of one's own work, such a choice may in time subtly mould one's perspective on events to the conclusion that "exploitation" or "power" are relatively unimportant (or even non-existent) phenomena. Similarly, an analysis conducted entirely in terms of "segments" or "classes" can easily lose sight of the importance of individual voluntary choices at the micro-level.

Most economists would argue that one's choice of theory should depend on how well a research tradition stacks up when measured against the evidence. The pure theory of choice, however, offers no clear prediction until one specifies the constraints to which choice is subject. The pure theory of class struggle offers no clear predictions until a specific historical context is provided. Pure theory of any description offers virtually no unambiguous, unqualified predictions. Applied theory of any description must be framed so as to be consistent with the same underlying social reality — hence it may use different terms and offer different interpretations but it must still produce the same predictions of empirical events.

A recurring regularity of a study of inequality is the similarity of the economic position of parents and children (see Chapter 6). One may explain this in terms of parental investment in "child quality" or in terms of the inheritance of class status. One may interpret this in terms of the choices parents make or in terms of the constraints parents face. To the child, of course, it makes little difference, and to fit the data, one's theories must produce the same prediction, a high correlation between parent and child in socio-economic status. The most striking conclusion of Chapters 7 and 8 was that despite their vast methodological differences both the radical and the neoclassical approach agree that inequality of result and inequality of opportunity are inevitable in an unconstrained capitalist market system. Indeed, in such a system inequality of result in one generation must always produce inequality of opportunity in the next generation — hence the very distinction between inequalities of "result" or of "opportunity" is somewhat misleading.

However, inheritance between generations is, in Knight's phrase, most "convenient" when it takes the form of the transfer of property. The inheritance of property has therefore long been of concern for those who value "equality of opportunity," and Chapter 10 examined the role of inheritance versus "life-cycle" saving in the accumulation of property. "Life-cycle" saving appears to be a reasonable picture of wealth acquisition only for the middle classes. A substantial fraction of the population have neither private pensions nor much personal property to live on in old age while most of the owners of "large fortunes" inherit the bulk of their wealth — and

Chapter 3 indicated that a majority of Canada's wealth is held by the top 10 per cent of Canadian families.

Since considerable attention has focused, in Canada, on government's redistributive policies as an explanation for our recent slow growth, Chapter 11 examined the connection between growth and inequality while Chapter 12.1 examined the redistributive impact of government policies in Canada. It was concluded that the economic connection (if any) between economic growth and economic inequality is, in general, not an obvious one. Above a fairly low level of income, richer nations tend to be more equal economically than poorer ones. Among OECD nations there appears to be little systematic pattern — and little theoretic reason to expect one. In any event, the "increased redistribution" of Canadian governments in the 1970s is a myth. Causes for Canada's recent slow growth (and the slow growth of other OECD nations) must therefore be found elsewhere.

Inequality may not be necessary for the production of economic growth but is growth necessary for the toleration of economic inequality? Marxists and conservatives alike have emphasized that capitalism's historic justification has been the increase in material wealth it has produced. But, in 1980/81, after half a decade of "stagflation" and with almost universal pessimism for the immediate future, it appears that the prospects for ever-rising average standards of living under capitalism have become rather remote. And when the engine of growth falters and individuals can no longer expect to become better off in absolute terms year by year with a constant share of a larger pie, will there not be increasing pressure for larger shares of a constant pie? And if existing economic institutions cannot satisfy the economic aspirations of much of the populace, if indeed some groups are net losers in the increasing struggle over distributive shares, will there not be increasing pressure for changes in existing economic institutions?

What form those changes will take is a topic far beyond the scope of this book. One possibility is that existing members of the elite will consolidate their economic and political positions, that economic inequality will increase while political repression smothers the discontent that would otherwise emerge. Another possibility is that political pressures will force a greater attention to equality of opportunity and equality of result. Whether Canada will tend towards a "Latin American" or a "Scandinavian" model in future years, and just how such models would be adapted to the uniqueness of Canada's situation, is an issue that would certainly require a study of its own.

This book has therefore concentrated on description and analysis of economic inequality in Canada as it now exists, and on reforms within existing institutions. If such description and analysis of the current situation contributes to greater understanding and a more informed debate as to our future path, the purpose of this book will have been well served.

Bibliography

Adams, Ian. *The Poverty Wall*. Toronto: McClelland and Stewart, 1970.

Adams, Ian, W. Cameron, B. Hill, P. Penz. *The Real Poverty Report*. Edmonton: M. C. Hurtig Ltd., 1971.

Addison, J. T. and W. S. Siebert. *The Market for Labor: An Analytical Approach*. Santa Monica: Goodyear Publishing Co., 1979.

Ahamad, Bill, J. Greenberg, et al. *Degree-Holders in Canada: An Analysis of a Highly-Qualified Manpower Survey of 1973*. Ottawa: Education Support Branch, Department of the Secretary of State, 1979.

Ahluwalia, M. S. "Inequality, Poverty and Development." *Journal of Development Economics* 3 (1976a): 307-342.

Ahluwalia, M. S. "Income Inequality — Some Dimensions of the Problem," pp. 3-37 in Chenery et al. (1976).

Aigner, P. J. and G. C. Cain. "Statistical Theories of Discrimination in Labor Markets." *Industrial and Labor Relations Review* 30 (1977): 175-187.

Aitchinson, J. and J. Brown. *The Log-Normal Distribution*. Cambridge: University Press, 1957.

Akerlof, G. A. "The Market for 'Lemons': Qualitative Uncertainty and the Market Mechanism." *Quarterly Journal of Economics*, August 1970, p. 488.

Akerlof, G. A. "The Economics of Tagging." *The American Economic Review*, March 1978, pp. 8-19.

Akerlof, G. A. "A Theory of Social Custom, of which Unemployment may be one Consequence." *Quarterly Journal of Economics*, June 1980, pp. 749-776.

Akin, J. and I. Garfinkel. "The Quality of Education and Cohort Variation in Black/White Earnings Differentials: Comment." *American Economic Review*, March 1980, pp. 186-191.

Allen, V. L., ed. "Psychological Factors in Poverty." Institute for Research on Poverty Monograph. Chicago: Markham Publishing Co.,1970.

Allen, V. L. "Personality Correlates of Poverty." Institute for Research on Poverty Monograph. Chicago: Markham Publishing Co., 1970, pp. 242-266.

Armstrong, D. A.; P. H. Friesen, and D. Miller. "The Measurement of Income Distribution in Canada: Some Problems and Some Tentative Data." *Canadian Public Policy*, Autumn 1977, pp. 479-488.

Armstrong, D. A.; P. H. Friesen, and D. Miller. "Income Distribution in Canada: A Reply to Needleman and Shedd." *Canadian Public Policy*, Autumn 1979, pp. 510-517.

Arrow, K. J. "Higher Education as a Filter." *Journal of Public Economics*, July 1973.

Arrow, K. J. "Models of Job Discrimination," in A. Pascal, ed. (1972).

Asimakapulos, A. "Profits and Investment: A Kaleckian Approach," pp. 328-342 in Harcourt, ed. (1977).

Atkinson, A. B. "On the Measurement of Inequality." *Journal of Economic Theory* 2 (1970): 244-263.

Atkinson, A. B., ed. *Wealth, Income and Inequality.* Harmondsworth: Penguin Books, 1973.

Atkinson, A. B. *The Economics of Inequality.* Oxford: Clarendon Press, 1975.

Atkinson, A. B., ed. *The Personal Distribution of Incomes.* London: George Allen and Unwin, 1976.

Auer, L. and K. McMullen. "Changes in Poverty Levels in Canada Between 1967 and 1976. An Exploratory Analysis." Conference on Canadian Incomes, May 1979. Mimeographed.

Auld, D., L. Christofides, R. Swidinsky and D. Wilton. "The Impact of the Anti-Inflation Board on Negotiated Wage Settlements." *The Canadian Journal of Economics*, May 1979, pp. 195-213.

Barer, M. L.; R. C. Evans, and C. L. Stoddart. "Controlling Health Care Costs by Direct Charges to Patients: Snare or Delusion?" Ontario Economic Council, Occasional Paper No. 10, Toronto, 1979.

Baron, J. N. and W. T. Bielby. "Current Research on Segmentation and Stratification: Substance in Search of a Method." Paper presented at N.S.F. conference on The Structure of Labor Markets, Athens, Georgia, March 1980. Mimeographed.

Becker, G. *The Economics of Discrimination.* Chicago: University of Chicago Press, 1957.

Becker, G. *Human Capital.* New York: Columbia University Press, 1964.

Becker, G. "A Theory of Social Interaction." *Journal of Political Economy* 82 (1974): 1063-93.

Becker, G. and N. Tomes, "Child Endowments and the Quality and Quantity of Children." *Journal of Political Economy*, August 1976, pp. 5143-5162.

Becker, G. and N. Tomes. "An Equilibrium Theory of the Distribution of Income and Intergenerational Mobility." *Journal of Political Economy*, December 1979, pp. 1153-1189.

Bendix, R. and S. M. Lipset. *Class, Status and Power — Social Stratification in Comparative Perspective,* 2nd ed. New York: The Free Press, 1966.

Ben-Porath, Y. "The Production of Human Capital and the Life-Cycle of Earnings." *Journal of Political Economy*, August 1967.

Bergmann, B. "The Effect on White Incomes of Discrimination in Employment." *Journal of Political Economy*, 19 (1971).

Berkowitz, S. D., Y. Kotowitz, L. Waverman. "Enterprise Structure and Corporate Concentration." Study No. 16, Royal Commission on

Corporate Concentration, Ministry of Supply and Services, Ottawa, 1977.

Berkowitz, S. D., P. J. Carrington, Y. Kotowitz, and L. Waverman. "The Determination of Enterprise Groupings Through Combined Ownership and Directorship Ties." *Social Networks* 1 (1978/79): 391-413.

Bhatia, K. "Capital Gains and the Inequality of Personal Income: Some Results from Survey Data." *Journal of the American Statistical Association,* September 1976, pp. 575-580.

Blau, F. "Women's Place in the Labor Market." *American Economic Review,* May 1972.

Blaug, Mark. "Human Capital Theory — A Slightly Jaundiced Survey." *Journal of Economic Literature,* September 1976, pp. 827-855.

Blinder, A. S. "A Model of Inherited Wealth," *The Quarterly Journal of Economics,* November 1973, pp. 608-626.

Blinder, A. S. *Toward an Economic Theory of Income Distribution.* Cambridge: MIT Press, 1977.

Blinder, A. S. "On Dogmatism in Human Capital Theory." *Journal of Human Resources,* Winter 1976, pp. 8-22.

Blinder, A. S. and R. M. Solow, ed. *The Economics of Public Finance,* Washington D.C.: The Brookings Institution, 1974.

Bliss, C. J. *Capital Theory and the Distribution of Income.* Amsterdam, North Holland: Oxford 1975.

Blumberg, Paul. "White Collar Status Panic." *The New Republic,* December 1, 1979.

Blunn, R. "Salaries Soar at the Top: Jumps of 30% to 60% in wake of controls." *The Financial Times,* May 26, 1980, pp. 1, 20-21.

Booth, A. "Paul Desmarais: At the Ready." *The Financial Post,* March 15, 1980, p. 19.

Boserup, E. *Woman's Role in Economic Development.* London: George Allen and Unwin, 1970.

Boulet, J. A. and D. W. Henderson. "Distributional and Redistributional Aspects of Government Health Insurance Programs in Canada." Economic Council of Canada, Discussion Paper No. 146, December 1979.

Bowles, S. "Schooling and Inequality from Generation to Generation." *Journal of Political Economy,* May/June 1972, pp. 219-251.

Bowles, S. and H. Gintis. *Schooling in Capitalist America: Educational Reform and the Contradictions of Economic Life.* New York: Basic Books, 1976.

Bradley, C. F., S. E. Ross and J. M. Warnyca. "Parent's Choice. A Comprehensive Perinatal Programme." Vancouver Perinatal Health Project, November 1978.

Break, George F. "The Incidence and Economic Effects of Taxation," in Blinder, ed. (1974).

Brittain, J. A. *The Inheritance of Economic Status.* Washington D.C.: The Brookings Institution, 1977.

Brittain, John A. *Inheritance and the Inequality of Material Wealth.* Washington, D.C.: The Brookings Institution, 1978.

Bronfenbrenner, M. "Neo-Classical Macro-Distribution Theory," pp. 476-500 in Marchal and Ducros, eds. (1968).

Brown, J. A. C. "The Mathematical and Statistical Theory of Income Distribution." (Comments By Shorrocks and Muelbauer) pp. 72-97 in Atkinson, A. B. (1976).

Brown, J. C. *Prevention of Handicap: A Case for Improved Prenatal and Perinatal Care.* Ottawa: Canadian Institute of Child Health, 1978.

Brown, Lester R. *By Bread Alone.* New York: Praeger Publishers for the Overseas Development Council, 1974.

Butler, N. R. and D. G. Bonham. Perinatal Mortality: The First Report of the 1958 British Perinatal Mortality Survey, Edinburgh & London: E. and S. Livingstone, 1963.

Buttrick, J. "Who Goes to College," in Martell (1974), pp. 65-68.

Cain, G. "The Challenge of Segmented Labor Market Theories to Orthodox Theory: A Survey." *Journal of Economic Literature,* December 1976, pp. 1215-1257.

Calvo and Wellisz. "Hierarchy, Ability and Income Distribution." *Journal of Political Economy.* October 1979.

Canadian Intergovernmental Conference Secretariat. "The Income Security System in Canada — Report for the Interprovincial Conference of Ministers Responsible for Social Services." Ottawa, September, 1980.

Canterbury, E. R. "A Vita Theory of the Personal Income Distribution." *Southern Economic Journal,* July 1979, pp. 12-48.

Caskie, Donald M. *Canadian Fact Book on Poverty.* Ottawa: Canadian Council on Social Development, 1979.

Champernowne, D. G. "A Model of Income Distribution." *Economic Journal,* June 1953, pp. 318-51.

Champernowne, D. G. "A Comparison of Measures of Inequality of Income Distribution." *The Economic Journal,* December 1974, pp. 788-816.

Chenery, H., M. S. Ahluwalia, C. Bell, J. Duloy, and R. Jolly. *Redistribution With Growth.* World Bank, London: Oxford University Press, 1976.

Chiplin, B. and P. J. Sloane. *Sex Descrimination in the Labour Market.* London: Macmillan, 1976.

Chiswick, B. R. "The Average Level of Schooling and Intraregional Inequality of Income." *American Economic Review,* June 1968, pp. 495-500.

Chiswick, B. R. *Income Inequality.* New York: National Bureau of Economics Research, 1974.

Chiswick, B. R. and J. Mincer. "Time Series Changes in Personal Income Inequality in the United States from 1939 with Projections to 1985." *Journal of Political Economy,* May/June 1972.

Clairmont, D., M. MacDonald, and F. Wien. "A Segmentation Approach to Poverty and Low Wage Work in the Maritimes." Institute of Public Affairs, Dalhousie University, Halifax, 1978.

Clark, J. B. *The Distribution of Wealth — A Theory of Wages, Interest and Profit.* New York: MacMillan, 1908.

Clement, W. *The Canadian Corporate Elite.* Carleton Library No. 89, Toronto: McClelland and Stewart, 1975.

Cloutier, J. E. "The Distribution of Benefits and Costs of Social Security in Canada 1971-75." Discussion Paper 108, Economic Council of Canada, 1978.

Cohen, M. "Property and Sovereignty," (1927) pp. 153-176 in C. B. Macpherson, ed. 1978.

Coleman, R. P. and L. Rainwater. *Social Standing in America: New Dimensions of Class.* New York: Basic Books, 1978.

Comanor, W. S. and R. H. Smiley. "Monopoly and the Distribution of Wealth." *Quarterly Journal of Economics,* May 1975, pp. 177-194; "Revisited." *Quarterly Journal of Economics,* February 1980, pp. 195-198.

Cooper, G. *A Voluntary Tax? New Perspectives on Sophisticated Estate Tax Avoidance.* Washington D.C.: The Brookings Institution, 1979.

Cornwall, J. *Modern Capitalism: Its Growth and Transformation.* New York: St. Martin's Press, 1978.

Courchene, T. J. *Migration, Income and Employment: Canada 1965-68.* Montreal: C. D. Howe Research Institute, 1974.

Cunningham, J. "Where There's a Will There's a Way." *Manchester Guardian Weekly,* May 20, 1979, p. 5.

Cowell, F. A. *Measuring Inequality.* Oxford: Philip Allan Publishers, 1977.

Cowell, F. A. "On the Structure of Additive Inequality Measures." *The Review of Economic Studies,* April 1980, pp. 521-532.

Crow, J. F. "Do Genetic Factors Contribute to Poverty?" pp. 147-160 in Allen ed. (1970).

Danziger, S., R. Haverman, and E. Smolensky, eds. "The Measurement and Trend of Inequality: Comment." *American Economic Review,* June 1977, pp. 505-512.

Davies, J. B. and A. F. Shorrocks. "Assessing the Quantitative Importance of Inheritance in the Distribution of Wealth." *Oxford Economic Papers,* March 1978, pp. 138-149.

Davies, J. B. "On the Size Distribution of Wealth in Canada." *Review of Income and Wealth,* September 1979, pp. 237-260.

Davies, J. B. "Life-Cycle Savings, Inheritance and the Distribution of Income and Wealth in Canada." Ph.D. thesis presented to the University of London, 1979b.

Davies, J. B. "On the Relative Quantitative Importance of Inheritance and Other Sources of Economic Inequality," Research Report #8012, Economics Department, University of Western Ontario, London, 1980.

Davies, J. B. "Uncertain Lifetime Consumption and Dissaving in Retirement." *Journal of Political Economy,* forthcoming 1981.

Davies, H. T. *The Theory of Econometrics.* Bloomington, 1941.

de Jesus, M. C. *Child of the Dark.* New Jersey: Mentor Books, 1962.

Dodge, David A. "Impact of the Tax Transfer and Expenditure Policies of Government on the Distribution of Personal Income In Canada." *Review of Income and Wealth,* March 1975, pp. 1-52.

Doeringer, P. B. and M. J. Piore, *Internal Labor Markets and Manpower Analysis.* Lexington, Mass.: D. C. Heath and Co., 1971.

Dore, R. *British Factory — Japanese Factory: The Origins of National Diversity in Industrial Relations.* London, 1973.

Dun's Review. "Politics: The New Anti-Merger Strategy." *Dun's Review,* July 1970.

Economic Council of Canada. "Trends and Regional Differences in Education." *Sixth Annual Review,* Ottawa, 1969.

Economic Council of Canada. *People and Jobs.* Ottawa: Information Canada, 1976.

Edwards, R. *Contested Terrain: The Transformation of the Workplace in the Twentieth Century.* New York: Basic Books, 1979.

Edwards, R. C. "The Social Relations of Production in the Firm and Labor Market Structure", pp. 3-26, in Edwards, Reich & Gordon, eds. 1975.

Edwards, R. C., M. Reich, D. Gordon, eds. *Labor Market Segmentation.* Lexington, Mass.: D. C. Heath & Co., 1975.

Elias, T. O. *Nigerian Land Law and Custom.* London: Routledge and Kegan Paul Ltd., 1962.

Feinstein, C. H. "Changes in the Distribution of the National Income in the United Kingdom since 1860." pp. 115-138 in Marchal and Ducros, 1968.

Finance Canada. *Economic Reviews.* Ottawa: Ministry of Supply and Services, April 1980.

Financial Post (1979). "The 1979 Ranking of Canada's 500 Largest Companies." *The Financial Post,* June 16, 1979.

Forcese, D. *The Canadian Class Structure.* Toronto: McGraw-Hill Ryerson, 1975.

Freedman, M. *Labor Markets: Segments and Shelters.* New York: Allanheld, Osmun and Co., Universe Books, 1976.

Freeman, R. B. "Decline of Labor Market Discrimination and Economic Analysis," *American Economic Review,* 1973.

Freeman, R. B. "The Exit-Voice Tradeoff in the Labor Market: Unionism, Job Tenure, Quits and Separations." *Quarterly Journal of Economics,* June 1980, pp. 643-674.

Friedman, M. "Choice, Chance and the Personal Distribution of Income." *Journal of Political Economy* 61 (1953): 277-290.

Friedman, M. *Capitalism and Freedom.* Chicago: University of Chicago Press, 1962.

Fuchs, V. R. "Redefining Poverty and the Redistribution of Income." *The Public Interest,* Summer 1967, pp. 88-95.

Galbraith, J. K. *The New Industrial State.* New York: Signet Books, 1967.

Garfinkel, I., and R. H. Haveman. *Earnings Capacity Inequality and Poverty.* Institute for Research on Poverty Monograph Series, New York: Academic Press, 1977.

Gianessi, L. P. and H. M. Peskin and E. Wolff. "The Distributional Implications of National Air Pollution Damage Estimates," pp. 201-226 in T. F. Juster, ed., 1977.

Gibrat, R. *Les Inegalites Economiques,* Paris: Sirey, 1931.

Gillespie, W. I. "The Incidence of Taxes and Public Expenditures on the Canadian Economy." Studies of the Royal Commission on Taxation, No. 2, Ottawa: Queen's Printer, 1966.

Gillespie, W. I. "On the Redistribution of Income in Canada." *Canadian Tax Journal,* July/August 1976, pp. 419-450.

Gillespie, W. I. *In Search of Robin Hood, The Effect of Federal Budgetary Policies During the 1970s on the Distribution of Income in Canada.* Montreal: C. D. Howe Institute, 1978.

Gillespie, W. I. "Taxes Expenditures and the Redistribution of Income in Canada, 1951-1977." *Reflections on Canadian Incomes.* Ottawa: Economic Council of Canada, 1980, pp. 27-50.

Gini, C. *Variabilita e mutabilita, contributo alla studio delle distrubugioui e della relazioni statisticle,* Bologna 1912.

Goldberger, A. S. "The Genetic Determination of Income: Comment." *American Economic Review,* December 1978, pp. 960-969.

Goldberger, A. S. "Heritability." *Economica* 46 (1979): 327-347.

Gooding, Wayne "Little Firms are Really Big Business." *The Financial Post,* April 5, 1980, p. 51.

Gordon, D., R. Edwards, and M. Reich. "Labor Market Segmentation in American Capitalism." Paper presented at NSF conference on labour market stratification, Athens, Georgia, 1980. Mimeographed.

Granovetter, M. S. *Getting a Job: A Study of Contacts and Careers.* Cambridge, Mass.: Harvard University Press, 1974.

Grant, E. K. and J. Vanderkamp. *The Economic Causes and Effects of Migration: Canada 1965-71.* Ottawa: Economic Council of Canada, 1976.

Gray, A. D. "Suppliers Worry as Bay Moves in on Zeller's." *The Financial Times,* December 15, 1980.

Griliches, Z. "Wages of Very Young Men." *Journal of Political Economy,* August 1976, pp. 569-586.

Griliches, Z. "Estimating the Return to Schooling: Some Econometric Problems." *Econometrica,* January 1977, pp. 1-22.

Gronau, R. "Leisure, Home Production and Work." *Journal of Political Economy,* December 1977, pp. 1099-1125.

Gronau, R. "Home Production a Forgotten Industry." *Review of Economics and Statistics,* August 1980, pp. 408-416.

Gunderson, M. "Decomposition of the Male/Female Earnings Differential: Canada 1970." *Canadian Journal of Economics,* August 1979, pp. 479-484.

Gunderson, M. *Labour Market Economics: Theory Evidence & Policy in Canada.* Toronto: McGraw-Hill Ryerson, 1980.

Hagerbaumer, J. B. "The Gini Concentration Ratio and the Minor Concentration Ratio: A Two-Parameter Index of Inequality." *The Review of Economics and Statistics,* August 1977, pp. 337-339.

Haley, B. F. "Changes in the Distribution of Income in the United States." pp. 3-28 in Marchal and Ducros (1968).

Harbury, C. D. "Inheritance and the Distribution of Personal Wealth in Britain." *Economic Journal,* December 1962.

Harbury, C. D. and P. C. McMahon. "Inheritance and the Characteristics of Top Wealth Leavers in Britain." *Economic Journal,* September 1973, pp. 810-833.

Harbury, C. D. and D. Hitchens. "The Inheritances of Top Wealth Leavers: Some Further Evidence." *Economic Journal,* June 1976, pp. 321-326.

Harcourt, G. C. *The Microeconomic Foundations of Macroeconomics.* Boulder, Colorado: Westview Press, 1977.

Harp, J. and J. Hofley, eds. *Poverty in Canada.* Scarborough: Prentice-Hall, 1971.

Harris, D. J. *Capital Accumulation and Income Distribution.* Stanford: Stanford University Press, 1978.

Harrison, A. 1979 "The Distribution of Wealth in Ten Countries." Background Paper No. 7, Royal Commission on the Distribution of Income and Wealth, London: H.M.S.O., 1979.

Hearnshaw, L. S. *Cyril Burt, Psychologist.* Ithaca: Cornell University Press, 1979.

Henderson, D. W. and J. C. R. Rowley. "The Distribution and Evolution of Canadian Incomes 1965-1973." Economic Council of Canada Discussion Paper No. 91, Ottawa, July 1977.

Henderson, D. W. and J. C. R. Rowley. "Structural Changes and the Distribution of Canadian Family Incomes 1965-1975." Economic Council of Canada Discussion Paper No. 118, July 1978.

Henle, P. and P. Ryscavage. "The Distribution of Earned Income Among Men and Women, 1958 - 77." *Monthly Labor Review,* April 1980, pp. 3-10.

Hess, R. D. "The Transmission of Cognitive Strategies in Poor Families: The Socialization of Apathy and Underachievement." pp. 73-92 in V. L. Allen (1970).

Hicks, J. R. (1946). "Income". pp. 74-82 in R. H. Parker & G. C. Harcourt (eds.) *Readings in the Concept and Measurement of Income,* Cambridge: Cambridge University Press, 1969.

Hill, C. R. and F. P. Stafford. "Family Background and Lifetime Earnings." pp. 511-549 in F. T. Juster (1977).

Hoffman, S. D. "Black-White Life Cycle Earnings Differences and the Vintage Hypothesis: A Longitudinal Analysis." *American Economic Review.* December 1979, pp. 855-867.

Holmes, R. (1976). "Male-Female Earnings Differentials in Canada." *Journal of Human Resources,* Winter 1976, pp. 109-112.

Hughes, David and Pamela. "Canada's Top 500 Companies." *Canadian Business,* July 1979.

Hum, D. P. J. "Negative Income Tax Experiments: A Description with Special Reference to Work Incentives," in Economic Council of Canada, *Reflections on Canadian Incomes,* 1980.

Humphreys, E. H. "Equality? The Rural/Urban Disparity in Ontario Elementary Schools." *Education Canada,* Vol. 11, No. 1, March 1971, pp. 34-39.

Husen, T. *Talent Opportunity and Career.* Stockholm: Almquist and Wicksell, 1969.

Hutchison, T. W. *The Signifigance and Basic Postulates of Economic Theory.* New York: A. M. Kelley, 1960.

Irvine, Ian. "Pitfalls in the Estimation of Optimal Lifetime Consumption Patterns." *Oxford Economic Papers,* July 1978, pp. 301-309.

Irvine, Ian. "The Distribution of Income and Wealth in a Lifecycle Framework." *Canadian Journal of Economics.* August 1980, pp. 455-479.

Jencks, C. et al. *Inequality: A Reassessment of the Effect of Family and Schooling in America.* New York: Basic Books, 1972.

Jencks, C. et al. *Who Gets Ahead? The Determinants of Economic Success in America.* New York: Basic Books, 1979.

Jensen, A. R. "How Much Can We Boost I.Q. and Scholastic Achievement?" *Harvard Educational Review,* Winter 1969, pp. 1-123.

Jensen, A. R. "Learning Ability, Intelligence and Educability." pp. 106-132 in V. L. Allen (1970).

Johnson, H. G. and P. Mieszkowski. "The Effects of Unionization on the Distribution of Income: A General Equilibrium Approach." *The Quarterly Journal of Economics,* November 1970, pp. 539-561.

Johnston, B. F. and P. Kilby. *Agriculture and Structural Transformation — Economic Strategies in Late Developing Countries.* New York: Oxford University Press, 1975.

Juster, F. T. ed. "The Distribution of Economic Well-Being, Studies in Income and Wealth." Vol. 41, National Bureau of Economic Research, Cambridge, Mass.: Ballinger Publishing Co., 1977.

Kakwani, W. "On a Class of Poverty Measures." *Econometrica,* March 1980, pp. 423-436.

Kamin, L. J. *The Science and Politics of I.Q.* New York: John Wiley and Sons, 1974.

Kanbur, S. M. "Of Risk Taking and The Personal Distribution of Income." *Journal of Political Economy,* August 1979, pp. 769-797.

Kerr, C. "Labor Markets: Their Character and Consequence." *American Economic Review*, May 1950.

Kessler-Harris, A. "Stratifying By Sex — Understanding the History of Working Women." Ch. 8 in Edwards, Reich, Gordon, eds., 1975.

Kimber, S. "Michelin Tire Rolls On." *Financial Post Magazine*, April 26, 1980, p. 34.

Knight, F. H. "The Ethics of Competition." *Quarterly Journal of Economics*, August 1923, pp. 579-624.

Knight, F. H. "The Role of Principles in Economics and Politics," *American Economics Review*, March 1951, pp. 1-29.

Kolko, G. *Wealth and Power in America: An Analysis of Social Class and Income Distribution*. New York: Praeger, 1962.

Koopmans, T. C. "The Construction of Economic Knowledge," in *Three Essays on the State of Economic Science*. New York: McGraw-Hill, 1957.

Koopmans, T. C. "Examples of Production Relations based on Micro-Data." pp. 144-171 in Harcourt, ed., 1977.

Kotz, D. M. "The Significance of Bank Control over Large Corporations." *Journal of Economic Issues*, June 1979 pp. 407-426.

Kravis, I. "Relative Income Shares in Fact and Theory." *American Economic Review*, (49) 1959.

Kuch, P. J. and W. Haessel. "An Analysis of the Determinants of the Size Distribution of Male Earnings in Canada," 1977. Mimeographed.

Kuhn, T. S. *The Structure of Scientific Revolutions*. 2nd ed. Chicago: University of Chicago Press, 1970.

Kuznets, Simon. "Demographic Aspects of the Size Distribution of Income: An Exploratory Essay." *Economic Development and Cultural Change* 25 (1976): 1-99.

Kuznets, S. "Economic Growth and Income Inequality." *American Economic Review*, March 1955, pp. 1-28.

Kuznets, S. *Modern Economic Growth*, New Haven, Conn.: Yale University Press, 1966.

Lacroix, R. and C. Lemelin. "Higher Education and Income." *Reflections on Canadian Incomes*, Economic Council of Canada, 1980, pp. 465-488.

Layard, R. and C. Psarchopoulous. "The Screening Hypothesis and the Returns to Education." *Journal of Political Economy*, September/October 1974, pp. 995-8.

Layard, R. and A. Zabalya. "Family Income Distribution-Explanation and Policy Evaluation." *Journal of Political Economy*.

Lazear, E. "The Narrowing of Black-White Differentials is Illusory." *American Economic Review*, September 1979, pp. 553-565.

Lazear, E. P., and R. T. Michael. "Family Size and the Distribution of Real Per Capita Income." *American Economic Review*, March 1980, pp. 91-107.

Lebergott, S. *Wealth and Want*. Princeton: Princeton University Press, 1975.

Leff, N. H. "Entrepreneurship and Economic Development: The Problem Revisited." *Journal of Economic Literature*, March 1979, pp. 44-64.

Leibowitz, A. "Home Investments in Children." *Journal of Political Economy,* March/April 1974, pp. S111-S131.

Leibowitz, A. "Parental Inputs and Children's Achievement." *Journal of Human Resources,* Spring 1977, pp. 242-251.

Leigh, D. E. "Occupational Advancement in the late 1960s: An Indirect Test of the Dual Labor Market Hypothesis." *Journal of Human Resources,* Spring 1976, pp. 155-171.

Lenin, V. I. *Imperialism, The Highest Stage of Capitalism.* New York: International Publishers, 1939.

Lewis, H. G. *Unionism and Relative Wages in the United States.* Chicago: University of Chicago Press, 1963.

Lillard, L. A. "Inequality: Earnings as Human Wealth." *American Economic Review,* March 1977, pp. 43-54.

Link, C., E. Ratledge, and K. Lewis. "The Quality of Education and Cohort Variation in Black-White Earnings Differentials." *American Economic Review,* March 1980, pp. 196-203.

Lipsey, R. G. "Wage Price Controls: How To Do A Lot of Harm by Trying to Do A Little Good." *Canadian Public Policy,* Winter 1977, pp. 1-13.

Lipsey, R. G., C. R. Sparks, and P. O. Steiner. *Economics.* 3rd ed. New York: Harper and Row, 1979.

Lipset, S. M. "Value Patterns Class and the Democratic Policy: The United States and Great Britain," in R. Bendix and S. M. Lipset, eds., 1966.

Lorenz, M. O. "Methods of Measuring the Concentration of Wealth." *Quarterly Publications of the American Statistical Association* (1905): 205-219.

Love, R. and M. Wolfson. *Income Inequality: Statistical Methodology and Canadian Illustrations.* Ottawa: Statistics Canada Cat. No. 13-559, 1976.

Lucas, R. E. B. "Hedonic Wage Equations and Psychic Wages in the Returns to Schooling." *American Economic Review,* September 1977a, pp. 549-558.

Lucas, R. E. B. "Is There a Human Capital Approach to Income Inequality?" *Journal of Human Resources,* 1977b, pp. 387-395.

Lydall, H. F. "The Distribution of Employment Incomes." *Econometrica* 27 (1959): 110-115.

Lydall, H. F. *The Structure of Earnings.* Oxford: Oxford University Press, 1968.

Lydall, H. F. "Theories of the Distribution of Earnings," pp. 15-46 in A. B. Atkinson, ed., 1976.

Macpherson, C. B., ed. *Property: Mainstream and Critical Positions.* Toronto: University of Toronto Press, 1978.

MacLeod, N. and K. Horner. "Analyzing Post-War Changes in Canadian Income Distribution." *Reflections on Canadian Incomes.* Ottawa: Economic Council of Canada, 1980.

Malles, P. *The Institutions on Industrial Relations in Continental Europe.* Ottawa: Labour Canada, 1973.

Mandel, E. *An Introduction to Marxist Economic Theory.* New York: Merit Publishers, 1969.

Mandelbrot, B. "Paretian Distributions and Income Maximization." *Quarterly Journal of Economics*, February 1962.

Manga, P. "The Income Distributional Effects of Inflation on Canadian Households. Ottawa: Anti-Inflation Board, 78.03, 1977.

Manga, P. "The Income Distributional Effect of Medical Insurance in Ontario." *Ontario Economic Council Occasional Paper No. 6*, Toronto, 1978.

Marchal, J. and B. Ducros, eds. *The Distribution of National Income*, London: Macmillan-St. Martin's Press, 1968.

Marfels, C. "Concentration Levels and Trends in the Canadian Economy 1965-1973." Study No. 31 for the Royal Commission on Corporate Concentration. Ottawa: Ministry of Supply and Services, 1976.

Marfels, C. "The Gini Ratio of Concentration Reconsidered." *Statistiche Hefte/ Statistical Papers, International Journal for Theoretical and Applied Statistics* 13, No. 2, (1972a): 160-179.

Marfels, C. "On Testing, Concentration Measures." *Zeitschrift fur National-ekonomie* 32 (1972b): 461-486.

Marglin, S. "What Do Bosses Do? The Origin and Functions of Hierarchy in Capitalist Production." *Review of Radical Political Economy* No. 2, 1974.

Marshall, A. *Principles of Economics*. 8th ed. New York: The Macmillan Co., 1913.

Martell, G. ed. *The Politics of the Canadian Public School*. Toronto: James Lewis and Samuel, 1974.

Marx, K. *Capital: A Critique of Political Economy*. Volumes I-III. New York: International Publishers, 1967.

Marx, K. *"Economic and Philosophic Manuscripts,"* in L. D. Easton and K. H. Guddat. *Writings of the Young Marx on Philosophy and Society*. Garden City: Anchor Books, Doubleday, 1967.

Marx, K. "Value, Price and Profit," in *The Essential Left*. London: Unwin Books, 1960.

Maslove, A. M. *The Pattern of Taxation in Canada*. Economic Council of Canada, Ottawa: Information Canada, 1972.

Mayhew, K. and B. Rosewell. "Labour Market Segmentation in Britain." Oxford University Institute Bulletin of Economics and Statistics, 1979, pp. 81-115.

McKenzie, J. C. "Poverty: Food and Nutrition Indices," pp. 64-85 in Townsend, ed. *The Concept of Poverty*. New York: American Elsevier, 1970.

McRoberts, H. "An Income Attainment Model for Native Born Canadian Male Wage Earners," pp. 489-510 in *Reflections on Canadian Incomes*. Economic Council of Canada, 1980.

Meade, J. E. *The Just Economy*. London: George Allen and Unwin, 1976.

Mehmet, O. "Who Benefits From the Ontario University System?" Occasional Paper No. 7, Toronto: Ontario Economic Council, 1978.

Menchik, P. L. "Inter-generational Transmission of Inequality: An Empirical Study of Wealth Mobility." *Economica*, November 1979, pp. 349-362.

Menchik, P. L. "Primogeniture, Equal Sharing and the U.S. Distribution of Wealth." *Quarterly Journal of Economics,* March 1980, pp. 299-316.

Mill, J. S. *Principles of Political Economy.* Vol. I. New York: The Colonial Press, 1900.

Minarik, J. "The Size Distribution of Income During Inflation." *The Review of Income and Wealth,* December 1979, pp. 377-392.

Mincer, J. "The Distribution of Labor Incomes — A Survey: With Special Reference to the Human Capital Approach." *Journal of Economic Literature,* March 1970, pp. 1-26.

Mincer, J. *Schooling Experience and Earnings.* New York: National Bureau of Economic Research, 1974.

Mincer, J. "Progress in Human Capital Analyses of the Distribution of Earnings," p. 136 in A. B. Atkinson, ed. 1976.

Mincer, J. and S. Polachek. "Family Investments in Human Capital: Earnings of Women." *Journal of Political Economy,* March/April 1974, pp. 576-S108.

Morishima, M. *Marx's Economics,* Cambridge: Cambridge University Press, 1973.

Moss, Milton. "Income Distribution Issues Viewed in a Lifetime Income Perspective." *Review of Income and Wealth,* June 1978, pp. 119-136.

National Council of Welfare. "Poor Kids." Ottawa, March 1975.

National Council of Welfare. "The Working Poor — A Statistical Profile." Ottawa, June 1977a.

National Council of Welfare. "Jobs and Poverty." Ottawa, June 1977b.

National Council of Welfare. "Women and Poverty." Ottawa, October 1979.

Needleman, L. "Income Distribution in Canada and the Disaggregation of the Gini-Coefficient of Concentration." *Canadian Public Policy,* Autumn 1979, pp. 497-505.

Nelson, E. R. "The Measurement and Trend of Inequality Comment." *American Economic Review,* June 1977, pp. 497-501.

Newman, Peter C. *The Canadian Establishment.* Toronto: McClelland and Stewart, 1975.

Newman, Peter C. *The Bronfman Dynasty.* Toronto: McClelland and Stewart, 1978.

Newton, K. and N. Leckie. "What's QWL? Definition, Notes." Economic Council of Canada Discussion Paper No. 100, Ottawa 1977.

Niosi, J. *The Economy of Canada.* Montreal: Black Rose Books, 1978.

Nordhaus, W. D. "The Effects of Inflation on the Distribution of Economic Welfare." *Journal of Money Credit and Banking.* February 1973, pp. 465-504.

Nyman, S. and A. Silberston. "The Ownership and Control of Industry." *Oxford Economic Papers,* March 1978, pp. 74-101.

Oi, W. "Labour as a Quasi-Fixed Factor." *Journal of Political Economy,* December 1962, pp. 538-555.

Oja, Gail. "Inequality of the Wealth Distribution in Canada 1970 and 1977." *Reflections on Canadian Incomes.* Economic Council of Canada, Ottawa, 1980.

Okun, A. *Equality and Efficiency: The Big Tradeoff.* Washington, D.C.: The Brookings Institution, 1975.

Orcutt, C., S. Caldwell and R. Wertheimer. "Policy Exploration through Micro-analytic Simulation." Washington, D.C.: The Urban Institute, 1976.

Orwell, George. *The Road to Wigan Pier.* London: Penguin Books, 1962.

Osberg, L. S. "A Structural Approach to the Distributions of Earnings." Ph.D. dissertation, Yale University, 1975.

Osberg, L. S. "Stochastic Process Models and the Distribution of Earnings." *Review of Income and Wealth* 23(1977): 205.

Osman, Thomas. "The Role of Intergenerational Wealth Transfers in the Distribution of Wealth over the Life Cycle: A Preliminary Analysis." pp. 397-412 in T. F. Juster, ed., 1977.

Osterman, P. "An Empirical Study of Labor Market Segmentation." *Industrial and Labor Relations Review,* July 1975.

Ostry, S. and M. Zaidi. *Labour Economics in Canada.* 3rd ed. Toronto: Macmillan of Canada, 1979.

Oulton, N. "Inheritance and the Distribution of Wealth." *Oxford Economic Papers,* March 1976, pp. 86-101.

Paglin, Morton. "The Measurement and Trend of Inequality: A Basic Revision." *American Economic Review,* September 1975, pp. 598-609.

Papanicolaou, J. and G. Psarchopoulos. "Socio-Economic Background, Schooling and Monetary Rewards in the United Kingdom." *Economica* 46 (1979): 435-439.

Pareto, V. *Cours d'Economie Politique.* Geneve: Librarie Droz, 1964.

Parsons, D. O. "Intergenerational Wealth Transfers and Educational Decisions of Male Youth." *Quarterly Journal of Economics,* November 1975, pp. 603-617.

Parsons, T. *Essays in Sociological Theory.* Glencoe: The Free Press, 1954.

Pascal, A. *Racial Discrimination in Economic Life,* Lexington: D. C. Heath, Lexington Books, 1972.

Pasinetti, L. *Growth and Income Distribution — Essays in Economic Theory.* Cambridge: Cambridge University Press, 1974.

Pen, J. *Income Distribution.* Harmondsworth: Penguin Books, 1971.

Perkins, S. "Malnutrition and Mental Development." International Union of Child Welfare Conference, 1974.

Perlman, Richard. *The Economics of Poverty,* New York: McGraw-Hill, 1976.

Phelps-Brown, J. *The Inequality of Pay.* Oxford: Oxford University Press, 1977.

Pigou, A. C. *The Economics of Welfare.* London: Macmillan and Co., 1932.

Piore, M. J. "Comments" on M. L. Wachter (1974), Brookings Papers on Economic Activity, No. 3, p. 685, 1974.

Piore, M. J. "Notes for a Theory of Labor Market Stratification," p. 125 in Edwards, Reich and Gordon, eds., 1975.

Piore, M. J. *Birds of Passage: Migrant Labor and Industrial Societies.* New York: Cambridge University Press, 1979.

Pissarides, C. A. "Risk, Job Search and Income Distribution." *Journal of Political Economy,* November/December 1974, pp. 1255-1267.

Podoluk, J. R. *Incomes of Canadians.* Ottawa: Dominion Bureau of Statistics, 1968.

Podoluk, J. R. "Measurement of the Distribution of Wealth in Canada." *Review of Income and Wealth,* June 1974.

Podoluk, J. R. *Poverty and Income Adequacy, Reflections on Canadian Incomes.* Ottawa: Economic Council of Canada, 1980.

Poole, A. "The Reclusive Reichmanns." *The Financial Times,* July 1980.

Porter, John. *The Vertical Mosaic.* Toronto: University of Toronto Press, 1965.

Rainwater, Lee. *What Money Buys: Inequality and the Social Meanings of Income.* New York: Basic Books, 1974.

Rawls, J. *A Theory of Justice.* Cambridge: Belknap Press, 1971.

Rees, A. *The Economics of Trade Unions.* Chicago: University of Chicago Press, 1962.

Rees, A. "Information Networks in Labor Markets." *American Economic Review,* May 1966, pp. 559-566.

Reid, F. "The Effects of Controls on the Rate of Wage Change in Canada." *The Canadian Journal of Economics,* May 1979, pp. 214-227.

Rein, Martin (1970). "Problems in the Definition and Measurement of Poverty," pp. 46-63 in Townsend, ed., 1970.

Reinemer, V. "Stalking the Invisible Investor." *Journal of Economic Issues,* June 1979, pp. 391-405.

Reuber, G. L. "The Impact of Government Policies on the Distribution of Income in Canada." University of Western Ontario, 1976, Mimeographed.

Reuber, G. L. "The Impact of Government Policies on the Distribution of Income in Canada: A Review." *Canadian Public Policy,* Autumn 1978, pp. 505-528.

Reynolds, Lloyd. *The Structure of Labor Markets: Wages and Labor Mobility in Theory and Practice.* Westport, Conn.: Greenwood Press, 1951.

Ricardo, D. *The Principles of Political Economy and Taxation.* New York: Dent, Everyman's Library, 1969.

Richardson, K. and D. Spears. *Race and Intelligence.* Baltimore: Pelican Books, 1972.

Riley, John C. "Testing the Educational Screening Hypothesis." *Journal of Political Economy,* October 1979, pp. 5227-5252.

Rist, R. C. "Student Social Class and Teacher Expectations: The Self-Fulfilling Prophecy in Ghetto Education." *Harvard Educational Review,* August 1970.

Roach, J. L. and J. K. Roach, eds. *Poverty.* U.K.: Penguin Books, 1972.

Robb, L. "Earnings Differentials in Ontario 1971." *Canadian Journal of Economics.* May 1978, pp. 350-359.

Roberti, P. "Income Distribution — A Time Series and Cross-Section Study." *The Economic Journal,* September 1974, pp. 629-638.

Robinson, A. "It Pays to be at the Top." *Financial Post,* June 7, 1980, pp. 1-19.

Robinson, J. and J. Eatwell. *An Introduction to Modern Economics.* London: McGraw-Hill, 1973.

Robinson, S. "A Note on the Hypothesis Relating Income Inequality and Economic Development." *The American Economic Review.* June 1976, pp. 437-440.

Rosenmayr, Leopold "Cultural Poverty of Working Class Youth," pp. 165-183 in Townsend, 1970.

Ross, D. P. *The Canadian Fact Book on Income Distribution.* Ottawa: Canadian Council on Social Development, 1980.

Ross, Irwin. "The Boy Wonder of Canadian Business." *Fortune,* January 29, 1979, p. 66.

Ross, S. E. and A. C. Rutter. "Healthiest Babies Possible: An Outreach Program," Vancouver Perinatal Health Project, November 1978.

Rossi, J. W. "Two Essays on Income Distribution: Problems of Measurement and Trends in Brazilian Income Inequality." Ph.D. dissertation, Dalhousie University, Halifax, 1979.

Rothman, P. A. *Inequality and Stratification in the United States.* New Jersey: Prentice-Hall, 1978.

Rowntree, B. S. *Poverty and Progress: A Second Social Survey of Yale.* London: Longmans, 1941.

Roy, A. D. "The Distribution of Earnings and of Individual Output." *The Economic Journal,* September 1950, p. 489.

Rutherford, R. S. G. "Income Distribution — A New Model." *Econometrica,* July 1955, pp. 277-294.

Ryan, J. "I.Q. — The Illusion of Objectivity," pp. 36-55 in K. Richardson and D. Spears, eds., 1972.

Ryder, N. B. "Comment." *Journal of Political Economy,* March/April 1973, pp. 556-570.

Sahota, C. S. "Theories of Personal Income Distribution: Survey." *Journal of Economic Literature,* March 1978, pp. 1-55.

Sattinger, M. "Comparative Advantage and The Distribution of Earnings and Abilities." *Econometrica,* Vol. 43, May 1975, pp. 455-468.

Sattinger, M. "Comparative Advantage in Individuals." *Review of Economics and Statistics,* May 1978, pp. 259-267.

Sawyer, M. "Income Distribution on OECD Countries." Occasional Paper, OECD Economic Outlook, Paris, July 1976.

Schiller, Bradley R. *The Economics of Poverty and Discrimination.* Englewood Cliffs, New Jersey: Prentice-Hall, 1976.

Schnitzer, M. *Income Distribution: A Comparative Study of the United States, Sweden, West Germany, East Germany, and Japan.* New York: Praeger, 1975.

Schultz, T. P. "Long-Term Change in the Personal Income Distribution: Theoretical Approaches, Evidence and Explanations." Rand Corporation, 1971. Mimeographed.

Schumpeter, J. A. *The Theory of Economic Development.* London: Oxford University Press, 1969.

Schumpeter, J. A. *Capitalism, Socialism and Democracy.* New York: Harper Torchbooks, 1962.

Schwartz, J., ed. *The Subtle Anatomy of Capitalism.* Santa Monica: Goodyear Publishing Co., 1977.

Scitovsky, T. *The Joyless Economy.* New York: Oxford University Press, 1976.

Sen, Amartya. "Issues in the Measurement of Poverty." *Scandinavian Journal of Economics,* 1979, pp. 285-307.

Shockley, W. "A 'Try Simplest Cases' Approach to the Heredity-Poverty-Crime Problem," pp. 141-146 in V. L. Allen, 1970.

Shorrocks, A. F. "Income Mobility and the Markov Assumption." *Economic Journal,* September 1976, p. 566.

Shorrocks, A. F. "On the Structure of Inter-Generational Transfers Between Families." *Economica,* November 1979, pp. 415-423.

Shorrocks, A. F. "The Class of Additively Decomposable Inequality Measures." *Econometrica,* April 1980, pp. 613-626.

Simons, H. C. "The Definition of Income," (1938) pp. 63-73 in R. H. Parker and G. C. Harcourt, *Readings in the Concept and Measurement of Income,* Cambridge: Cambridge University Press, 1969.

Smith, Adam. *The Wealth of Nations* (edited by E. Cannan, two volumes). London: University Paperbacks, Methuen, 1961.

Smith, A. M. M., J. E. Cloutier, and D. W. Henderson. "Poverty and Government Income Support in Canada 1971-1975: Characteristics of the Low Income Population." Economic Council of Canada Discussion Paper No. 130, Ottawa, April 1979.

Smith, J. P. "Family Labour Supply Over the Life Cycle." Explorations in Economic Research, NBER Vol. 4, B, Spring 1978.

Smith, R. S. "Compensating Wage Differentials and Public Policy: A Review." *Industrial and Labor Relations Review,* April 1979, p. 339.

Solow, R. M. "Some Long-Run Aspects of the Distribution of Wage Incomes." *Econometrica* 19 (1951).

Solow, R. M. "On Theories of Unemployment." *American Economic Review,* March 1980, pp. 1-11.

Spence, A. M. "Job Market Signalling." *Quarterly Journal of Economics.* August 1973, pp. 355-379.

Spence, A. M. *Market Signalling.* Cambridge: Harvard University Press, 1974.

Staehle, Hans. "Ability, Wages and Income." *Review of Economics and Statistics* 25 (1943): 77.

Stamp, Sir Josiah. *The Science of Social Adjustment.* London, 1937.

Stark, T. "The Distribution of Personal Income in the United Kingdom 1949-63." Cambridge: Cambridge University Press, 1972.

Starr, G. *Union-Non-union Wage Differentials.* Toronto: Ontario Ministry of Labour, 1973.

Starr, G. "Union-Non-union Wage Differentials in Ontario," pp. 283-294 in Hameed, ed., 1975.

Starret, D. "Social Institutions and Imperfect Information." *Quarterly Journal of Economics.* May 1976, pp. 261-284.

Statistics Canada. "Distributional Effects of Health and Education Benefits." Canada 1974. Cat. No. 13-561 Occasional, Ottawa, 1977.

Statistics Canada. "Income Distributions by Size in Canada 1978." Catalog No. 13-207 (Annual), Minister of Supply and Services, April 1980.

Statistics Canada. "Intercorporate Ownership." Cat. No. 61-517, (Occasional).

Statistics Canada. "Family Incomes: Census Families." Cat. No. 13-208, (Annual).

Statistics Canada. "Incomes, Assets and Indebtedness of Families in Canada, 1969." Cat. No. 13-547, (Occasional).

Stigler, G. S. and G. Becker. "De Gustibus non est Disputandum." *American Economic Review* 67(2)(1977): 76-90.

Stiglitz, J. "The Theory of 'Screening', Education and the Distribution of Income." *American Economic Review,* June 1975a, p. 269.

Stiglitz, J. "Incentives Risk and Information: Notes Toward a Theory of Hierarchy." *Bell Journal of Economics,* Autumn 1975b, pp. 552-579.

Starrett, D. "Social Institutions, Imperfect Information and the Distribution of Income." *Quarterly Journal of Economics,* May 1976, pp. 261-284.

Stone, K. "The Origins of Job Structures in the Steel Industry." pp. 27-84 in R. Edwards, M. Reich and D. Gordon, eds., 1975.

Stone, L. O. and M. J. MacLean. "Future Income Prospects of Canada's Senior Citizens." Scarborough: Butterworth and Co. for the Institute for Research in Public Policy, 1979.

Sweezy, P. M. *The Theory of Capitalist Development: Principles of Marxian Political Economy.* New York: Oxford University Press, 1942.

Taubman, Paul. "The Determinants of Earnings: Genetic Family and Other Environments; A Study of White Male Twins." *The American Economic Review,* December 1976, pp. 858-870.

Taubman, P. "Schooling, Ability, Non-Pecuniary Returns, Socio-economic Background and the Lifetime Distribution of Earnings," pp. 419-500 in T. F. Juster ed., 1977.

Taubman, P. and T. Wales, "Education, Mental Ability and Screening." *Journal of Political Economy.* January/February 1973.

Tawney, R. H. (1920), "Property and Creative Work," pp. 135-151 in C. B. MacPherson (1978).

Tawney, R. H. *Equality.* 4th ed. London: George Allen and Unwin, 1952.

Tebbel, J. *The Inheritors: A Study of America's Great Fortunes and What Happened to Them.* New York: C. P. Putnam's Sons, 1962.

Theil, Henri. *Economics and Information Theory.* Amsterdam: North-Holland Publishing Co., 1967.

Thomas, L. G. "Monopoly and the Distribution of Wealth. A Reappraisal." *Quarterly Journal of Economics,* February 1980, pp. 185-194.

Thurow, Lester C. *Generating Inequality — Mechanisms of Distribution in the U.S. Economy.* New York: Basic Books, 1975.

Titmuss, R. M. *Income Distribution and Social Change.* London: George Allen and Unwin, 1962.

Tomes, N. *The Family, Inheritance and the Intergenerational Transmission of Inequality.* Research Report 8001, University of Western Ontario, January 1980.

Toole, D. "Olympia and York Takes Aim at Brinco: Reichmanns Into Resources." *The Financial Times,* August 11, 1980, p. 3.

Townsend, Peter. ed., *The Concept of Poverty.* New York: American Elsevier, 1970.

Ulman, C. and J. Flanagan. *Wage Restraint.* California: University of California Press, 1975.

United Nations Educational, Scientific and Cultural Organization, 1978 Statistical Yearbook, New York, 1979.

Van der Eyken, W. *The Pre-School Years.* Harmondsworth: Penguin Books, 1977.

Vanderkamp, J. "Industrial Mobility: Some Further Results." *Canadian Journal of Economics,* August 1977, pp. 462-471.

Van Loon, R. and M. Whittington. *The Canadian Political System: Environment Structure and Process.* 2nd ed. Toronto: McGraw-Hill Ryerson, 1976.

Varian, H. R. *Microeconomic Analysis.* New York: W. W. Norton.

Vernon, P. E. *Intelligence: Heredity and Environment.* San Francisco: W. H. Freeman and Co., 1979.

Virmani, B. R. *Workers, Participation in Management — A Select Annotated Bibliography.* London: Commonwealth Secretariat, 1979.

Viscusi, K. "Wealth Effects and Earnings Premiums for Job Hazards." *Review of Economics and Statistics,* August 1978, pp. 408-416.

Wachter, M. L. "Primary and Secondary Labour markets: A Critique of the Dual Approach." *Brookings Papers on Economic Activity* C (1974): 637-689.

Wayand, Otto. *The Measurement of Poverty.* Memorandum A9 Social Security Research Division, Research and Statistics Directorate, Health and Welfare Canada, Ottawa, 1973.

Wedderburn, D., ed. *Poverty Inequality and Class Structure,* Cambridge: Cambridge University Press, 1974.

Wedgwood, Josiah. *The Economics of Inheritance.* London: George Rutledge and Sons, 1929.

Weisskoff, F. "Women's Place in the Labour Market." *American Economic Review,* Papers and Proceedings, May 1972.

Welch, F. "Black-White Differences in Returns to Schooling." *American Economic Review,* December 1973, pp. 893-907.

Welch, F. "Effects of Cohort Size on Earnings: The Baby Boom, Babies' Financial Bust." *Journal of Political Economy,* October 1979, pp. 565-598.

Welch, J. P., E. J. Winson and S. M. MacKentosh, "The Distribution of Height and Weight, and the Influence of Socio-Economic Factors, in a Sample of Eastern Canadian Urban School Children." *Canadian Journal of Public Health,* September/October 1971, pp. 373-381.

Whalley, J. "Estate Duty as a 'Voluntary' Tax: Evidence from Stamp Duty Statistics." *The Economic Journal,* September 1974, pp. 638-644.

Whalley, J. "The Worldwide Income Distribution: Some Speculative Calculations." *Review of Income and Wealth,* September 1979.

White, B. B. "Empirical Tests of the Life Cycle Hypotheses." *American Economics Review,* September 1978, pp. 547-560.

Wien, F. and J. Browne. "Blacks in the Economic Structure in Southwest Nova Scotia," Institute of Public Affairs, Dalhousie University, Halifax, 1977.

Williamson, O., M. L. Wachter, and J. E. Harris. "Understanding the Employment Relation: the Analysis of Idiosyncratic Exchange." *Bell Journal of Economics,* Spring 1975, pp. 250-278.

Willis, R. J. "A New Approach to the Economic Theory of Fertility Behaviour." *Journal of Political Economy,* March/April 1973, pp. 514-565.

Wise, D. A. "Personal Attributes Job Performance and Probability of Promotion." *Econometrica,* September/November 1975, pp. 913-932.

Wold, H. O. A. and P. Whittle. "A Model Explaining the Pareto Distribution of Wealth." *Econometrica,* (25), pp. 591-595.

Wolff, E. N. "The Distributional Effects of the 1969-75 Inflation on Holdings of Household Wealth in the United States." *Review of Income and Wealth.* June 1979, pp. 195-208.

Wolff, E. N. "The Rate of Surplus Value, the Organic Composition and the General Rate of Profit in the U.S. Economy." *American Economic Review,* June 1979, pp. 329-342.

Wolfson, M. C. "The Causes of Inequality in the Distribution of Wealth, a Simulation Analysis." Ph. D. Thesis, Cambridge University, 1977. Also: "The Bequest Process and the Causes of Inequality in the Distribution of Wealth." N.B.E.R., 1977. Mimeographed.

Wolfson, Michael C. "Wealth and the Distribution of Income, Canada 1969-70." Series 25 No. 2, June 1979, pp. 129-140.

Woodbury, S. A. "Methodological Controversy in Labor Economics." *Journal of Economic Issues,* December 1979, pp. 933-955.

Yntema, D. B. "Measures of the Inequality in the Personal Distribution of Wealth or Income." *Journal of the American Statistical Association,* Vol. XXVIII, 1933.

Index